The Works of Edmund Spenser

A Variorum Edition

THE LIFE OF EDMUND SPENSER

LONDON: HUMPHREY MILFORD
OXFORD UNIVERSITY PRESS

THE WORKS

OF

EDMUND SPENSER

A Variorum Edition

EDITED BY

EDWIN GREENLAW

CHARLES GROSVENOR OSGOOD

FREDERICK MORGAN PADELFORD

RAY HEFFNER

Baltimore

THE JOHNS HOPKINS PRESS

PRINTED IN THE UNITED STATES OF AMERICA
BY J. H. FURST COMPANY, BALTIMORE, MARYLAND

THE LIFE

OF

EDMUND SPENSER

BY

ALEXANDER C. JUDSON

Baltimore

THE JOHNS HOPKINS PRESS

1945

PREFACE

NOT SINCE the publication of Alexander B. Grosart's edition of Spenser's works in 1884 has a "full-length" life of the poet appeared. The need of a new life scarcely admits of argument. The present life differs most from its predecessors in the attention given to the atmosphere in which Spenser moved. I have undertaken to place him in his environment, surround him with his friends and associates, and study the influences both physical and human upon him.

It is a pleasure to acknowledge the assistance that I have received from many sources, and I only wish it were possible to mention here all who have aided me in various ways. For help on particular points, and for encouragement in the early stages of this project, I owe a debt of gratitude to certain of my colleagues at Indiana University, particularly to Professors Arthur B. Leible, John Robert Moore, and Henry Holland Carter; and I owe also a similar debt to the late Professor Ray Heffner, to whose generosity of spirit and true devotion to scholarship it is a sad privilege to testify now that he is gone. To Mrs. Ray Heffner I am thankful for the opportunity to examine papers of her husband's concerned with Spenser's life, including copies of a number of documents that had been available to me only in an abbreviated form. I am grateful to the late Professor Robert B. Mowat, of the University of Bristol, for reading my chapter on Cambridge, and to Dr. Rudolf Gottfried, Professors Ernest A. Strathmann and Charles G. Osgood, and the late Professor Frederick M. Padelford for reading the whole of my manuscript and for giving me many valuable suggestions and criticisms. To Dr. Gottfried and to Professor Osgood I am further indebted for their kindness in reading the proofs. I am thankful to Professor Samuel C. Chew for helpful suggestions. Finally I wish to express my deep appreciation for numerous courtesies received in the libraries where this life was principally written—the Indiana and Yale University Libraries and especially the Huntington Library, where I was privileged to spend the equivalent of over two years.

I make grateful acknowledgment to the University of Chicago Press for permitting quotations from *The Life and Correspondence of Lodowick Bryskett*, by Henry R. Plomer and Tom Peete Cross; and to Mrs. W. L. Renwick for allowing me to quote from her husband's edition of Spenser's *A View of the Present State of Ireland*, issued by Eric Partridge, Ltd., at the Scholartis Press (Professor Renwick, when my request was made, was in China).

A. C. J.

CONTENTS

CONTENTS

ILLUSTRATIONS

For courtesies in connection with the illustrations, thanks are due: to the Huntington Library for "Althorp," "The Merchant Taylors' School," "Cambridge," "Gate of Dublin Castle," "Plan of Cork," "Elizabeth Tynte to Sir Richard Boyle," and "Essex House"; to the New York Public Library for "The Bishop's Palace at Bromley, Kent"; to the Harvard College Library for "The village of Kilcullen" and "A sketch of New Abbey"; to Professor Charles G. Osgood for "The site of Fort del Oro, on Smerwick Harbour" and "The FitzHardinge miniature"; to the Newberry Library for "Spenser's monument in Westminster Abbey"; and to the British Museum for "Mezzotint by J. C. Le Blon" and "The Kinnoull portrait."

I

THE SPENCERS

ON JUNE 29, 1552, there was born to Sir John and Lady Katherine Spencer, of Wormleighton and Althorp, their third daughter, whom they named Elizabeth. During not improbably the same year, Edmund Spenser first opened his eyes upon the sunlight and fogs of London. Though he was modestly to claim relationship with this noble family of the Midlands—the present distinction between the spelling of his name and theirs came later—and to praise, almost reverently, the virtue and beauty of Elizabeth and of her younger sisters Anne and Alice, there awaited him a fame, even in his own day, far higher than theirs.

The children of Sir John, like other children, must sometimes have asked for stories about their ancestors, and one may believe that such stories most often concerned their great-grandfather Sir John Spencer, for he it was who had first made the family illustrious. His wealth and prominence had come to him from just such sheep as they could see grazing by the thousand over the hills and slopes of their father's lands. A Warwickshire man, the first Sir John had attained great wealth in Henry VII's time through sheep-raising. In 1504 he had been granted a coat of arms. In 1506 he had purchased the lordship of Wormleighton, near the southeastern border of Warwickshire, and two years later the manor of Althorp, twenty miles away in Northamptonshire, not to name many other less important properties. In or after 1519 he had been knighted.[1]

Those were the days when large profits from wool were causing the conversion of arable lands to pasture and the enclosure of common lands, with the result that many farmhouses and even whole villages were disappearing. Governmental disapproval and popular indignation were expressed in laws, but the vigorous trend toward sheep could not easily be checked by statute.

Wormleighton included lands that the previous owner, William Cope, had enclosed. Sir John seems more than once to have been ordered to undo the work of his predecessor, for petitions exist in which the wealthy grazier protests vigorously against decreasing the extent of his pastures and uprooting his hedges. In one of these, an undated petition to Henry

[1] Round, *Studies in Peerage and Family History*, p. 286.

VIII, he points out that the enclosures had been made long before by another; he tells of his worthy deeds—of his purchase of cross, books, cope, vestments, chalices, and censers for the church, of his erecting four houses (and " men, women, and children dwelling in them "), and of his planting trees, some from the acorn, in a treeless region; finally he describes the great injury to himself if hedges are removed and pastures returned to tillage.[2]

Sir John died in 1522. In his will he had inserted a curious provision, indicative of a conscience somewhat more tender than popular opinion would accredit to the great sheep-owners of that day. His executors were to recompense all who could prove, or would take oath, that they had been hurt by him in any way. He said he could remember none, but preferred that their souls rather than his own should be in danger.[3]

The Spencer family continued to derive its wealth from grazing, and to increase its possessions in lands and manors. " Alone, perhaps, among the English nobility," says J. H. Round, " the Spencers owed their riches and their rise, neither to the favour of a court, nor to the spoils of monasteries, nor to a fortune made in trade, but to successful farming." [4]

Prior to the civil wars of the seventeenth century, the Spencers' two principal seats were Wormleighton and Althorp, but the partial destruction of the Wormleighton manor-house in 1646 caused the family to make Althorp its permanent home. When Sir John Spencer purchased Wormleighton, he erected a noble mansion there. The Wormleighton manor-house is said to have surrounded a quadrangle and to have possessed two great state rooms; a portion of it, now remaining as a farmhouse, testifies to what must have been its fine architectural detail and its magnificence. It had indeed to be large to provide space for the builder's household of nearly sixty persons. Wormleighton is situated on high, windy land excellent for sheep-raising, and flocks of sheep still add their picturesqueness to that created by little stone villages with winding streets and by untouched country lanes.[5]

The better known mansion of Althorp, a large structure with wings extending forward at each side, is now thought to have been built by Sir John's grandson, though its Tudor details are effectually concealed by additions and alterations made by successive owners.[6] It stands in a

[2] Leadam, *The Domesday of Inclosures* 2. 485-489.

[3] Baker, *The History and Antiquities of the County of Northampton* 1. 107.

[4] P. 281.

[5] Harris, *Unknown Warwickshire*, pp. 82 ff.

[6] Gotch, *The Old Halls & Manor-Houses of Northamptonshire*, p. 68; Tipping, *English Homes, Period VI—Vol. I*, pp. 299-302.

ALTHORP, seat of the Spencers, as it appeared in 1669 when visited by Cosmo III, grand duke of Tuscany. From *Travels of Cosmo the Third*, London, 1821.

handsome park of five hundred acres, three hundred of which Sir John was permitted to enclose by Henry VIII in 1512. In earlier times the park offered an unobstructed approach to the mansion, and " deer could be fed from the windows."[7] Today the park is much admired for its avenues and clumps of noble trees. A stone, with the motto " Up and be doing, and God will prosper," records the planting of trees in the park, and reminds one of the energy that had lifted the Spencers so rapidly into their enviable position of wealth and prominence. Situated on higher land than the mansion stands Great Brington Church, its square tower rising above the trees that surround it. Here the Spencers chose to be buried, and ten of their effigies, excellently preserved, grace the church. Those of the first Sir John and his wife, Isabel, are of admirable workmanship, and are evidently intended to be faithful likenesses. His strong, lean, wrinkled face might well be that of a successful farmer. The dress of both—her neck is adorned with three heavy gold chains—hints at their wealth.[8]

The grandson of these first Spencers of Wormleighton and Althorp, father of the sisters whom Spenser celebrated, inherited his grandfather's talent for business, and along with it a love of entertaining which prompted him in his will to direct that the hospitalities he had maintained at his two residences should after his death be continued by his heir.[9] In his liberality he may have been fortified by his marriage to Katherine Kytson, a daughter of the vastly wealthy London merchant Sir Thomas Kytson, whose life well illustrates the romantic possibilities within reach of his occupation. Kytson had been apprenticed to a London mercer in his youth. At twenty-two he was admitted a freeman of the company. At thirty-six he was rich enough to purchase two manors from the duke of Buckingham, and at forty he began the erection of a magnificent manor-house at Hengrave, in Suffolk. At forty-eight he was knighted. He belonged to the Merchant Adventurers' Company, and in his warehouses at his death were " cloth of gold, satins, tapestry, velvets, furs, fustians, bags of pepper, cloves, madder " worth nearly twelve hundred pounds—an inventory that would have pleased Keats.[10]

Because of the special bond that existed between three daughters of this distinguished family and Edmund Spenser, we may profitably glance at the career of each of the three, and at the means used by Spenser to

[7] " Lord Spencer's Library," p. 5, in *Tracts . . . Relating to Northamptonshire.*

[8] *The Victoria History of the County of Northampton* 1. 414.

[9] Colvile, *The Worthies of Warwickshire*, p. 708.

[10] *DNB.*

2

win their favor and to show his appreciation of their friendship and patronage. Of the thirteen children born to Sir John and Lady Katherine Spencer, Elizabeth, Spenser's coeval, was the sixth.[11] At the age of twenty-two, she married Sir George Carey, who in 1570 had been knighted after praiseworthy conduct in the Scottish expedition of that year, and who in 1596 succeeded his father as second baron Hunsdon. In 1582 he became captain-general of the Isle of Wight and kept a watchful eye over the island at the time of the Armada. At Carisbrooke Castle, his residence when on the Isle of Wight, he played the part of liberal host, and here the writer Thomas Nashe experienced and immensely enjoyed his hospitality. Sir George Carey was favorably known as a patron of learning, as was also his wife. She was lauded by several poets, particularly by Nashe, who dwells on the generosity of her patronage, referring, for example, to her purse " so open to her poor beadsmen's distresses." [12]

Since in that day a writer could expect little return from his publishers, he was obliged to appeal, for at least a part of his reward, to rich and influential patrons. The first evidence we have of Spenser's interest in the Spencer family is his inclusion of Elizabeth Carey among the distinguished company of those whom he honored with dedicatory sonnets in *The Faerie Queene.* In language typical of Elizabethan dedications, which were rarely marred by understatement, he alludes to her " glorious ornaments of heuenly grace " and asserts that he needs a golden pen and silver pages to do her justice. There is in the sonnet no hint of past favors, and indeed it is quite likely that he first met her at court in the winter of 1589-1590 shortly before this sonnet was composed. Evidence of her cordial response appears in certain phrases used by him some months later when he dedicated to her his fanciful mock epic *Muiopotmos: or The Fate of the Butterflie*; here he addresses her as " bountiful lady " and refers to the " excellent favours " received at her sweet hands and to her " great bounty " to himself. In *Colin Clouts Come Home Againe*, written the following year, he calls her " *Phyllis* the faire " and dwells on her dazzling beauty. Through her he may well have met her sisters Anne and Alice.

Anne Spencer, the sixth of the Spencer daughters, born in 1557, married William Stanley, Lord Monteagle, and, after his death, Henry Lord Compton. In 1589 her second husband died. In 1591 Spenser dedicated to this beautiful young widow—beauty surpassing hers, he declared, he had seen neither in nor out of court [13]—his racy animal satire *Mother*

[11] Genealogical table by Welply, *NQ* 162. 112.

[12] Strathmann, *ELH* 2. 41 and *passim.*

[13] *Colin Clouts Come Home Againe* 556-559.

Hubberds Tale. In his dedication he says he is making a present of this tale, composed long before in his youth and lately discovered among other papers, that she may know of the duty he has always professed to her house. Did she reward him for this courtesy? Perhaps, for in *Colin Clouts Come Home Againe*, published in 1595, he calls her " bountifull *Charillis*."

On December 4, 1592, she had married Robert Sackville, who was to succeed his father in 1608 as second earl of Dorset, and in *Colin Clouts Come Home Againe* Spenser warmly congratulates her husband on being the sole possessor of " so chaste a brest." At the time of her third marriage, Anne was thirty-five; her husband, thirty-one. He was a graduate of Oxford. A contemporary says of him: " He was a man of singular learning in many sciences and languages, Greek and Latin being to him as familiar as his own natural tongue." [14] He was interested also in politics and trade.

What was in store for these two in whom our interest flickers up after all these years merely because a great poet saw fit to devote a dozen or so lines of melodious laudatory verse to them and their marriage? Not enduring happiness, for after sixteen years of married life the earl sought a separation, then quickly offered to live again with his wife, terrified, it would seem, at the thought of having to pay as alimony £1400 a year.[15] Their domestic problems were settled by an unexpected arbiter, for the earl died in less than two months.

Alice Spencer, the eighth and youngest daughter of Sir John and Lady Spencer, when she was twenty years old, married Ferdinando Stanley, Lord Strange. He was about her own age, a slight, fair, blue-eyed youth, whose portraits reveal an amiable, intelligent face. In blood he was allied to Queen Elizabeth, and he had connections with many of England's noblest families. His presence at court had been requested by the queen when he was still a boy, and he had later made New Year's gifts to her—an enameled earpick of gold and a golden jewel in the form of a squirrel, set with small diamonds, emeralds, rubies, and pearls. Lord Strange had varied interests. He was a poet (though no poem of consequence by him is known today). He was a friend and patron of poets and dramatists; Shakespeare perhaps was associated with his company of players. He hunted and hawked and tilted. At the time of the Armada he raised a large force of horsemen for the protection of Liverpool, of which he was

[14] Milles, *The Catalogue of Honor*, p. 414.
[15] *C. S. P. Dom.* (1603-1610), pp. 477 (66, 68), 484 (8).

mayor. On September 25, 1593, he succeeded his father as earl of Derby, but died on April 16 of the following year.[16]

The death of this popular and versatile nobleman at the age of thirty-five must have been sincerely mourned by many. In 1591 Spenser had dedicated his *Teares of the Muses* to Lady Strange. In his dedication he had enumerated the three things that had made her so much honored by the world: her " excellent beauty," her " virtuous behavior," and the " noble match with that most honourable lord, the very pattern of right nobility." Spenser had also mentioned her " particular bounties " to himself. When he had completed *Colin Clouts Come Home Againe* late in that same year, he had evidently included Lord Strange in his catalogue of the poets who were helping to make brilliant the court of Elizabeth, but the earl's death necessitated a revision, so that when the poem was published in 1595, Spenser made the passage read:

> There also is (ah no, he is not now)
> But since I said he is, he quite is gone,
> *Amyntas* quite is gone and lies full low,
> Hauing his *Amaryllis* left to mone.
> Helpe, O ye shepheards helpe ye all in this,
> Helpe *Amaryllis* this her losse to mourne:
> Her losse is yours, your losse *Amyntas* is,
> *Amyntas* floure of shepheards pride forlorne:
> He whilest he liued was the noblest swaine,
> That euer piped in an oaten quill:
> Both did he other, which could pipe, maintaine,
> And eke could pipe himselfe with passing skill.

When, in the same poem, Spenser mentioned the three Spencer sisters, he said of Lady Strange:

> But th'youngest is the highest in degree.

She alone of the three at the time was a countess. In 1600 she became the second wife of Lord Chancellor Ellesmere, friend of Elizabeth and James, of Essex and Bacon and Donne. It was in her honor that Milton wrote his masque *Arcades*. She died in 1637, at the unusually ripe age, for that time, of seventy-seven.

With this noble family of Wormleighton and Althorp, Spenser, as we have seen, claimed relationship, and they acknowledged the connection.[17]

[16] Raines, *Lancashire Funeral Certificates*, pp. 63 ff.

[17] Dedications to *Muiopotmos* and *The Teares of the Muses*; Harington, " Apology," p. 30, in *The Metamorphosis of Ajax*.

Precisely what this connection was, diligent research has failed to reveal.[18] Spenser's most outspoken claim occurs in these lines of *Colin Clouts Come Home Againe*:

> Ne lesse praisworthie are the sisters three,
> The honor of the noble familie:
> Of which I meanest boast my selfe to be,
> And most that vnto them I am so nie.

Again in his *Prothalamion*, written in 1596, a poem describing a barge trip on the Thames to London, he says:

> At length they all to mery *London* came,
> To mery London, my most kyndly Nurse,
> That to me gaue this Lifes first natiue sourse:
> Though from another place I take my name,
> An house of auncient fame.

Spenser's use of the expression "An house of auncient fame" for the family that he had previously called merely "noble" no doubt indicates that he was aware of a new coat of arms, granted by Clarencieux King-of-Arms Lee in 1595, which connected the Spencers of Althorp with the ancient baronial Despencers. The late Dr. J. H. Round was sure that the new pedigree is erroneous. To those who admire the family chiefly for its rapid rise through its own virility and industry, the main point of interest is that Spenser was closely enough in touch with it to learn promptly of the new coat of arms.

The importance of his relationship with this vigorous noble family of the Midlands ought to be emphasized. How early the connection began to have meaning for him we do not know, but early or late, his knowledge of alliance with it, coupled with the gracious attitude toward him of at least three of its members, must have heightened his dignity and increased his ambition and sense of power.

[18] Welply, *NQ* 162. 110 ff.; Hamer, *ibid.*, p. 380.

II

MERRY LONDON

THANKS TO a brief passage in *Prothalamion*, already quoted, we know that Spenser was born in London and that he lived there as a boy. The exact year of his birth, like many other facts of his life, we do not know. Persons concerned with later periods sometimes forget how immature was the art of biography in England at the close of the sixteenth century. One cannot help wishing that a man like Thomas Heywood, instead of industriously compiling an encyclopedic history of women that contains hardly a reference to the ladies of his own day, had chronicled the stirring lives of some of his fellow dramatists, and that Raleigh had written during his tedious years of confinement in the Tower, not a history of the world, but a narrative of his own life and times. However, where facts are lacking, inferences are sometimes possible. In his *Amoretti* Spenser remarks that the one year he has been courting his reluctant mistress seems longer than all the forty of his previous life. The manuscript of *Amoretti* was dispatched to the publisher in the autumn of 1594, and sonnet LX, in which occurs the reference to his tedious year of courting, was very likely written late in 1593. If the round number forty is to be taken literally, then Spenser was probably born in 1552. But we cannot be certain.

Of his family, our knowledge is also meager enough. Indeed, of his parents nothing is surely known except that they were not people of means, that his mother's name was Elizabeth,[1] and that they were related, as we have seen, to the noble Spencers of Wormleighton and Althorp. It is sometimes conjectured that he was the son of a certain John Spenser, a " free journeyman " in the " art or mystery of cloth-working " known to have been connected with the Merchant Taylors' Company of London in 1566. Spenser was educated at Merchant Taylors' School, which was founded by the Merchant Taylors' Company. During the eight years when Spenser was probably attending the school, three men of that name were associated with the company, and of these the free journeyman John Spenser seems most likely to have been the poet's father,[2] for he alone

[1] *Amoretti* LXXIV.

[2] R. B. Knowles in Historical Manuscripts Commission, *Fourth Report*, p. 407.

of the three, because of his modest circumstances, would have entered his son in the school as a " poor boy," and Edmund Spenser appears in that category. But after all, we have here only a guess. The name Spenser was common in that day, and the statutes of Merchant Taylors' School do not indicate that even its poor boys had to be the sons of tailors.

Spenser had a sister Sarah, as has been demonstrated by Mr. Welply,[3] and he had perhaps one or more brothers, since Gabriel Harvey once referred to him as his mother's eldest son, though the jesting tone of the remark leaves the matter in some doubt.[4]

According to tradition, Spenser was born in East Smithfield. The best evidence appears to be a statement by the versatile eighteenth-century engraver and antiquary George Vertue, in an unpublished manuscript of 1731. Here Vertue says that he has seen, " printed in Latin and English " below Hollar's perspective view of London that was published in 1647, the following sentence: " East Smithfield near the Tower: the birth place of Edmund Spencer that Famous poet, and our Second Chaucer." Efforts to confirm Vertue's assertion in regard to Hollar's 1647 bird's-eye view of London have proved futile.[5] Probably Vertue meant merely that some one had thus inscribed a copy of Hollar's view—but who, and on what authority? Evidently the location in London of Spenser's birthplace, like the year of his birth, has yet to be proved.

It is pleasant to turn from these conjectures to the more certain evidence of Spenser's own verse. His boyhood seems to have been free, happy, zestful. That he considered himself fortunate to have been reared in London is at least hinted at in his reference to " mery London," his " most kyndly Nurse "; and that he had an unrepressed, joyous youth is surely implied by the December eclogue of his *Shepheardes Calender.* Here, in its earlier stanzas, we find a highly engaging picture of Colin Clout, " under which name," says E. K., annotator of the *Calender,* " this poet secretly shadoweth himself." Of course we need not assume that we have in this fearless, madcap boy racing through the woods, gathering nuts for Christmas, hunting the young buck and the hare, or climbing an oak to drive a raven from her nest a literal picture of the young Spenser, but

[3] *NQ* 165. 93; 179. 74.

[4] *Letter-Book*, p. 60. Of a John Spenser who entered Pembroke Hall as sizar in 1575 and graduated B. A. in 1578, Venn says: " Perhaps brother of Edmund, the poet " (*Alumni Cantabrigienses*) ; not to be confused with a John Spenser (son of John Spenser, gentleman) who was admitted to Merchant Taylors' School August 3, 1571, and who attended Corpus Christi College, Oxford, and afterwards became its president (see Robinson, *A Register of the Scholars Admitted into Merchant Taylors' School* 1. 18).

[5] Grosart, ed. of Spenser 1. 4-5; Heffner, *HLQ* 2. 84; Hind, *Wenceslaus Hollar and His Views of London*, p. 44 and plate 20.

the spirit, the temper of his boyhood, as here depicted we need not question. Liberty, enthusiasm, joy, these must all have characterized his early years.

Will some one object that Spenser's "December" is based on Clément Marot's *Eglogue au Roy*, and therefore should not be accepted as autobiographic, even as to the spirit of Spenser's youth? Actually but half Spenser's poem is derived from Marot; Spenser's intention and tone are quite different. Here, as elsewhere, Spenser seems to have taken, in accordance with the literary ethics of his day, what met his needs, what expressed his thoughts, and no more. Certain features of Marot's poem live again in Spenser's English verse, but the habits of imitation to which the age was devoted did not, we may be sure, cramp the powerful, articulate Muse of Spenser, or lead him to say what he did not wish to say.

The city of one's birth and earlier years is likely to anchor itself deeply in the affections, and Spenser's writings show that he considered London a delightful and beautiful city. Of all its features, he refers most often to the Thames. The setting of *Prothalamion*, his one London poem, is the Thames, whose gentle current provides the closing line for each stanza. As we move with the poet on the river toward London, we can imagine the stately buildings on the north bank sweeping into view. They formed a long, impressive panorama, of which Spenser mentions only the brick towers of the Temple, then as today occupied by "studious Lawyers," and Essex House, once the palace of the earl of Leicester. Here, years before Spenser wrote this poem, when in the service of Elizabeth's first great favorite, he had come to know its glamorous interior.

The Thames was spanned at London in those days by only one bridge, a structure very generally regarded as the city's greatest marvel. Its twenty-one piers, massive enough to support two rows of tall houses, confined the river to a series of narrow channels, through which, at ebb and flood tide, the water flowed in turbulent rapids. On the Southwark end stood Bridge Gate, through which traffic passed to and from the great highway to the south. The gate, surmounted by a forest of poles, each bearing a traitor's or heretic's head, resembled, if we may trust contemporary engravings, a gigantic pincushion. Spenser mentions the "roring rage" of the water beneath the bridge, whose billows "all men feare to tempt," and he declares that the structure, because of its height, is celebrated in foreign lands as "a wonder of the world."[6]

The skyline of old London as seen from the Thames must have possessed great beauty and interest. Take, for instance, William Smith's

[6] *F. Q.* 3. 9. 45.

view of London published in 1588. This drawing is from such an angle that the Tower, with its lofty keep and maze of battlements and lesser towers, does not form part of the horizon, nor for that matter do any of the buildings lining the river all the way to Westminster. Yet sharply etched against the sky rise thirty towers or steeples of varied design, the most impressive being the huge tower of old St. Paul's. Perhaps this picturesque London skyline, seen often by Spenser from the river as well as from other points, was partly responsible for the coronet worn by Thames in the great river pageant in *The Faerie Queene.* Thames will be recalled as a beautiful youth in a robe of pale blue, woven to imitate the gleam of waves, and wearing a crown encircled, as with golden fretwork, by towers and battlements. This diadem, "embattild wide With hundred turrets," is indeed, says Spenser, the famous Troynovant; in other words, London.[7]

Geoffrey of Monmouth's story of the conquest of England (then a savage wilderness) by Brutus, the grandson of Aeneas, was an amazing piece of fiction that Spenser, like many other patriotic Elizabethans, loved to repeat. Troy, Rome, London—it was agreeable to think of these cities as links in a single chain. Thus bound to her more famous sisters, this young northern city acquired a share in a very ancient and noble past. And this New Troy, says Spenser, will dare to equal "in all glory and great enterprise" its two predecessors.[8]

London's glory for Spenser lay no doubt partly in its outward beauty—its great river, its palaces and churches and endless winding streets of tall, narrow, half-timbered houses, with green hills and fields in surprising proximity—but even more, one may imagine, in the mental life of the place, in the sense of power and great destiny beginning to be felt alike by merchant and statesman and poet. Yet, as a young boy, he was perhaps but dimly conscious of this stimulating atmosphere. For the normal boy, pleasure, recreation come first. Have we any means of knowing, or guessing, how he spent his idle hours, or what most interested his active, curious mind?

In "October" of *The Shepheardes Calender* he has Piers remark that Cuddie formerly led the shepherd lads in rhymes and riddles. These two recreations may well have claimed Spenser's especial interest. It is difficult to believe that he did not begin very early to compose poetry, or at least to make rhymes. While still a schoolboy he had mastered the art of versification, as his translations for van der Noot's *Theatre* prove. Whether, like Abraham Cowley, he was already writing poetry at the age of ten, we

[7] *Ibid.* 4. 11. 27-28. [8] *Ibid.* 3. 9. 44.

shall probably never know, but we can be certain that he took up his poet's pen early and plied it with boyish ardor. In riddles he surely excelled. *The Faerie Queene* reveals a mind prone to express itself through symbols and indirections, and few of his writings are quite free from enigmas—for many readers a fascinating element. One may easily imagine his leading in the fireside tales and riddles of the long winter evenings. Of outdoor pastimes, fishing and hawking were, or were destined to become, favorites, an inference justified by their frequent mention in his poetry. Indeed his imagery would suffer a real loss if robbed of the expressive terms of angling and falconry.

May Day and Christmas, with their spontaneous emotion and their pageantry, must have delighted him. The fact that a number of cantos of his great epic are scarcely more than descriptions of masques or pageants proves the absorbing interest felt by him in such entertainments. Indeed his genius for conceiving elaborate masques and designing appropriate costumes fitted him to become a veritable Inigo Jones if he had cared to follow such a profession. Though Spenser nowhere describes the Christmas masquers and mummers, he does in "May" of *The Shepheardes Calender* depict vividly the May Day festivities, from which Londoners were not barred by the size of their city. Not only do we see the singing, shouting throng hastening to the greenwood, but we are made to feel the exuberant spirits of the revellers.

Sometimes on a holiday afternoon Spenser may have been ferried across the Thames to Paris Garden to watch the baiting of bulls or bears. There, in its heyday, as many as three bulls, twenty bears, and seventy mastiffs were kept. This "sweet and comfortable recreation," as one of its proponents termed it, was very generally approved and enjoyed, though the Puritans condemned it on various grounds, including its brutality. In half a dozen instances, Spenser's mind seems to have reverted to this Elizabethan pastime when he wished to give color and emphasis to the account of a combat. His knights, striking and parrying terrible blows, their armor perhaps red with their blood, are momentarily dismissed, and in their place a savage bull tosses and tramples the fierce attacking mastiffs. Bear-baiting apparently seemed less suitable as an illustration of knightly combat, for he has but one simile based on this sport.

A boy's hours of play, of naïve observation—these are an essential part of any education, and these we may assume Spenser made the most of. But the more formal education of hornbook and Latin declensions was, of course, also his. And so, turning from the shadowy, yet important, influences just depicted, let us look briefly at Spenser the Elizabethan schoolboy.

III

THE SCHOOLBOY

NARROW, CROOKED Suffolk Lane, near the heart of old London, runs from upper Thames Street north to Cannon Street. In the year 1561 a noteworthy transformation was wrought in the Manor of the Rose, a famous old mansion on the east side of this lane. It had been built by the wealthy merchant Sir John Pulteney, mayor of London in the reign of Edward III, and among its owners had been the duke of Buckingham and the earls of Sussex. A portion of this historic mansion was bought by the Merchant Taylors' Company for £566, and was remodeled for the purpose of housing their newly founded grammar school.[1] The aim of the school was simply stated as "the better education and bringing up of children in good manners and literature," but the statutes for its regulation were elaborate, and permit us to form an accurate picture of the early life of the school.[2]

Shortly before seven o'clock in the morning, Suffolk Lane must have been thronged with boys entering from Thames Street on the south and Candlewick Street, as Cannon Street was then called, on the north, for the Merchant Taylors' School was, and still is, primarily, a day-school. Some must have been young, for the only admission requirements were the ability to read perfectly, write competently, and repeat the catechism in English or Latin. Since the founders opened their school to children of all nationalities, and since they admitted a hundred poor boys without tuition,[3] one might have seen a sprinkling of non-English faces and a democratic variety in cost of dress. The statutes do not indicate that the sons of tailors enjoyed any preference, but no doubt there was a tendency to favor them in choosing boys to be admitted free.[4] From seven till eleven, we may think of the lane as comparatively quiet except for a studious murmur from within the school. Then came the pandemonium of two hundred and fifty boys suddenly released from four hours of repression. At one they returned and remained till five.

[1] Farr, *Merchant Taylors' School*, pp. 34-35; Wilson, *The History of Merchant-Taylors' School*, p. 1.

[2] *Ibid.*, pp. 6-21.

[3] Besides the hundred admitted free, fifty children of poor men paid 2*s.* 2*d.* a quarter, and the remaining hundred, of "rich or mean" men, 5*s.* (*ibid.*, pp. 12-13).

[4] R. B. Knowles in Historical Manuscripts Commission, *Fourth Report*, p. 407.

For Elizabethan schoolboys, education was a serious business. The founders of Merchant Taylors' School explicitly provided that there should be no eating and drinking in the school, no cock-fighting or tennis playing, no "disputing abroad" on the part of the scholars, "which is but foolish babbling and loss of time." If no holiday occurred during the week, they were to have only Tuesday or Thursday afternoon for play.

We may think of the school as being conducted in one large room, with the head-master and his three assistants teaching their classes at the same time in different parts of the room. Three times during the day, "in the morning, at noon, and at evening," the boys knelt in prayer. From November till March artificial warmth was provided as needed, and also wax candles "for the poor children to read on their books by in the winter mornings and evenings."

Their chief study was, of course, Latin, but Greek and Hebrew were also taught. At a public examination held in the school in 1572, the boys were examined not only in Horace and Cicero, but also in Homer and the Hebrew psalter.[5] In 1611, fifty years after the Merchant Taylors' School was founded, its curriculum had very likely undergone little or no change. At that time, though Latin was taught in all the forms, we find the boys of the fourth form beginning the study of Greek, and the senior boys studying Hebrew. Writing and "very elementary arithmetic" may have been taught during an hour or two a week. But for two hundred years, the curriculum was to consist "almost entirely of Latin and Greek."[6] The question as to whether Spenser had a real command of Greek has been debated; he seems, at any rate, to have had the opportunity to ground himself early in that language. The occasional presentation of plays between 1572 and 1583 must have been a welcome diversion from the monotony of the regular school program, which went steadily forward during summer as well as winter, but we have no record of performances while Spenser was in attendance.[7]

Because of the long hours at their desks, the boys assuredly found the two-hour interval at noon precious, and may have devoted part of it to exploring the City, just as we know a majority of their successors did many years later.[8] Even the immediate neighborhood contained much of interest. In Candlewick Street, for instance, but a few steps away, was London Stone, so strong and so deeply set into the earth that carts striking

[5] Wilson, *The History of Merchant-Taylors' School*, pp. 39-40.

[6] Farr, pp. 43, 62. See *infra*, pp. 106, 107.

[7] Chambers, *The Elizabethan Stage* 2. 75-76.

[8] Farr, p. 67.

The Merchant Taylors' School, Suffolk Lane, London. From *The Beauties of England and Wales*, Vol. X, Part II, London, 1814.

it broke their wheels. Stow could not guess its origin, but Camden believed it to be the central milestone, like the Milliarium on the Roman forum, from which all British highways had radiated and had their distances measured. Perhaps, however, the boys wandered most often southward to the Thames. Emerging from Suffolk Lane, they had before them across Thames Street two churches, Allhallows the More and Allhallows the Less, as Stow calls them, and just to the right of these the Steelyard. This was a large establishment of the German merchants of the Hanse, which extended quite to the river's edge. Their hall contained two great pictures by Holbein representing the triumphs of Riches and Poverty, with a symbolism obvious even to a boy. A few steps to the left brought the boys through a narrow lane to Swan Stairs, a landing place for travelers down the river by water who preferred to walk around London Bridge rather than brave the Thames as it surged beneath. Then there was the bridge itself close by, leading over to Southwark, but leading also to Dover, to France, to Italy, just as the Thames led to a still vaster and more mysterious world. Only the thought of the inevitable birching for the tardy could have hurried the boys back by one o'clock to the confining walls of their big schoolroom.

Our knowledge that Spenser was a Merchant Taylors' boy rests entirely on two entries in an old Elizabethan account-book, which records the spending of money left by Robert Nowell, of Gray's Inn. Here we learn that Spenser was one of thirty-one " poor scholar[s] of the schools about London " who received gowns paid for from this fund, and that on going to Pembroke Hall he was given ten shillings, as well as two smaller sums while he was at the university. In the first two of these four entries he is described as a scholar of Merchant Taylors' School.[9] Was he one of those who flocked to the school soon after its doors were opened? Such an inference seems justified from the fact that the record of poor boys admitted, which dates from nine months after the school was started, lacks his name. We may therefore suppose that Spenser got all his early schooling at the Merchant Taylors' School, and that he enjoyed throughout this period of his life the wholesome, stimulating influence of its first great head-master, Richard Mulcaster.

Mulcaster came of border stock. He had been educated at Eton, at King's College, Cambridge, and at Christ Church, Oxford. When offered the head-mastership of Merchant Taylors' School, he was about thirty years old, and had had several years' experience as a schoolmaster. After

[9] Grosart, *The Spending of the Money of Robert Nowell*, pp. xvi-xvii, 28, 160.

considering the offer for less than a day, he accepted, took up his residence in the school, and remained as head-master for twenty-five years.[10] Of his methods, Thomas Fuller remarks:

> In a morning he would exactly and plainly construe and parse the lessons of his scholars; which done, he slept his hour (custom made him critical to proportion it) in his desk in the school; but woe be to the scholar that slept the while! Awaking, he heard them accurately; and Atropos might be persuaded to pity as soon as he to pardon, where he found just fault.[11]

In Mulcaster's two treatises on education, *Positions* and *The First Part of the Elementarie*, we may perceive something of the man as well as his educational ideals. One of his principal traits seems to have been a love of order, system, thoroughness. Logical procedure we admire, though we may question a degree of system that advocates the master's having "in his table a catalogue of school faults," such as swearing, lying, truancy, tardiness, and so on, with the number of stripes, "immutable though not many," to be administered for each.[12] Yet when system is applied wisely, results follow. He knew what he wanted, and must have held an unwavering course toward his objectives.

In various respects he was definitely ahead of his time; for example, in his notions on the education of women. Although he would not violate English custom so radically as to allow them to attend grammar schools or universities, and although he says they have not time to learn much "because they haste still on toward husbands," he is aware that they are molded from the same clay as men, for he does not doubt their capacity, and where their station and circumstances permit, he approves of higher education for them.[13] His ideas on physical training also were advanced. He devotes many pages to the subject. The soul and body, he says, are copartners in good and ill, and we cannot afford to have one strong and the other feeble. In this part of his book, however, he is much indebted to a treatise by a contemporary Italian physician, so that one is left in some doubt whether he actually organized a definite scheme of physical training for the Merchant Taylors' boys.[14] In a day when music received scant consideration in English grammar schools, he defended it as a school subject and taught it to his boys.[15]

[10] Wilson, *The History of Merchant-Taylors' School*, pp. 22, 12.

[11] *The History of the Worthies of England* 3. 308.

[12] *Positions*, p. 274.

[13] *Ibid.*, pp. 167, 177.

[14] *Ibid.*, p. 40; cf. Oliphant, *The Educational Writings of Richard Mulcaster*, p. 17.

[15] *Positions*, pp. 36-40; Watson, *The English Grammar Schools to 1660*, pp. 210-212.

He believed in self-expression, and advocated placing "pen and penknife, ink and paper, compass and ruler, a desk and a dust-box" at the child's disposal.[16] In spite of his mastery of the classics, he had an unusually high regard for English, and considered it essentially as good as Greek or Latin.[17]

Mulcaster lacked a clear and graceful style, so that his books are little read today. But they are, as James Oliphant has pointed out, the work of one who was "at once a thinker and a practical expert in matters of education," and Mr. Oliphant has "little hesitation in admitting the claim of Richard Mulcaster to be considered the Father of English Pedagogy." [18]

It is tempting to speculate on Mulcaster's influence on Spenser. To Spenser's brilliant young mind, the intelligent, liberal outlook of Mulcaster could hardly have been other than stimulating; and as the years passed, Spenser must have rejoiced that no mere taskmaster, but a philosopher, was sitting at the head-master's desk. Spenser's enthusiasm for the broadly trained individual, his faith in English and his desire to enrich English poetical diction and to produce illustrious works in English, his appreciation of music, and finally his patriotism may all have owed something to Mulcaster. Fortunately Mulcaster believed in discovering a boy's talents and ministering to them. Boys with a gift for poetry, he thought, should study the poets; boys with a gift for history, the historians.[19] Moreover, Mulcaster's theory of poetry was strikingly like Spenser's practice: when poets write soberly, without disguise, declares Mulcaster, they are not true poets, but only when they "cover a truth with a fabulous veil." [20] The December eclogue of *The Shepheardes Calender* alludes to Spenser's boyhood delight in verse-composition, and then occur the lines:

> A good olde shephearde, *Wrenock* was his name,
> Made me by arte more cunning in the same.

Entirely plausible is the conjecture that Wrenock is indeed Mulcaster.

On Friday morning, August 16, 1562, the school must have been fluttering with excitement, for the first visitation, as provided by its statutes, was about to take place. The dignified company of the examiners, including the learned Edmund Grindal, bishop of London, assembled in what had been the chapel when the Manor of the Rose was a town house. Unfortunately Mulcaster was ill in bed, but the examination went forward.

[16] *Positions*, p. 34.

[17] *Mulcaster's Elementarie*, pp. 267 ff.

[18] Pp. 210, 245.

[19] *Positions*, p. 269.

[20] *Ibid.*

First, the undermasters were questioned as to their learning and methods of teaching, and then the scholars were tested, from form to form. The pronunciation of the boys, affected, it was thought, by that of their teachers, who were for the most part Northern-born men, occasioned some criticism, but in general the report was highly favorable to the school, and cheering to Mulcaster.[21] During such visitations, Spenser may have had his first sight of Edmund Grindal and John Young, later bishop of Rochester, to both of whom he was destined to make kindly allusions in his *Calender*. Quite possibly his interest in these distinguished men began at this time, and perhaps also theirs in him.

On March 12, 1564, a son of Mulcaster was christened Sylvanus in St. Laurence Pountney, the parish church of the school, a fact that gains interest from the choice of this unusual name for Spenser's own son years later.[22]

Toward the end of Spenser's last year at Merchant Taylors' School, on February 6, 1569, the prominent and wealthy London lawyer, Robert Nowell, died. His brothers, including Alexander Nowell, dean of Paul's, as executors under their brother's will, arranged a stately funeral. Many sheets were needed to itemize the funeral expenses, including the long lists of those to whom gowns were given. While the recipients of the gowns were in all probability expected to contribute to the pageantry of the occasion by marching in the funeral procession, the giving of the gowns must have been inspired largely by benevolence. Not mere mourning robes were these, but a type of garment much worn in that day and made of a good quality of wool, costing five shillings or more a yard, and many of them were not black.[23]

The long funeral procession winding through the London streets to St. Paul's can be easily pictured. If the arrangements were like those, for example, of Sir Christopher Hatton's funeral, the poor who received gowns preceded the bier. Perhaps the grief of the two hundred and forty "very poor" men whose gowns were paid for from the Nowell fortune was tempered by the pleasant feeling of a warm new gown on a February day, not to mention the thought of the sixpence that Master Aske, goldsmith of Cheapside, was directed to pay to each one.[24] The account-book

[21] Wilson, *The History of Merchant-Taylors' School*, pp. 23-25; Long sees the probable influence of the Northern-born teachers on the dialect Spenser was later to use in the *Calender* (*MLN* 32. 59).

[22] Millican, *ELH* 6. 214-215.

[23] Grosart, *The Spending of the Money of Robert Nowell*, pp. 10-30, 49.

[24] *Ibid.*, p. 48.

also records gowns given to the poorer sort, to certain women of wealth, to the poorer sort of women, and to thirty-one poor scholars in five of the schools about London. Spenser's name heads the list of six Merchant Taylors' boys.[25] If we had been there, we might perhaps have seen him marching in his gown of "the new color"—Grosart surmises blue or crimson—at the head of his little band of schoolmates.

Robert Nowell, thanks to many lucrative appointments during the last ten years of his life, had amassed a large fortune. A few hours before he died, he reminded Alexander Nowell that the poor were to receive "all his goods" after his debts, legacies, and funeral expenses had been discharged, and a similar statement appears in his will.[26] The old paper account-book in its vellum wrapper is the record of how Alexander Nowell, the acting trustee of the will, complied with his brother's desires. To a great number of individuals small sums were given over a period of years. And Spenser, as we have seen, was one of these. When, his Merchant Taylors' days over, he departed for Cambridge, he received on April 28, 1569, ten shillings from the fund.[27] Possibly ten shillings, in spite of the greater purchasing power of such a sum in that day, appears to us a paltry contribution, but to a sixteenth-century boy who expected to maintain himself at the university largely through his own efforts, it may have seemed a heartening gift.

[25] *Ibid.*, p. 28. To each of the six boys a shilling was given then or later (*ibid.*, p. 160).
[26] *Ibid.*, pp. xxxvii, xlix.
[27] *Ibid.*, p. 160.

IV

VAN DER NOOT'S *THEATRE*

A YOUNG WRITER'S first publication is likely to have an importance for him quite beyond its intrinsic merit. Once his composition is actually in print, it gains a fateful sort of permanence, and the writer himself has, as it were, crossed a portentous threshold into a new world.

What we may suppose was Spenser's first experience with publication occurred in 1569, the year he went to the university. In that year there came from the press of Henry Bynneman in London a small book with a title well calculated to excite the interest of ultra Protestants—*A Theatre wherein be represented as wel the miseries & calamities that follow the voluptuous Worldlings, As also the greate ioyes and plesures which the faithfull do enioy*, by Jan van der Noot. For this book Spenser had been employed to make twenty-two short verse translations, or that at any rate is the inescapable inference from the fact that seventeen of these—with alterations, including such changes as were needed to cast them into the form of sonnets—appeared twenty-two years later in his *Complaints*.[1] His name, to be sure, does not occur in the *Theatre,* but presumably van der Noot secured the boy's services, paid him, and felt under no obligations to give the youthful translator public recognition, an omission that would surely have been avoided could van der Noot have guessed the enduring fame his book would acquire from the collaboration of an obscure schoolboy.

A closer glance at this curious book may be worth while. Its author, a wealthy citizen of Antwerp, had been led by his ardent Calvinism to seek refuge in England in 1567, and had employed the leisure of exile in preparing this treatise, Flemish and French versions of which he caused to be issued in 1568. In 1569 he widened his circle of readers by the publication of an English version. Though the volume is ostensibly an exhortation against worldliness, much of it is aimed directly at the shortcomings of the Roman Catholic Church. To heighten the appeal of his book, he begins with a series of "visions," brief allegorical descriptions in verse introduced generally by the words "I saw," accompanied by woodcuts. The object of these visions, he says, is to set the vanity and inconstancy of

[1] Stein, *Studies in Spenser's Complaints*, pp. 114-125; Introduction by Friedland in Jan van der Noot, *Theatre for Worldlings.*

worldly things more vividly before his reader's eyes.[2] First appear six visions of Petrarch, which mirror the death of Laura; for example, a ship of ivory and ebony, with golden sails and silver tackle, suddenly foundering on a rock. Next occur ten visions of du Bellay, in which the fall of Rome is symbolized. The series ends with four visions of van der Noot himself—for he was a competent poet—drawn from the Revelation of St. John. Then follows a commentary of two hundred and fourteen pages upon these visions, translated by Theodore Roest from the French edition.

Those who today pick up van der Noot's book are likely to read the Epistle to Elizabeth, which serves as introduction, examine the twenty crude but vigorous woodcuts, and read the accompanying verse translations by Spenser, yet quail before the long commentary in black letter. The modern fish, therefore, after devouring the bait of pictures and verses, would slip off the hook and be counted by van der Noot as virtually lost. And such a reader would indeed miss a lively presentation of the sixteenth-century anti-Catholic position.

Van der Noot's four visions, as we have seen, are based on certain passages in the Apocalypse, and to the elucidation of these passages one hundred and forty pages of his commentary are devoted. One may easily perceive what he considered the marrow of his volume. From that mysterious last book of the Bible, four more memorable pictures could hardly have been chosen: the beast of seven heads and ten horns, the woman in scarlet seated on the beast, the Word of God riding on a white horse, and the New Jerusalem coming down from God out of heaven.[3] In his eyes, these were all manifestly concerned, not with the Roman empire, but with the Catholic Church of his day; in them he saw clearly blazoned both its description and a prophecy of its destruction. Toward the beginning of his commentary he tells how the bishop of Rome, forgetting simplicity, introduced many "superstitions and traditions of men": the Latin service, bells, organs, cymbals, incense, palms, candles, and so on. This attack upon Catholic forms and ceremonies, so typical of the Puritan disputation of that day, has many echoes throughout his treatise, along with graver accusations; and in places the full bitterness of Reformation controversy flares up, as when he maintains that the Pope alone has "more contaminated God's holy temple than all the infidels together that ever were."[4] His prediction of the overthrow of Roman Catholicism seems to him supported by the progress that the Reformation has already made. Remember, he says, what God has

[2] Leaf 12ᵛ. [3] Rev. 13, 17, 19, 21. [4] Leaves 19ᵛ, 23ᵛ.

wrought by his servants; and then he calls the long roll of the reformers, beginning with Wyclif, Huss, and Luther.[5]

Nothing in van der Noot's book is more interesting than the allusions to himself and to his own country. Not always, he declares, has he been a Protestant; once indeed he was counted among those who upheld Catholicism by force; and he thanks God for having called him, with St. Paul, out of the shadow of death and the company of God's enemies. He tells at length of the great moral revival that the Reformation brought to the Netherlands, during which wickedness melted like dew before the sunlight of the Reformed Faith. But he speaks also of godly preachers burned and teachers banished, persecuted, and silenced "in our native country of low Germany," and refers to "that wicked tyrant the duke of Alba, with all his adherents, very hangmen and cruel murderers of the Pope."[6] Since van der Noot fled to England in the same year that Alva with ten thousand troops was sent to the Netherlands to root out heresy, and since Alva's ruthless measures were at their height at this time, we cannot wonder at van der Noot's characterization of the duke. No doubt van der Noot, as he says in the Epistle to Elizabeth, prepared this treatise partly to avoid idleness; yet every word was surely prompted by the deepest feeling, and a solemnity seems to pervade the whole from the fact that just across the narrow northern sea his native land was even then suffering from Alva's merciless regime.

In providing woodcuts for his visions, van der Noot really made of his treatise an emblem book. Remarkable was the vogue enjoyed, during the Renaissance, by collections of little fables or moral allegories, each accompanied by a picture. While these so-called emblem books, picture books for grown people, as they have been termed, attained their greatest popularity in Italy, France, and Germany, a number, of course, appeared also in England; and it is worth noting that Spenser, by contributing to van der Noot's *Theatre,* had a part in the earliest English emblem book.[7]

So meager is our knowledge of Spenser's youth that the glimpse of him afforded by this queer old volume is precious indeed. The mere fact that he was commissioned to make translations for it suggests the high regard which his older associates held for his poetic ability, even in his boyhood, and his translations show how well that confidence in him was justified. Two of these translations—the only ones written originally in the sonnet form—were deemed by the mature Spenser worthy to be reprinted almost without change. Since Spenser's translations are from the French (in the

[5] Leaf 49^{r-v}.

[6] Leaves 44^{r}, 71^{v}, 28^{r-v}, 105^{v}.

[7] Thompson, *Literary Bypaths of the Renaissance*, p. 64.

case of the visions of Petrarch, from Marot's rendering), it is evident that the schoolboy's preoccupation with Latin, Greek, and Hebrew did not hinder his acquiring, outside the regular school curriculum, some mastery of French. Clearly the youth suffered from no lack of initiative and industry.

Not all authors remember their juvenile publications with satisfaction, but Spenser's reprinting of his early translations suggests at least no regret over his first modest entry into the world of letters. However he viewed the *Theatre,* it could scarcely have failed to exert an influence upon him. For one thing his interest in vision literature was probably awakened. Without this early experience, he might never have written his two original series of visions, one for *The Ruines of Time*, in which the deaths of his famous friends Sidney and Leicester are symbolized, the other entitled *Visions of the Worlds Vanitie*, in which the power of small creatures over large is pictured—the ability of a gadfly, for instance, to ruin the complacency of a lordly bull—in order to illustrate that thought so dear to both the Medieval and the Renaissance mind, the insecurity of greatness, and to teach the love of low degree. Is it fanciful to wonder, moreover, whether Spenser's tendency to muse on the ephemeral character of all earthly things, which, as long as he lived, intermittently touched his poetry with a melancholy beauty, may not owe something to these early translations, or to speculate on whether his fondness for allegory and symbolism may not have been heightened, at least to a small extent, by his cooperation in van der Noot's undertaking?

In still another and more specific way Spenser may show the influence of the *Theatre*. We can hardly suppose, for example, that he did not remember van der Noot's vision of the woman in scarlet on her beast (as well as St. John's vision) when he described Duessa " High mounted on her manyheaded beast," or that van der Noot's vision of the New Jerusalem was altogether forgotten when Spenser had the aged hermit Contemplation lead the Red Cross Knight up " to the highest Mount " from which " The Citie of the great king " was visible,[8] or that van der Noot's allusions to Alva's campaign in the Netherlands were not recollected when Spenser described the sorrows of Lady Belge in Book V of *The Faerie Queene*. Van der Noot's linking of the stupendous visions of the Apocalypse with the realities of sixteenth-century Europe is not something to be erased quickly from the memory, and it may well be that too little weight has been given to the effect of this zealous pamphlet on the plastic mind of Spenser.

[8] *F. Q.* 1. 8. 6; 1. 10. 53, 55.

V

CAMBRIDGE

SPENSER'S REFERENCES to his university are few but kindly. He alludes to it as "My mother Cambridge," and speaks of its possession of "many a gentle Muse, and many a learned wit." Cambridge and Oxford, he says, are "Englands goodly beames," but, taking sides in a controversy that raged in his day, he calls Cambridge the elder sister.[1] Though his allusions are few, his university years were surely of profound importance in his development. The breadth of his learning, everywhere apparent in his writings, suggests a highly intelligent use of the opportunities for study and contemplation then offered. We feel justified, therefore, in examining with some care his physical surroundings, the methods and materials of his learning, and the chief events that occurred at Cambridge from 1569 to 1576.

At that time Cambridge was, of course, far more lonely and isolated than it is today. On the north lay the vast, unreclaimed district of the Fens, reedy, wooded, or productive of coarse grass, intersected by numberless watercourses, and supporting the rude fen-dwellers, who waded on stilts and subsisted in part on the abundant fish and fowl. During the summer, according to Camden, the fenland was of a pleasant green, but in winter the rising waters almost turned it into a lake. We must not, however, think of the Fens as utterly desolate. Ely, for example, was within their boundaries, the beautiful octagonal lantern of its cathedral celebrated then as today; and farther to the north, Wisbech, with its castle erected by the bishops of Ely and soon to become a famous prison for Catholics.[2] To the south of Cambridge lay London only fifty miles away; yet the poorer students at least must have visited it rarely, for good roads were still unknown, and travel was slow and costly. As winter journeys were especially difficult, many students remained during the Christmas holidays, making the colleges animated places, full of the gaiety of the season.[3]

In spite of nearly four centuries of growth and change, the Cambridge of 1569 would not have seemed altogether strange to those who know it today. Let the reader picture a small, compact town, largely of red

[1] *F. Q.* 4. 11. 34, 35, 26.

[2] Camden, *Britain*, pp. 491, 494, 495.

[3] Venn, *Early Collegiate Life*, p. 127.

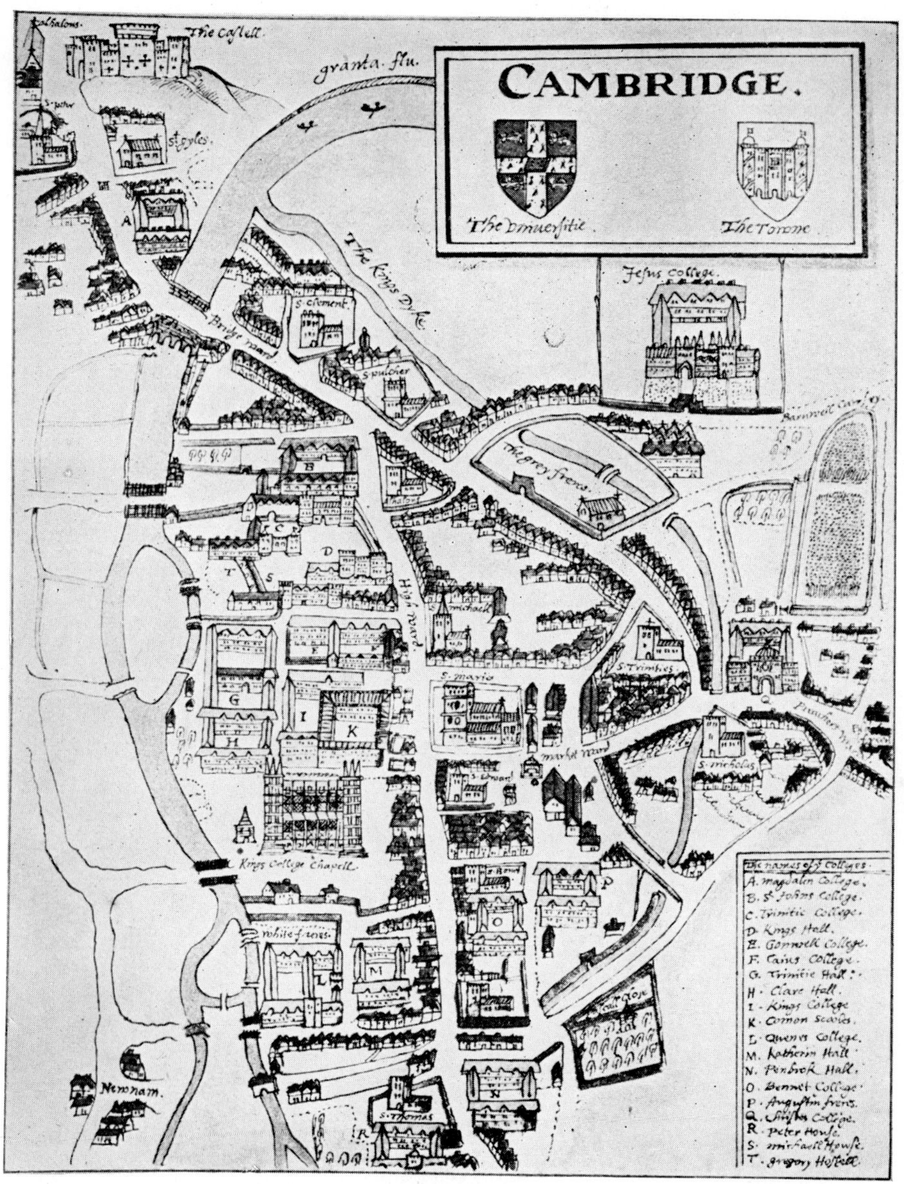

CAMBRIDGE. Pembroke College is at the lower right-hand corner. From William Smith's *The Particular Description of England*, 1588; reprinted, London, 1879.

brick and clunch, built mainly on one bank of a gently flowing stream, which is spanned by half a dozen bridges. Fourteen colleges, most of them housed in one or two low quadrangles, are scattered through the town and especially along the river. Across the river on elevated ground stands a ruined Norman castle. Trinity College, largest then as now, has not yet acquired the dignity and beauty of its present design, but possesses its handsome entrance tower of today. Great St. Mary's, the church of the university, its tower not yet completed, furnishes a place for important disputations and graduation exercises as well as religious services. Opposite St. Mary's across Trumpington Street stands the Schools Quadrangle, where the public disputations and all the university lectures are held. Dominating Cambridge then as now is King's College Chapel. The growing taste for the new architecture does not prevent the men of the Renaissance from enjoying its Gothic splendor. How could any age be unmoved by its great windows or the fan-tracery of its vaulting? Travelers to Cambridge were deeply impressed by the chapel, and Elizabeth, marveling at its beauty, " greatly praised it, above all other within her realm." [4] May we not suppose that Spenser's undoubted interest in architecture [5] brought him often to wonder at its " massy roofe, and riches huge "?

To Camden the city offered an agreeable prospect, with its " fair streets orderly ranged," its numerous churches, and its colleges. Only the air might be improved, for it was somewhat unhealthful, he thought, by reason of the neighboring Fens.[6] He might have added that, small though the town was, its streets were insanitary, and it was not immune to the plague.

In turning from the physical aspects of the university to its organization and daily life, let us first glance at a contemporary account by William Soone in a letter from Cologne written in 1575. Soone knew whereof he wrote: a Cambridge man, he had served briefly as Regius Professor of the Civil Law, but had gone abroad in 1563 on account of his Catholic sympathies.

The common dress of all is a sacred cap; (I call it sacred, because worn by priests); a gown reaching down to their heels, of the same form as that of priests. None of them live out of the colleges in the townsmen's houses; they are perpetually quarreling and fighting with them. . . . They go out in the night to show their valour, armed with monstrous great clubs furnished with a cross piece of iron to keep off the blows, and frequently beat the watch. When they walk the

[4] Nichols, " Entertainments at Cambridge, 1564," p. 11, in *The Progresses . . . of Queen Elizabeth*, Vol. I.

[5] Hard, *Sewanee Review* 42. 308.

[6] *Britain*, p. 486.

streets they take the wall, not only of the inhabitants, but even of strangers, unless persons of rank. . . . In standing for degrees, the North country and South country men have warm contests with one another. . . . In the months of January, February, and March, to beguile the long evenings, they amuse themselves with exhibiting public plays, which they perform with so much elegance, such graceful action, and such command of voice, countenance, and gesture, that if Plautus, Terence, or Seneca, were to come to life again, they would admire their own pieces, and be better pleased with them than when they were performed before the people of Rome; and Euripides, Sophocles, and Aristophanes, would be disgusted at the performance of their own citizens. . . . When the different ranks are assembled in the senate house, which is done by the Marshal going round to all the colleges and halls, and standing in the court with his gilded staff in one hand and his hat in the other, and with a loud voice proclaiming the day and hour of the congregation, you would think the wisest and gravest senators of some great republic were met together. To conclude, the way of life in these colleges is the most pleasant and liberal: and if I might have my choice, and my principles would permit, I should prefer it to a kingdom.[7]

In 1570, the year after Spenser matriculated, Elizabeth approved a revised body of statutes for the university.[8] From them we gain a satisfactory notion of a student's formal instruction, which was derived principally from college and university lectures and from disputations. The university lectures were delivered at the Schools Quadrangle, each professor lecturing as a rule daily from Monday till Thursday. Attendance on these lectures was rigidly enforced, and students were not allowed to arrive late or leave early. Absences were punished by fines, a third absence, for example, requiring from the culprit the price of a week's commons. At a time when Latin was still the language of formal university functions and even in theory at least the language of conversation in the halls during dinner, the statutes wisely provided that the books lectured on were to be explained and interpreted in English in accordance with the capacity of the hearers. The disputations offered the student a golden opportunity to show what he had learned.

If we may assume that the program laid down in the statutes was respected, the student devoted his first year to rhetoric, being guided by lectures on Quintilian, Hermogenes, or Cicero's orations. In his second and third years he studied logic, and heard lectures on the *Sophistici Elenchi* of Aristotle or the *Topica* of Cicero. His last year was devoted to philosophy, with lectures on the *Problems*, *Ethics*, and *Politics* of Aristotle,

[7] Cooper, *Annals of Cambridge* 2. 329 f.

[8] Latin original in *Documents Relating to the University and Colleges of Cambridge* 1. 454-495; translated as *The Statutes of Queen Elizabeth for the University of Cambridge.*

on Pliny, or on Plato. In addition to the university lectures at the Schools, lectures were delivered in the various colleges, and a student was expected to pursue the same subject in both places. During these four years he was required to dispute twice in the Schools and to defend a thesis twice in his own college. And now, his quadrennium completed, he was duly examined and became a bachelor of arts.

His next three years, leading to the degree of master of arts, were not notably different. He continued to attend lectures on philosophy, and heard lectures also on drawing, astronomy, and Greek. Though Copernicus, the father of modern astronomy, had been dead some thirty years, the professor of astronomy still lectured on the crystal spheres and static earth of Ptolemy, and he dealt also with arithmetic, geometry, and cosmography. The professor of Greek translated Homer, Isocrates, Demosthenes, Euripides, or some earlier author, and did not omit instruction in the Greek language. The student continued also to participate in disputations, and whenever the masters of arts disputed, he was expected to be in faithful attendance, with head uncovered. Our present restless age perhaps wonders at the Elizabethan enthusiasm for orations, declamations, and disputations. It was a taste inherited from the medieval universities. Such exercises were, of course, valued primarily as an educational discipline, but that they really gave enjoyment may be inferred from the almost unbroken succession of them to which Elizabeth was treated upon a memorable visit to Cambridge in 1564.

An examination of the eighteen authors prescribed for the university lectures in all fields, including law and medicine, shows how largely Elizabethan higher education was based on the learning of antiquity. Only two of these authors lived later than the second century of our era—Girolamo Cardano and Bishop Tunstall, Renaissance scholars who wrote on arithmetic. Indeed, the only subject besides arithmetic that professedly made use of contemporary material was the law, which taught the newly formulated ecclesiastical laws of England. But though French and Italian had no formal recognition in the statutes of 1570, we cannot question the influence of recent Continental letters and learning both within and without the lecture halls.

The curriculum as set forth in these statutes may suggest to some an arduous intellectual life. But Soone's picture of the university, slightly idealized in all probability by the nostalgia of an exile, emphasizes its pleasures. In addition to the recreations named by him, we know that football and tennis were enjoyed by some, and the mild pleasure of walking in the college gardens by others. Then there were many amusements that could be enjoyed only *sub rosa*, or at least in violation of the university regulations. The statutes of 1570 forbade playing at quoits, loitering in the town, attending fencing or dancing schools, being present at cock-fights or at bull- and bear-baitings, and, save with special permission, visiting Stourbridge Fair. They also forbade dice and, except at Christmas, cards. In 1571 swimming and bathing in the waters about Cambridge were prohibited,[9] and there was at this time no boating.[10] Though the university authorities did their best to keep a firm hand on their charges, many of whom were younger than college students of today, the task must have been difficult indeed when bears were baited outside the town on Gogmagog Hills or at Chesterton, or when in September Stourbridge Fair was in progress. This fair, the greatest in England, was held but a mile or so from Cambridge, near a brook called the Stour. Was it in memory of jolly forbidden hours spent at Stourbridge Fair that Spenser dignified this tiny stream by placing it in his river pageant in *The Faerie Queene*? A bear, it appears, was baited at Chesterton on a certain Sunday afternoon in 1581, and "a great multitude of young scholars" were looking on. University officials were dispatched to stop it, but with poor success, one of them, a bedell, being shoved and thrust upon the bear by the crowd "in such sort that he could hardly keep himself from hurt."[11] The prohibition of attendance at such sports was no doubt caused quite as much by the fear of riots or of the spread of disease as by a desire to conserve the student's time and protect his morals.

The paternalism of the university extended to the student's dress as well as to his amusements. In a day of exceptionally colorful and elaborate costume, for men as well as for women, the university sought to cultivate sobriety in dress.[12] The square cap and gown, which have remained the formal academic costume to this day, were prescribed for those holding degrees when they walked forth from their colleges. Plumed caps were forbidden, as also very full trunk-hose, or breeches, and the latter could not be reticulated, slashed, silk-sewn, padded, or stuffed. Students supported by college or church revenues were not permitted to wear plaited ruffles at the wrist, but they were allowed a modest ruff. We are not, however, to think of a body of Cambridge college youths as altogether lacking in rich and fantastic costumes, for the sons of lords and the heirs of knights were fully exempted from these regulations; so that,

[9] Cooper, *Annals of Cambridge* 2. 277.

[10] Venn, *Early Collegiate Life*, p. 124.

[11] Heywood and Wright, *Cambridge University Transactions* 1. 306-307.

[12] *The Statutes*, Chap. 46.

even if unable to shine in learning, they could at least adorn their colleges with the latest and most gorgeous novelties in dress from France or Italy.

Through streets dotted by students wearing such garb, we may imagine Spenser's making his way as he paid his first visit to Pembroke Hall on a spring day in 1569. A boy's visit to the college he is about to enter is likely to be a tour of deeply interested inspection. Let us try to reconstruct what Spenser may have seen. Entering from Trumpington Street and pausing as he steps on to the pavement of the court, he is able to view all the buildings then constituting Pembroke Hall, for the college at that time occupied but a single small quadrangle about half the size of the present first court (Old Court).[13] Directly before him, toward the east, rises the largest building of the group, a Gothic structure containing the hall and kitchen, the fellows' parlor, the master's quarters, and above the hall, well away from the damp of the ground story, the commodious library, where he will spend many an hour over books chained to their sloping desks.[14] The building at his right, as also the building behind him, contains chambers for students. At his left are more chambers and the college chapel. Dormer windows, chimneys, and a low battlemented tower concealing a spiral stairway break the horizontal lines of the simple buildings.

Further exploration will reveal Pembroke Hall Orchard behind the college. To reach it, he must cross a plot of ground and a public lane. A wall surrounds the orchard. If we may trust Lyne's plan of Cambridge published in 1574, near the center of the orchard rises a large pigeon-house, from which many a bird surely finds its way to the college table. A pigeon-house, says Willis, was considered, during the fifteenth and sixteenth centuries, a college necessity.[15] The college accounts record the building of a tennis court in 1564; and in the southwest corner of the orchard, next the lane, a tennis court is shown on Hammond's map, of 1592. This court has high, solid walls but no roof, for the tennis of that day must not be confused with its later offshoot, lawn tennis. On two sides of the orchard lies open pasture, in which Lyne has depicted several huge swine busily rooting, but in the very year of Spenser's arrival, an effort was made to banish hogs from the greens and pastures of the town.[16]

Small as this Pembroke seems when compared with the college of today, it had already received the mellowing touch of age, for it had been founded in 1347,[17] 221 years before Spenser matriculated. Its snug little

[13] Willis and Clark, *The Architectural History of the University of Cambridge* 1. 121 ff.

[14] *Ibid.* 3. 416, 429.

[15] *Ibid.*, p. 592.

[16] Cooper, *Annals of Cambridge* 2. 240.

[17] Attwater, *Pembroke College*, p. 7.

quadrangle had probably been laid out during the lifetime of the foundress, Mary de St. Pol, countess of Pembroke; and its chapel had been standing for perhaps two centuries. Today the only buildings of Spenser's time rise on the north and west sides of the Old Court, and so extensively has their fabric been patched and resurfaced that probably little except their height and proportions reminds us of the Pembroke that Spenser knew.[18] Perhaps we should be grateful to time for sparing even so much.

On May 20 Spenser matriculated as a sizar in Pembroke Hall.[19] The total number of persons in the college at that time was probably well under a hundred. Dr. John Caius, when he compiled his history of the university four years later, gave the number as 87, divided as follows: the master, 24 major fellows, 6 minor fellows, 7 inferior ministers (servants), 36 pensioners (students who paid their way), and 13 sizars (poor students).[20] The fellows were unmarried men supported on the foundation for the pursuit of advanced study. They aided in the routine work of the college, and with the master they formed its governing body. The university statutes of 1570 end with an interesting chapter of regulations affecting the colleges. Here we learn that an entering student must be fourteen years old, and have adequate preparation for the study of mathematics and logic. Having been duly examined and admitted, he becomes answerable to his tutor, who is expected to teach him diligently, correct his faults, and see to it that he does not wander idly in the town. The student's day begins with chapel at five, followed twice a week by a short homily delivered by a graduate. Much of the rest of the day is devoted to college and university lectures, to disputations, and to private study. Dinner and supper are taken in hall. At eight in winter and at nine in summer, the college gates swing shut, and the long day has virtually come to an end. Religion is carefully fostered. There are evening as well as morning prayers. On the first day of each term, a communion service is held, and the students are urged by the master or his representative to apply themselves to literature and to piety. Twice a year the master exhorts the students to give some attention to the study of the Scriptures, and especially to read them and to pray on Sundays and on feast-days. At the end of every term, a special chapel service is held in each college in honor of its founder and benefactors, with a sermon, songs, and a prayer befitting the occasion.

Spenser, as we have seen, entered Pembroke as a sizar. For several

[18] Willis and Clark 1. 132,135.

[19] Venn, *Alumni Cantabrigienses.*

[20] Cooper, *Annals of Cambridge* 2. 316.

years at least his status was probably unchanged, since on November 7, 1570, he was one of " two poor scholars " of Pembroke Hall to receive six shillings each from the Nowell fund; and since again on April 24, 1571, he received two shillings sixpence from the same fund.[21] The word *sizar* seems to have come from " size," a portion of bread and ale, which the poor students had free. In addition to their board, the sizars received lodging and instruction, in return for the discharge of certain duties. They assisted in kitchen or buttery, ran errands for the master and fellows, thus acquiring more freedom in the town than the other young students, and waited at table. After the fellows had been served, the sizars sat down to what was left. The butler and steward at Gonville and Caius College were sizars. Many were " proper," or private, sizars, and performed various personal services for the fellows. According to Willis, a sizar upon entrance was usually attached to some fellow, shared his room, and slept beneath his master in a trundle-bed. Out of 1813 members of the university in 1573, Dr. Caius lists 250 as sizars or subsizars. Apart from the services they performed, they lived a life similar to that of the other students, and they seem not to have felt any sense of indignity in having to render menial services. Many men afterwards highly distinguished began their careers as sizars.[22]

At the time Spenser went to Cambridge, sharp differences of opinion in respect to religion were agitating the university community. Although Elizabeth, soon after becoming queen, had turned the country from the Catholicism of her sister Mary back to the Protestantism of her brother Edward, she had honestly sought a religious settlement that would content the majority of her people. With characteristic diplomacy she had approved a ritual and organization that would remind her Catholic subjects of a church they still venerated, and had provided a system of doctrine satisfactory to her Protestant subjects. Yet throughout her long reign her church leaders were always concerned with extremists, who had to be compelled, outwardly at least, to respect the established church. Men who were devoted to the mass and to the offices of a Catholic priest, and men to whom an archdeacon or a bishop, an organ or a surplice, were alike painful reminders of Antichrist—these had to be gently persuaded or forcibly pushed into the arms of a church that the religious and political thought of the time believed should comprehend all.

[21] Grosart, *The Spending of the Money of Robert Nowell*, pp. 172, 164.

[22] For sizars, see Willis and Clark 1. lxxxvi; *The Statutes*, Chap. 47; Venn, *Caius College*, p. 192; id., *Early Collegiate Life*, p. 131; id., *Biographical History of Gonville and Caius College* 3. 271-275; Cooper, *Annals of Cambridge* 2. 315-316.

The year 1569, Spenser's first at Cambridge, was memorable for the emergence of a leader capable of representing well the Puritan element in the university. Thomas Cartwright had enjoyed a successful career, chiefly at St. John's and at Trinity College, and finally, in 1569, had become Lady Margaret Professor of Divinity. He was an impetuous, eloquent, learned man; in church discipline, a Presbyterian. He commenced his professorship with lectures on the first two chapters of the book of Acts, which deal with the simple beginnings of the Apostolic church. To Cartwright, the contrast between the unassuming, democratic character of the early church and the episcopal organization of his day was painful, and he could not forgo a severe criticism of the existing church system. He disapproved, for instance, of the office of archbishop, archdeacon, bishop, and deacon, and of the fact that a congregation had no part in the election of its minister.[23] The man's courage, united with an eloquence which, according to an early biographer, made the sexton of St. Mary's wish he could remove the windows in order to accommodate the multitudes when Cartwright's turn came to preach, brought crowds to his lecture room.[24]

Cartwright's bold attack was bound to be challenged. Among those whom it distressed were John Whitgift, master of Trinity College, William Chaderton, president of Queen's College, John Mey, vice-chancellor, and even the gentle Grindal, at this time archbishop of York. Of these, John Whitgift claims our particular attention. At one time opposed to the use of the surplice in the college chapels,[25] he was now passionately loyal to Elizabeth's religious establishment, and was tireless through his long life in its support, especially during his twenty-one years as archbishop. Like Cartwright, he was an eloquent preacher: Elizabeth called him her "White-gift" after listening delightedly to one of his sermons. To this small, dark man, intelligent and resolute, fell the task of opposing the forces that rallied about Cartwright. In 1572 the two schools of thought took to their pens, and for five years a pamphlet warfare of "Admonitions to Parliament," "Answers," and "Replies" raged, in which these two men loomed well above the rest.

But we must return to the beginning of the contest. On June 11, 1570, Dr. Chaderton wrote a letter to Cecil in which he declared that Cartwright, who had always been stubborn in the matter of vestments, was now teaching daily in his lectures doctrine not to be tolerated. Two weeks later,

[23] Pearson, *Thomas Cartwright and Elizabethan Puritanism*, pp. 26-29; Mullinger, *The University of Cambridge* 2. 207.

[24] Pearson, p. 23.

[25] *DNB*; Mullinger 2. 198.

Grindal wrote to Cecil in a similar vein, deploring the fact that Cartwright in his lectures was attacking the ecclesiastical polity of the realm. The youths who were flocking to Cartwright's lectures, Grindal thought, were in danger of being infected with a love of contention and a fondness for innovations. On June 29 it was expected that Cartwright would receive the degree of doctor of divinity, but Dr. Mey, the vice-chancellor, used his authority to prevent the granting of the degree, and early in August, Cartwright was suspended by the heads from lecturing. Meanwhile Cartwright and his supporters were not permitting Cecil to ignore their side of the case. Thoroughly alarmed by the size of Cartwright's following, the heads next, under Whitgift's leadership, drew up a revision of the university statutes, with the primary aim of bringing about a greater concentration of authority in themselves and the vice-chancellor. These statutes, to which reference has so often been made, passed the royal seal on September 25. On December 11, the heads deprived Cartwright of his professorship, with the result that he went abroad and taught for a time in the more congenial atmosphere of Geneva. In 1572 Whitgift struck a final blow as far as Cartwright's relationship with the university was concerned by depriving him of his fellowship in Trinity College.[26]

Probably to a majority of Cambridge students, the Cartwright-Whitgift battle provided the events of most absorbing interest in the years 1569 and 1570. Cartwright's powerful, provocative lectures, the crowds of eager listeners, the rumors of growing official disapproval, Cartwright's failure to receive his degree, the sudden cessation of his lectures, Whitgift's *coup d'état* in connection with the new statutes, and Cartwright's loss of his professorship—these would not soon be forgotten. The emotional life of large bodies of young men must find some outlet, and in the absence of important athletic contests, it probably concerned itself at this time with events such as we have been narrating. Spenser, we cannot doubt, was one of those who found these events deeply absorbing. Ten years later, in *The Shepheardes Calender*, his first work of consequence, he was to treat of kindred matters. Where his sympathies lay at this time we can only guess, but we need not doubt that he was stimulated to give new and serious thought to the organization of the church and the calling of a minister. Clear evidence of the strong impression left, first by the dispute over vestments, which was still unabated when Spenser entered Cambridge, and then by the new debate, over episcopacy, initiated by Cartwright, is found in a chance remark by Harvey in a letter dated 1580 to his friend

[26] Pearson, pp. 28-63.

Spenser: "No more ado about caps and surplices; Master Cartwright nigh forgotten."[27]

Perhaps the most interesting event in Cambridge during 1571 occurred at the end of August, when the French ambassador Paul de Foix, accompanied by Cecil (now Lord Burghley), the earls of Oxford, Bedford, and Hertford, Lord Buckhurst, and other distinguished persons, visited the university. De Foix was in England in connection with the proposed marriage of Elizabeth to the duke of Anjou, brother of the French king, Charles IX. Both in France and in England there were those who thought that such a marriage would cement the friendship of the two countries and provide a sorely needed balance to the great power of Spain. In the autumn of 1570 the match had therefore been proposed to Elizabeth, and for nearly a year negotiations had been in progress. The duke, a comely youth of twenty, perfumed, voluptuous, unstable, had veered back and forth under the influence of those who favored or opposed the marriage. Elizabeth had professed a lively, even a sentimental, interest in it, and had indeed agreed to it, but with conditions that could scarcely be met. No doubt she harbored no serious intentions of marrying the duke, but for purposes of state was glad to enter upon and prolong the negotiations.[28]

From Audley End, a few miles south of Cambridge, where the queen was holding her court, Burghley conducted the distinguished visitors for an inspection of the university, of which he was chancellor. Having entered the town, they rode from Corpus Christi College to Trinity College between members of the university, who stood along the street according to their degrees and ranks. At Trinity College, Vice-chancellor Whitgift received the party, and there they dined at the cost of the university, after which they inspected the other colleges, admiring especially Dr. Perne's celebrated library at Peterhouse. They were then entertained with disputations, and five of them were honored with the degree of master of arts.[29] The pageantry of such a visit, and the excitement attending it, must have been especially welcome during the languid days of August, when the university, if not so reduced in numbers as it would be today, was less active than in term time.

The year 1572 was not characterized at Cambridge by the harmony and quiet congenial to study. An element in the university was still smarting over the new statutes. Indeed a proposed letter thanking Burghley for

[27] Harvey, *Works* 1. 71.

[28] Hume, *The Courtships of Queen Elizabeth*, pp. 115 ff.

[29] Cooper, *Annals of Cambridge* 2. 278.

them was blocked by the younger men, and instead a petition of complaint, signed by one hundred and thirty-four names, was sent. Youth and crabbed age, for the moment, were not living well together. But age won, for a committee of arbitration pronounced the statutes satisfactory, and condemned the young men for going from college to college, without permission, to get names for their petition.[30]

Late in August the strongly Protestant feeling of Cambridge was shocked by reports of the Massacre of St. Bartholomew. Almost exactly a year before, Cambridge had done its best to honor the ambassador of Charles IX. Then a marriage between Elizabeth and the duke of Anjou had been in the air, and now a French marriage was again under discussion, this time between Elizabeth and the king's youngest brother, the duke of Alençon.[31] As the hideous details of the massacre, brought daily to the shores of England by Huguenot refugees, filtered into Cambridge, Spenser's opposition to Catholicism must have quickened, and we cannot doubt that he was one of those whose distaste for the French marriage was deepened. Henry, the third duke of Guise, who personally directed the assassination of the great Huguenot leader Coligny, was to be typified in *The Faerie Queene* by Guizor, "a groome of euill guize," whom Artegall, the knight of Justice, slays with a single blow;[32] and Catherine de' Medici's part in the massacre may well have been in Spenser's mind when in the same poem he wrote:

> Such is the crueltie of womenkynd,
> When they haue shaken off the shamefast band,
> With which wise Nature did them strongly bynd,
> T'obay the heasts of mans well ruling hand. . . .[33]

Sympathy for the French Protestants who had suffered so bitterly led to greater intolerance in England toward Catholics, and the tendency to deal more harshly with them unfortunately appeared at Cambridge. Dr. Caius, a distinguished physician, who in 1557 had refounded Gonville Hall as Gonville and Caius College, and who, soon after, had been made its master, was known to have Catholic leanings, which were perhaps the result of a period of study at the university of Padua. Though a great scholar and a munificent benefactor of his college, he was extremely unpopular with the fellows. Some of these may have passed on the word that he had, stored in his college, a large collection of Catholic chapel ornaments, kept presumably against the day when the Catholic faith

[30] Mullinger 2. 235-238. [31] Hume, pp. 143, 164. [32] 5. 6. 33; 5. 2. 6. [33] 5. 5. 25.

should once more prevail in England. On December 13, a strange scene was enacted. Vice-chancellor Byng, Dr. Whitgift, and Dr. Goad, the provost of King's, with no opposition from any member of the college, burned the books and such other objects as "served most for idolatrous abuses," and defaced the rest. It is easy to picture the scene, which took place during the early hours of the short winter afternoon. The iconoclasts or their aids bear out armfuls of massbooks, vestments, pyxes, holy-water stoups and sprinklers, censers, superaltars, portases, and images—enough wrote Dr. Byng to Burghley to provide for the conduct of divers masses at once. Some they heap on the flames; others they break in pieces with hammers.[34] And meanwhile, the proud, lonely old master, lurking perhaps in the shadows, is powerless to stop the destruction.

Ecclesiastical conformity may have been highly desirable, but it caused those who had to enforce it many an anxious hour, especially in cases involving the Puritans. Ten days before the Catholic bonfire at Gonville and Caius College, William Chark had preached a Latin sermon in St. Mary's in which he had held Satan accountable for the introduction into the church of bishops and other officers peculiar to Episcopacy. And on the Sunday before Christmas and again on January 27, Nicholas Brown, preaching also at St. Mary's, had seconded Chark's ideas. Nor were the young Puritan preachers always content with an impersonal discussion of church organization but enjoyed hurling satirical darts at prominent Cambridge figures, whom, as some of the heads complained to Archbishop Parker, they "also particularly describe and name."[35] Spenser's undergraduate days had begun in an atmosphere of religious controversy, and as they drew toward a close, differences as to ecclesiastical policy were still dominant.

In the spring of 1573 Spenser graduated a bachelor of arts. His order of seniority was eleventh in a list of 120.[36] Although the great importance later attached to the position in the class list was not at this time recognized, the late Dr. Venn believed that "some notion of merit, in the sense of intellectual superiority, must have been recognized all along; at least so far as the men towards the top of the list are concerned." With Spenser graduated eleven other Pembroke Hall men, Spenser being third in order of seniority in this group. Did his eleven college mates guess that he alone of the twelve would win real distinction in life?[37]

[34] John Venn, "Memoir of John Caius," pp. 37-38, in Caius, *Works.*

[35] Mullinger 2. 241; Cooper, *Annals of Cambridge* 2. 312-315.

[36] *Grace Book* Δ, p. 260; cf. also Millican, *HLQ* 2. 467-470.

[37] *Grace Book* Δ, p. ix; for the attainments of Spenser's Pembroke classmates, see Venn,

As was not unusual with men of scholarly tastes, Spenser stayed on at the university, his goal the degree of master of arts. His sympathies during this first year of graduate study must have gone out to his friend Gabriel Harvey if, as seems likely, the celebrated attachment between these two had already developed. Harvey, the son of a farmer and rope-maker of Saffron Walden, was several years older than Spenser. A Christ's College man, he had in the fall of 1570 been elected to a fellowship at Pembroke Hall. He possessed gifts, both physical and mental, which seemed to promise success. He was good-looking. Queen Elizabeth, a few years later, gazing at his tall, dark, comely person, remarked that he resembled an Italian, and her statement gave him so much pleasure that he hastened to celebrate the incident in Latin verse. He had a real passion for knowledge. While he was devoted to Latin and Greek literature, he did not neglect English and Italian authors, and his attitude toward his learning was sane and intelligent. With these qualities went ambition: he was conscious of his superiority and visioned for himself a great career. These were no doubt the qualities that endeared Harvey to Spenser. But clay was mixed with the gold: he was tactless, egotistical, arrogant, vain; beauty and fancy meant little to him; he was without self-criticism. When most anxious to shine, he was likely to be merely ridiculous, as when he "came ruffling it . . . in his suit of velvet" before the queen and her nobles at Audley End.[38] Spenser was prone to see the best in his friends. To him Harvey's defects may not have greatly mattered.

But they mattered to some of Harvey's companions, had indeed made him so unpopular that when he needed the votes of the fellows of Pembroke Hall in the process of becoming master of arts, the votes were not available. His associates had suffered from his eccentricity, from his self-conceit and love of argument; now they would get their revenge. Harvey appealed to the master, John Young, who at this time was following the not unusual custom of governing the little world of his college *in absentia*, from London, where he had several ecclesiastical preferments. But Harvey's colleagues did not scruple to disregard Young's letters. Presently, however, came Harvey's turn to smile. On May 14, 1573, which was Thursday, the master suddenly appeared in Cambridge. What did he mean to do? Till Monday he kept the fellows guessing, indeed scarcely mentioned Harvey and his degree. But on Monday Young acted. Harvey

Alumni Cantabrigienses (of the twelve, only Spenser has a biography in Cooper, *Athenae Cantabrigienses*).

[38] Smith in Harvey, *Marginalia*, pp. 10, 18-20; for Harvey's verses on being compared to an Italian, see *Works* 1. xxxvi, xxxix.

was nominated in the senate. In spite of objections from one Pembroke Hall man, opposition crumbled, and Harvey received his degree. Spenser was not a fellow, and his name does not appear in the letters by Harvey from which we learn of these doings.[39] Yet the story of this college quarrel throws at least a slender beam of light on college life in Spenser's day and increases our knowledge of two interesting personalities who had a part in shaping the career, and perhaps the character, of Spenser.

Allusion has been made to Harvey's correspondence with Spenser. A letter written by Harvey at Cambridge on April 7, 1580, has a bearing on Spenser's college days.[40] After a tedious discussion of earthquakes—one had shaken England on the preceding day—Harvey exclaims: "But, I beseech you, what news all this while at Cambridge?" And then he indulges in just such witty, caustic university gossip as one college man might enjoy from another. We learn among other things that Cicero and Demosthenes are less studied than formerly, that Aristotle is "much named, but little read," that Machiavelli, Castilio (Castiglione), Petrarch, Boccaccio, della Casa, Guazzo, and Aretino are greatly enjoyed. "The French and Italian, when so highly regarded of scholars? The Latin and Greek, when so lightly?" laments Harvey. Evidently we must not conclude that Cambridge men were indifferent to the Renaissance writers of France and Italy even if the university statutes failed to prescribe them. Turning from books to men, Harvey rails at some one whom he calls Spenser's "old controller," and who from a later reference of Harvey's we know was Dr. Perne, master of Peterhouse, who had just prevented Harvey from becoming university orator. Had Dr. Perne "controlled" Spenser, curbed him in some way, perhaps when Dr. Perne was vice-chancellor in 1574-1575? An amusing series of epithets is lavished by Harvey on Perne: a busy, dizzy head, a brazen forehead, a leaden brain, and so on; but oddly enough, none of these epithets alludes to Perne's notorious shifting of his religious position from reign to reign, which caused students to coin from his name a new verb, *perno, pernare*, "to change often."[41] War, says Harvey, continues as of old between heads and members. There is a touch of pathos in Harvey's exclamation: "*O amice, amicus nemo*"—"O friend, I have no friend." Harvey must indeed have felt the absence of such a friend as Spenser.

It is interesting to speculate on the effect of Harvey's friendship upon

[39] *Letter-Book*, pp. 1-54, especially pp. 40-43.

[40] Harvey, *Works* 1. 68-73; for taste in French and Italian writers, cf. Harvey, *Letter-Book*, pp. 78-79.

[41] Smith in Harvey, *Marginalia*, note, p. 30; Mullinger 2. 179.

Spenser. Though Nashe accused Harvey of being a Puritan, Harvey denied it, and Professor G. C. Moore Smith can discover no ground for Nashe's accusation. Indeed, Professor Smith considers Harvey too thoroughly a man of the Renaissance to have been even "a very fervent Christian."[42] We may therefore assume that Harvey's influence on Spenser's religious ideas was not important. In the field of letters, Harvey's influence must have been of more weight. Spenser, rightfully proud of being commissioned to contribute to van der Noot's *Theatre,* surely continued to write with enthusiasm at Cambridge, and his early efforts were greatly encouraged by Harvey—the Hobbinol of the *Calender.* Says Spenser in "December":

> Fro thence I durst in derring doe compare
> With shepheards swayne what euer fedde in field:
> And if that *Hobbinol* right iudgement bare,
> To *Pan* his owne selfe pype I neede not yield.
> For if the flocking Nymphes did folow *Pan,*
> The wiser Muses after *Colin* ranne.

But though Harvey stimulated the young poet's creative impulse and gave him confidence in his powers, we need not suppose that the results were much affected by Harvey's judgment and advice, for the literary fields in which Spenser liked to wander were not those in which Harvey was best qualified to play the critic. Assuming then that Harvey did not contribute much to the development of Spenser's religious thinking or his art, we may nevertheless easily believe that the older man awakened, or at least intensified, the ambition of the younger, urging him forward on the road to literary fame and implanting in his mind the hope of public service. Harvey, we know, was inordinately ambitious. He dreamed of a career in public life, says Smith, like those of Sir John Cheke, Sir Thomas Smith (a Saffron Walden man and a benefactor of Harvey's), and Lord Burghley.[43] Spenser also, as we shall see, thirsted for preferment, and indeed sought the patronage of the great throughout his life. Perhaps at times he too envisaged a career like those of Cheke, Smith, and Burghley, and we may easily imagine that his hopes were kindled during his college years by a spark from Harvey's.

Warmhearted and interested in people, Spenser must have acquired other friends during his college days. One of these may have been Edward Kirke, who became a sizar at Pembroke Hall two years and a half after Spenser matriculated, but who removed soon to Caius College, where he

[42] Harvey, *Marginalia,* p. 54. [43] *Ibid.,* p. 55.

graduated B. A. in 1575 and M. A. in 1578. We know little of Kirke except that he took holy orders, and on May 26, 1580, became rector at Risby, in Suffolk. It is of at least passing interest that he was preferred to this living by Sir Thomas Kytson, an uncle of the noble Spencer sisters, and that an account-book left by Kytson shows the purchase in 1583, for two shillings, of "a shepard's Calendar," which may or may not be Spenser's pastoral. In 1587, Kirke again benefited from Kytson's patronage when he became rector of the adjacent parish of Lackford.[44] He is remembered today solely because he is generally identified with the mysterious "E. K." who professed to be the editor of Spenser's *Shepheardes Calender.* Though several scholars have strongly contended that "E. K." is a mere disguise for Spenser himself, there remain certain obstacles to a full acceptance of this view. Perhaps Spenser, Harvey, and Edward Kirke all three cooperated in preparing the editorial material, working together as three young college friends might, to mystify the public and to accomplish certain ends, such as stimulating an interest in the works of both Harvey and Spenser. Since Kirke's precise part, if any, in the enterprise is impossible to define, and since we have no reason to suppose that he played any role in Spenser's life after the *Calender* period, we need not dwell further upon him.

Other Cambridge men who seem to have been members of Spenser's and Harvey's circle were the wise, learned Dr. John Still, at this time master of Trinity College, and Thomas Preston, a fellow of King's, who had dabbled in poetry and is remembered chiefly for his *Cambyses, King of Persia,* the bombast of whose opening lines was to arouse the merriment of Shakespeare. These men should perhaps be spoken of as Harvey's rather than as Spenser's friends, for our only evidence that Spenser knew them is a single sentence in a letter of his to Harvey, written in 1579, in which Harvey is warned to keep certain verses by Spenser in neo-classical meter "close to yourself, or your very entire friends Master Preston, Master Still, and the rest."[45]

Another man whom Spenser must have known was Dr. John Young, master of Pembroke Hall throughout the period of Spenser's study there. Even if Young was chiefly occupied with his ecclesiastical duties in London, his occasional visits to the college surely caused welcome ripples on the surface of its quiet routine. The students doubtless felt some awe of a man who was gifted enough to occupy the famous outdoor pulpits of St. Mary's Spital and St. Paul's Cathedral, and who indeed was occasion-

[44] Hamer, *NQ* 180. 222, 240. [45] Harvey, *Works* 1. 9.

ally called upon to preach before the queen herself. When he rode into Cambridge from the south, he must have seemed to bring with him a little gust of air from the great metropolis, and one can imagine that the sizars welcomed the privilege of serving him. Would the sizar Edmund Spenser have been surprised to know that the master would one day be a bishop and he himself his secretary?[46]

During midsummer of 1574, the plague appeared in Cambridge. By August it had become serious. Between July 26 and November 21, 115 persons died of it. The university and town cooperated in measures to control it; a hospital was constructed in certain old clay pits where those afflicted could be isolated with their keepers, and houses where it had broken out were quarantined. The regular work of the university was discontinued till after Christmas, and most of its members left for the country, those who remained being required to keep the gates of their colleges shut.[47]

Memories of this visitation of the plague doubtless flitted through Spenser's mind when he composed "July" of *The Shepheardes Calender* and also the opening lines of *Mother Hubberds Tale.* In "July" he says:

> And now the Sonne hath reared vp
> his fyriefooted teme,
> Making his way betweene the Cuppe,
> and golden Diademe:
> The rampant Lyon hunts he fast,
> with Dogge of noysome breath,
> Whose balefull barking bringes in hast
> pyne, plagues, and dreery death.

On November 21, Dr. Perne, then vice-chancellor, wrote at length to Burghley about the situation.[48] Though Perne felt sure that the principal cause of this and all other plagues was "our sins," he named as secondary causes the apparel of one who had come from London and died of the plague in neighboring Barnwell, and also the foul condition of the King's Ditch, which ran through Cambridge. The university, he was glad to report, had fared well; not two scholars had fallen ill.

Thomas Lodge, a physician as well as a novelist, published in 1603 a short *Treatise of the Plague.* After enumerating many remedies, he closes with Hippocrates' prudent rule: *Fuge longe.* The university was fortunate in being able to comply with this rule, although, as Perne remarked to

[46] Judson, *A Biographical Sketch of John Young*, pp. 5, 8, 12.
[47] Cooper, *Annals of Cambridge* 2. 321-324.
[48] *Ibid.*, pp. 322-323.

Burghley, the townspeople suffered sharp financial pains after the exodus. Sometimes members of a college gathered in the country and conducted their lectures and other exercises much as they would have done in Cambridge.[49] The colleges evidently felt some pecuniary responsibility for their members during a plague; and the Pembroke Hall accounts show that in this instance allowances were paid to seven fellows and eight boys "for their commons in the plague time." [50]

Probably Spenser obtained funds for leaving the university late in August. At any rate, the college accounts show that he was granted *aegrotat* allowances for the last six weeks of the college year, 1573-1574,[51] which extended to October 10. The so-called *aegrotat* ("he is sick") allowances paid to Spenser and other Pembroke Hall boys while Spenser was at Cambridge have given rise to interesting and various conclusions. The fact that Spenser on four occasions was granted such allowances, covering in the aggregate many weeks, led Grosart to the natural supposition that Spenser was sickly. Dr. Percy Long, whose wholesome skepticism has been of much value to Spenser scholarship, saw in the sick allowances a partiality on the part of the master, John Young, toward Spenser and, in general, toward boys from the Merchant Taylors' School, and indeed he went so far as to label these payments "Elizabethan graft." Finally, the late Aubrey Attwater, recent historian of Pembroke College, came to the conclusion that the term *aegrotat* was used at Pembroke Hall, with curious flexibility, to include disbursements to master and students in cases where no illnesses were involved, and that the boys from Merchant Taylors' School were perhaps relatively less favored than Dr. Long had supposed.[52]

Mr. Attwater considers it probable that Spenser did not return to Cambridge when the university reassembled in January. The Statutes of 1570, to be sure, required three years of resident study for the M. A. degree, but a tendency was apparent from the beginning to violate this provision, apparently on the theory that a young man could pursue his studies satisfactorily in private while he acted as curate or schoolmaster.[53] Did Spenser seek a fellowship in 1574 and fail to secure it? And if so, what must have been his feelings when four of his classmates were elected to fellowships in that year, three of whom were below him in the class list? [54] Was he weary of poverty? Did he decide that the time was ripe

[49] *The Statutes*, chap. 50, sec. 31. [50] Attwater, p. 48. [51] *Ibid.*

[52] Cf. Grosart, ed. of Spenser 1. 36; Long, *PMLA* 31. 717; Judson, *John Young*, p. 12, note 42; Attwater, p. 48.

[53] *Ibid.*, p. 49; cf. also *The Statutes*, Chaps. 7, 21, and Heywood and Wright 2. 230.

[54] Cf. *Grace Book* Δ, p. 260, and Venn, *Alumni Cantabrigienses*.

for making contact with the larger world beyond Cambridge? Or was love the exciting force, as "December" perhaps suggests? We have no means of knowing.

Whether he left Cambridge at this time or not, we know that he graduated M. A. in 1576, his grace being passed on June 26.[55] He was one of seven men of Pembroke Hall to receive the degree, and he stood this time, oddly enough, fourth from the end in a class list of 70.

The time had come finally to bid adieu to the little college that had been his home for perhaps the most critical years of his life. There must have been regrets at taking leave of the familiar quadrangle, with the pigeons circling above it; of the hall,—its walls brightened by freshly turned hangings,[56]—scene of such varied activities; of the chapel, where on feast-days the light had slanted in on surpliced figures while the organ played; and of the library above the hall, with its store of precious books. But there were doubtless also hopes for a distinguished future—literary fame, noble patrons, perhaps in the end a government post of great dignity and usefulness.

[55] *Grace Book* Δ, p. 290.

[56] Willis and Clark 1. 149, note 1.

VI

IN THE NORTH PARTS

THE EVENTS of Spenser's life from his leaving Cambridge—perhaps as early as the autumn of 1574—to the spring of 1578, when he became secretary to the bishop of Rochester, are largely concealed from our view. The biographer longs to push back the curtain, but at best he can only part it here and there for a brief look.

One of the plainest facts about Spenser, revealed by almost all his poetry, is his sensitiveness to the charm of women—surely from his heart came these lines:

> The loue of women not to entertaine;
> A lesson too too hard for liuing clay. . . .[1]

We are therefore not surprised that his first original work should tell a personal love story. Various subjects, to be sure, are dealt with in *The Shepheardes Calender,* but the fact that it begins with the account of his unsuccessful suit of Rosalind, returns to it from time to time, and ends with it, gives this theme sharp emphasis. Love, it would seem, was his most absorbing experience during this period.

Though Rosalind was certainly a real person, as is sufficiently indicated by the Spenser-Harvey correspondence,[2] Spenser took care that her identity should not be revealed. He expected his readers to believe that he had fallen in love with a beautiful, cultivated girl of good family living somewhere north of London; that his suit had seemed to prosper; but that he had then been supplanted by a rival—a blow from which it was hard to recover. The concealment of his mistress's identity under the name of Rosalind, we are informed in the " January " Gloss, has the sanction of tradition; as witness, for instance, Ovid's Corinna or Lucius Arruntius Stella's Asteris. If the name Rosalind were " well ordered," remarks E. K., it would " bewray the very name of his love and mistress," a statement which would hardly have been made had it provided a ready solution of the tantalizing mystery.

Ladies who are unresponsive sometimes change their minds. A sestina inserted at the end of " August," apparently after the *Calender* was finished, suggests the possibility of Rosalind's return " safe and sound "

[1] *F. Q.* 3. 4. 26.

[2] Harvey, *Works* 1. 6, 81.

to Colin, and recently a scholar, by retranslating a single Latin word in a letter of Harvey's, has developed the not unplausible theory that Rosalind did indeed return and became Spenser's first wife before he sailed with Lord Grey for Ireland in 1580.[3] But against this attractive hypothesis is Spenser's later reversion to the subject of Rosalind in *Colin Clouts Come Home Againe*, in which he defends her rejection of his suit. There he blames himself for looking so high, and hopes, since he may not have her love, that she will permit him to honor her pre-eminently and praise her worth.[4]

Rosalind lived, perhaps, not far from Cambridge, since Harvey knew her and seems to have been closely associated with Spenser while the affair was in progress, though the hills mentioned in " June " certainly suggest higher country farther north. Spenser quite evidently wished to be no more revealing about her dwelling place than about her person. Some have imagined that the Rosalind story is merely the idealization of a platonic friendship between Spenser and a patroness, in whose family he may have served as tutor or secretary. The true facts concerning Spenser's first serious experience with the powerful spell of woman we must reluctantly conclude are still, as he intended, a secret belonging to himself and Harvey and perhaps to other intimate friends.[5]

A virtual certainty in regard to these years is that Spenser was busy with his pen. Even the exacting demands of his government posts and varied business activities in Ireland were not destined to turn him from poetry, and we may rest assured that, however he was earning his bread after he left Cambridge, he found time to pursue the art he loved. His writing of poetry is several times alluded to in the *Calender*. In " June " Hobbinol says:

> *Colin*, to heare thy rymes and roundelayes,
> Which thou were wont on wastfull hylls to singe,
> I more delight, then larke in Sommer dayes. . . .

In " January " we are told of Rosalind's scorn of Colin's songs:

> Shepheards deuise she hateth as the snake,
> And laughes the songes, that *Colin Clout* doth make.

And in " April " we read of an interruption in his verse-making:

[3] Banks, *PMLA* 52. 335-337.

[4] 903-951.

[5] Professor Osgood summarizes the guesses as to Rosalind's identity, Variorum Edition, *Minor Poems* 1. 651-652. For a full discussion of " north parts," see *ibid.*, pp. 312-315.

> Shepheards delights he dooth them all forsweare,
> Hys pleasaunt Pipe, whych made vs meriment,
> He wylfully hath broke, and doth forbeare
> His wonted songs, wherein he all outwent.

On April 10, 1579, less than two years and ten months after Spenser received his master's degree, E. K. spoke of him, in the letter to Harvey prefixed to the *Calender*, as an accomplished writer and author of " sundry " works, seven of which are actually mentioned by title here or elsewhere in the editorial matter accompanying the *Calender.* One of these, *The English Poete,* suggests that Spenser was concerning himself rather ambitiously with the theory as well as the practice of his art. These seven are among the nineteen so-called " lost " works of Spenser, many of which are thought to have been more or less artfully incorporated in his later productions.[6] Indeed the facility revealed by the verse of the *Calender* offers in itself reasonable evidence that Spenser was zealously perfecting his art during this time.

Did Spenser in the course of these four obscure years make his first acquaintance with Ireland, the " savage island " that he was later to know so well? Irenius, one of the speakers in Spenser's lengthy prose dialogue *A View of the Present State of Ireland*, evidently represents Spenser, and when Irenius says, as he often does, " I have seen," I have " right well known," we may conclude that he is describing, generally at least, Spenser's own observations. In such a passage he tells of being present " at the execution of a notable traitor at Limerick called Morrogh O'Brien." [7] According to Irenius, O'Brien's foster mother took up her son's severed head while he was being quartered, and sucked the blood from it, saying that the earth was unworthy to drink it; and then, bathing her face and breast in his blood, tore her hair and uttered dreadful cries. The detailed account of this horrible event sounds like that of an eyewitness. Evidently there is ground for believing that Spenser may have been in Ireland on July 1, 1577, three years before he set foot there in the retinue of Lord Grey, although other evidence advanced for his being there at this time crumbles on close inspection, so that the inference must rest on this single passage.

The " June " eclogue of the *Calender,* devoted chiefy to a lament by

[6] Buck, *PMLA* 23. 80-99; Sandison, *ibid.* 25. 134-151. Five of the nineteen which were probably not so incorporated, and which may reveal one side of the young Spenser's poetic interests, are his *Ecclesiastes*, *Canticum canticorum* (translated), *The Seuen Psalmes*, *The howers of the Lord*, and *The sacrifice of a sinner*, all mentioned by Ponsonby in his Preface to the *Complaints*. Cf. Baroway, *JEGP* 33. 23-24.

[7] P. 81.

Colin over the loss of Rosalind, contains one autobiographical passage of unusual interest. Says Hobbinol to Colin:

> Then if by me thou list aduised be,
> Forsake the soyle, that so doth the bewitch . . .
> And to the dales resort, where shepheards ritch,
> And fruictfull flocks bene euery where to see.

E. K. can be startlingly explicit on occasion, and he obligingly leaves us in no doubt as to the meaning of this passage: "This is no poetical fiction, but unfeignedly spoken of the poet self, who for special occasion of private affairs, . . . and for his more preferment, removing out of the north parts, came into the south, as Hobbinol indeed advised him privately."

Why did Spenser go south and when? Harvey apparently felt that Spenser should escape from the locality that depressed him with memories of his ill success with Rosalind, and also that a better opening awaited him in the south. To judge by certain lines in "June" and "December," Spenser's means of supporting himself after leaving Cambridge had not been to his taste. A restless, dissatisfied young man, envious of Harvey's quiet security at the university, seems to speak in these lines, though to what extent his lack of tranquillity arose from Rosalind's hardness of heart is not clear. The first preferment in the south of which we have any real knowledge occurred in 1578, when Spenser became secretary to Bishop Young, whose official residence was at Bromley, Kent, ten miles from London. It is natural to connect this journey south with the preferment offered by Young, although we must remember that these four years may have contained many and varied activities, with sojourns in different parts of England, including one or more of the northern counties—Professor Osgood remarks that "it seems well-nigh certain that Spenser had some connection with the hilly country of the North of England"—and even preferment in the south of which no record remains. Possibly a connection was formed with either Sidney or Leicester by 1577 which led to Spenser's carrying dispatches to Sir Henry Sidney, then governor of Ireland, but this can be only a conjecture.[8] Of one thing, however, we may be sure: in 1578 Spenser was in Kent and in the employ of Bishop John Young.

[8] Cf. Jenkins, *PMLA* 47. 109.

VII

THE SOUTHERN SHEPHERD'S BOY

On March 16, 1578, Archbishop Parker's palace at Lambeth, across the Thames from Westminster, witnessed a solemn ceremony, the consecration of Dr. John Young, gifted London clergyman and master of Pembroke Hall, as bishop of Rochester.[1] To Young this preferment must have been the more gratifying because he had not been one to push himself forward. Indeed, he was wont to view with sorrow the rough-and-tumble struggle of clergymen for benefices and other preferments. He was doubtless aware that this great honor had come to him as a result of his fidelity to the task in hand and because of his learning and his rare gifts as a preacher.

Young was at this time forty-four years old. A bachelor of arts from Cambridge, he had begun a ten-year period as fellow at Pembroke Hall in the very year Mary had ascended the throne. Two years later he had received the degree of M. A., and with his temperamental inclination to bow to authority, had made the required profession of loyalty to the Roman Catholic faith, instead of following the more steadfast spirits across the Channel to Frankfort or Geneva. But his success as a clergyman under Elizabeth suggests that he had no difficulty in adapting himself to her reformed church, and, in fact, not many years after her reign began, he was bitterly assailing the Pope from St. Paul's Cross, the famous covered pulpit outside the cathedral. Preferment after preferment came to him, some of which may be accounted for by his association with Edmund Grindal, bishop of London, to whom Young had become chaplain by 1564. At one and the same time he was a prebend in three churches, rector of St. Magnus the Martyr, London Bridge, and master of Pembroke Hall.

Though Young was no starry-eyed spirit who would prefer exile to conformity, or heroically turn his back on sinecures that were dumped into his lap, he was undoubtedly an upright man. He discharged his duties conscientiously, was commendably firm where authority was his, and disliked pride, arrogance, and the pompous way of living to which wealthy prelates of his day were often tempted. Spenser in the "September" eclogue called him meek, merciful, and a careful tender of his flock. To

[1] Judson, *A Biographical Sketch of John Young.*

Archbishop Parker, both his pronunciation and his nature seemed princely, and Parker was eager to have him preach before Elizabeth; if his one published sermon is a fair sample of what he could do, we must approve the choice. And now in 1578 came the elevation of this man to a bishopric.

Since Young was installed on April 1, we may assume that he took up his residence about that time in the bishop's palace, which stood a quarter of a mile from the market place at Bromley, Kent. This rambling structure of two stories, with its many chimneys, had a hospitable, friendly look in keeping with Young's simple tastes. The ample park that surrounded it and the fine vistas made possible by its elevated situation would be attractive at any season, but especially so when adorned by the fresh greens of early April. Today Bromley is almost on the rim of Gargantuan London, but in 1578 it must have seemed a quiet haven, with miles of woods and fields separating it from the metropolis. And yet it had the advantage of being not too far away for easy communication. The road to London ran north toward Greenwich. Near this town, which boasted one of Elizabeth's principal residential palaces, it joined the great thoroughfare from Dover to London. Some two hours of riding must have brought the bishop to Southwark and London Bridge, so that there could have been no sense of isolation at Bromley.

Unfortunately it is impossible to speak with assurance about Young's household. A respectable retinue of servants may be assumed. If, as seems likely, Young at about this time married Grace Watts, the widow of his friend the archdeacon of Middlesex, the palace acquired a mistress, and was probably brightened by the laughter of a young girl, Susan Watts. Sometime during this first year, Edmund Spenser became Young's secretary.[2] Did he aid the bishop with his correspondence? Did he serve as tutor to Susan Watts? Did he enjoy alike the beautiful rolling country of Kent and the proximity of Bromley to both court and city? Did the ecclesiastical problems that had disturbed the calm of Cambridge acquire even a deeper significance when viewed over the shoulder of a bishop? No categorical answer, it appears, may be given to any of these questions.

Spenser was a secretary, but he was also a poet, and a very ambitious one. He was now about twenty-six years old. Since the appearance of the *Theatre* nine years before, he had published nothing, but, as we have seen, his pen had not been idle. He was now close to the great center of publication, and associated with a man who by virtue of his position had

[2] Gollancz in *Proceedings of the British Academy, 1907-1908*, p. 103.

access to the court. The time had surely come for Spenser to make his literary debut. His verses had delighted the small circle of his friends; now he would address himself to a wider circle and seek the rewards that awaited a poet.

Though we cannot tell when *The Shepheardes Calender* first took form in his mind, or was begun, we do know something of its genesis. So many other poets had made their bows with the lowly pastoral that tradition seemed to recommend that genre. E. K. reminds us that Virgil, Mantuan, Petrarch, Boccaccio, Marot, and Sannazaro, like young birds trying their wings, had started with pastorals before undertaking their loftier flights.

The pastoral genre chosen, the form, or structure, had next to be decided on. And here again E. K. confirms what might have been our guess. A popular work called *The Kalender of Shepherdes* suggested the title and presumably also the general plan.[3] Although this curious book had originated in France, it had soon been translated into English and had appeared often in both countries, at least eight English editions of it antedating Spenser's *Calender. The Kalender of Shepherdes* is a strange fusion of calendar, almanac, moral treatise, and manual of physiology, medicine, astrology, and astronomy. It contains both prose and verse and is copiously illustrated. In spite of the title and an occasional mention of shepherds, the special interests of real shepherds were not in the compiler's mind. The fact that this odd mélange of religion and science helped Spenser decide on the title and structure of his first important work proves his ability to discover literary hints in the most unpromising quarters.

The plan that he devised could hardly have been better. The pastoral form furnished him with an ostensible unity while allowing a great variety of subject-matter, and the naming of the eclogues for the months insured a measure of coherence, even though he did not in every case take the trouble to provide any very obvious connection between season and theme. Two subjects at once impress themselves on the reader as most vital—the story of unrequited love and the censure of the clergy, both traditional pastoral themes and yet evidently emphasized because they held for Spenser at the time a genuine and deep interest.

Of the half dozen eclogues on other subjects (aside from "December," which has been discussed in an earlier chapter), three have a special biographical significance. "April," with its graceful "laye Of fayre Elisa," is in a sense a prologue to the magnificent celebration of his queen

[3] For a facsimile edition of *The Kalender*, see Bibliography.

The Bishop's Palace at Bromley, Kent. Here Spenser served the bishop of Rochester as secretary in 1578. From Hasted's *The History and Topographical Survey of the County of Kent*, Vol. I, Canterbury, 1778.

that occupied him more or less constantly all the rest of his life. This eulogy of Elizabeth was moreover essential as a counterweight to the audacious handling of church affairs in the ecclesiastical eclogues. "October," a debate between two shepherds on the nature and rewards of poetry, is in reality a weighing of his own hopes and fears in regard to the calling on which he has entered, and may reveal, in two stanzas, that he is already wrestling with plans for a lofty romance which might honor Elizabeth or Leicester. And "November," consisting of a lament for the death of a maiden called Dido, portrays the grief of Colin and the other shepherds who have fed their flocks on Kentish downs over the loss of the fairest flower of their garland. According to the Argument of "November," Spenser steadfastly refused to reveal her identity even to E. K.[4]

To Spenser, the core of his book was probably the ecclesiastical eclogues. At any rate, when he bade his little volume adieu in an epilogue, he described its purpose as

> To teach the ruder shepheard how to feede his sheepe,
> And from the falsers fraud his folded flocke to keepe.

From the "May," "July," and "September" eclogues we gain a clear idea of Spenser's views on that absorbing topic of the day—the state of religion. Pride, pomp, devotion to wealth and pleasure, idleness, ignorance, and indifference to duty among the clergy he bitterly condemns. He considers the traffic in church livings a disgrace. He believes the greatest watchfulness is needed to circumvent Romanist activities. In "September" he introduces a portrait of Bishop Young as Roffy—a wise, mild, conscientious prelate, Argus-eyed in the matter of Catholic propaganda. Hobbinol is made to say:

> Shepheards sich, God mought vs many send,
> That doen so carefully theyr flocks tend.

And the eclogue closes with a fable in which Young demonstrates his watchfulness by uncovering the activities of an extraordinarily subtle Catholic who was operating in the diocese, and indeed had almost made a convert of one of Young's own most trusted officials.

Three other clergymen are introduced into the ecclesiastical eclogues with names so little disguised that they must have been easily recognized. The account of Roffy in "September" is preceded by a dialogue between Diggon Davie and Hobbinol. Diggon Davie, who, we are told, is "very friend to the author," has been recently identified, on plausible grounds,

[4] For speculation as to Dido's identity, see Variorum Edition, *Minor Poems* 1. 402-404.

with Richard Davies, the Welsh bishop of St. David's, and his "far country," where the church so suffers from poverty and many flagrant abuses, with Wales.[5] Aylmer, bishop of London, appears in "July" as the apologist for proud, rich prelates, and Spenser's readers must have thought of his princely household of eighty servants and of his personal accumulation of great wealth. With him is contrasted the unworldly Archbishop Grindal under the name Algrind, at this time suffering sequestration by Elizabeth because of his failure to forbid "prophesyings," or clerical conferences on the Scriptures, which he felt were useful as a sort of divinity school for the ministry. We marvel at Spenser's almost incredible boldness in appending a fable that clearly calls in question Elizabeth's treatment of Grindal. For like offence, men had been required to part with an ear or a hand. Prudence no doubt dictated the omission of Spenser's name from the book, a dedicatory poem to Sidney being signed merely "Immerito," a pseudonym which, according to Harvey, Spenser adopted after a certain undisclosed experience.[6]

Still another clergyman, John Piers, bishop of Salisbury, is introduced, it would seem, into "May" with no disguise of name. Learned, kind, and richly endowed with Christian humility, and at the same time vigorously Protestant, Bishop Piers was precisely the sort of man to excite Spenser's admiration. Since, moreover, he was Young's immediate predecessor as bishop of Rochester, his memory was green at Bromley.[7]

Though we do not know when the seed of the *Calender* began germinating in Spenser's mind, we can hardly doubt that its composition belongs in large part to the Bromley period. The description of Bishop Young, an allusion to the salt Medway, and repeated references to Kent, along with less obvious and concrete indications, seem to stamp much of it as the work of Spenser's leisure hours while he was Young's secretary.

On December 20, 1578, Spenser and Harvey were together in London. Just two days before, Harvey had been elected to a fellowship at Trinity Hall, Cambridge, a college where he could especially well satisfy a desire of his to pursue the study of the civil law.[8] We can easily imagine Harvey's pouring into the sympathetic ear of Spenser a full account of his election and of his future plans. An incident that occurred during this meeting gives a fleeting glimpse of the gay, whimsical side of Spenser's

[5] Hulbert, *JEGP* 41. 349-367. Cf. also P. E. McLane in Variorum Edition, *Minor Poems* 1. 354.

[6] Harvey, *Letter-Book*, p. 101.

[7] Cf. Percy W. Long and P. E. McLane in Variorum Edition, *Minor Poems* 1. 296.

[8] Smith in Harvey, *Marginalia*, p. 23.

character. Spenser presented his friend with four books—*Howleglas, Scoggin, Skelton,* and *Lazarillo*—with the proviso that, should Harvey fail to read them all through before January 1, he should forfeit to Spenser his Lucian in four volumes. This we learn from a notation by Harvey in his copy of *Howleglas.* Harvey goes on to remark that he was persuaded to trifle away the hours required for running through these four "foolish books." [9] All of them are jestbooks or tales of humorous adventure, for evidently Harvey refers, not to Skelton's acknowledged works, but to the *Merie Tales . . . by Master Skelton. Howleglas* is, of course, the adventures of Eulenspiegel, and *Lazarillo,* the best of the four, is the famous Spanish picaresque tale which, late in the Renaissance, started the popularity of that genre. Also in this year Spenser gave Harvey a copy of *The Traueiler of Ierome Turler*, a little book containing hints on oversea travel and a description of Naples. Unlike Ascham, Turler was a warm advocate of foreign travel, even going so far as to assert that "all that ever were of any great authority, knowledge, learning, or wisdom, since the beginning of the world unto this present, have given themselves to travel." [10] On the title-page Harvey recorded in Latin the fact that the book was a present from Edmund Spenser, secretary of the bishop of Rochester, 1578, a chance entry destined to give this undistinguished little volume a high significance, for only through this statement, noted by the late Sir Israel Gollancz in 1907, was Spenser's important relationship to Bishop Young established.

How long Spenser remained as Young's secretary we do not know. But apparently the connection had been terminated by the summer of 1579, for Harvey's *Letter-Book* makes it clear that by that time Spenser had exchanged the quiet of Bromley for the stir and bustle of London, with its better opportunities for contact with the great and for the type of preferment toward which his ambitions were spurring him.[11]

[9] *Ibid.*
[10] *The Traueiler of Ierome Turler*, p. 87.
[11] Pp. 64, 68.

VIII

GIFTS AND GRACE FROM LEICESTER

BY MIDSUMMER of 1580 Spenser was to place the waters of the Irish Sea between himself and England, and to enter upon a new life in the wild, remote confines of Ireland. The year preceding his departure from England must always have seemed to him one of the most memorable of his life. The documents which give us a glimpse of this *annus mirabilis*, aside from *Mother Hubberds Tale*, which appears to belong in part to this time, are chiefly letters, written by Harvey and Spenser to each other. One of these seems unfortunately not to be a genuine missive, and even the others may have been altered for publication. Yet we may reasonably suppose that the biographical facts relating to Spenser in all these letters are, in the main, authentic.

To begin with, there is a letter from Harvey to Spenser preserved in Harvey's "paperbook," or private letter-book.[1] This letter reproaches Spenser bitterly for the unauthorized publication of a volume of Harvey's virelays. Harvey pictures his mortification when his little volume shall be hawked for fourpence at Bartholomew and Stourbridge Fairs, with the recommendation that it is the work of a university man and a great scholar. What scorn his Cambridge colleagues will visit upon him when they learn that he is its author! The thought that these "slender and extemporal" verses of his were given to the world by "his very unfriendly friend" fills him with horror. Spenser must send him a portion of his beard to hide the blushes of his beardless face. In other countries poetry in the vernacular is honored, but, alas, not in England. The tone is gay and bantering. One guesses that Harvey planned to connive in the publication of his virelays and contemplated circulating or printing this letter partly to disarm hostile criticism, partly to display his wit. The letter purports to have been written on "the 10 of this present, and as beautiful a sunny day as came this summer—1579," and from a cancellation in the manuscript we may date the letter more definitely as of July.[2] There seems no good reason to suppose that the volume of virelays was ever published.

[1] *Letter-Book*, pp. 58-68; evidence that any of the letters on pp. 70-88 were addressed to Spenser is lacking (Bennett, *MP* 29. 163-186).

[2] Harvey substituted "sunny" for "July" (*ibid.*, p. 172).

If dependence may be placed on this curious letter, Spenser, by July, 1579, was living the life of a gallant in London and confidently seeking advancement among the great. He is addressed by Harvey as a "young Italianate signor and French monsieur," and his mustache and beard call forth endless witty comment from his friend. Apparently he was frequenting the theatres with lively companions. In the previous Easter he had had, we learn, a long conversation at Westminster with Harvey on how best to advance one's fortunes in England, and he was evidently bent on such an end.

Who, we may ask, were Spenser's associates in this new career of his in London? Fortunately the published letters of Spenser and Harvey furnish a partial answer. Among those with whom Spenser had at least some contact were three men of prominence—the earl of Leicester, Elizabeth's great favorite; Philip Sidney, Leicester's nephew, to whom the earl was deeply attached; and Edward Dyer, eleven years Sidney's senior, and a devoted friend of the Sidneys.

No one in England had attained greater eminence than Robert Dudley, earl of Leicester. When about sixteen, he had been introduced to the Princess Elizabeth, and a friendship had begun that lasted as long as he lived. The comeliness of his tall person, his customary gorgeous attire, his love of pomp, perhaps even his arrogance, combined to enchant her; and as the years passed, the parsimonious queen lavished such wealth upon him that even his genius for extravagance could not undermine his fortune. In one year alone she gave him sixteen estates.[3] On her accession she seriously considered marrying him. Though she made him a member of her privy council and assigned him various posts of responsibility, she probably recognized his limitations, for she did not permit him to displace her wise Secretary Cecil. Sometimes her anger flared up against him, especially when women were involved, but her true affection for him always allayed her resentment quickly. Even if we discredit the many attacks of his enemies, who insisted, for example, that he was an artist in the use of poison, we must admit that he was selfish and unprincipled. Perhaps his manifest love of Sidney and his encouragement of literary men prove that his nature had its better side.

The period that now concerns us was probably one of the most painful of Leicester's life. In his youth he had married Amy Robsart, whose death ten years later caused many sinister rumors concerning him. In 1573, when he was about forty-one, he is said to have contracted a secret marriage,

[3] Sir Sidney Lee in *DNB*.

which he never acknowledged, with Lady Sheffield. Finally in 1577 [4] he married the countess of Essex, taking pains that news of his act should not reach the queen. In addition to the anxiety he must have felt lest Elizabeth learn of his marriage, he was maddened in 1579 by the extraordinary sight of two foreigners insinuating themselves into the queen's affections.

On January 5, 1579, Jehan de Simier, Alençon's master of the wardrobe, arrived in London,[5] to be followed in August by Alençon himself (now also duke of Anjou). Some years before, it will be recalled, there had been talk of Elizabeth's marrying this young man. In most respects a less appropriate suitor could hardly be imagined. He was twenty-two years her junior, short of stature, swarthy, and thickly pitted with smallpox. Early in the negotiations, Elizabeth had written to Walsingham, her ambassador in France, that if she wedded the duke, she felt Calais should be ceded to England to make her forget his pockmarks.[6] Another drawback, for Englishmen, was his Catholic faith. Yet, thanks to the political interests of England and France, discussion of the marriage had been revived from time to time during the intervening years, but never so seriously as at present. Simier, an adept in the arts and graces of lovemaking, in which the French court was pre-eminent, so charmed Elizabeth that people thought he must have used magic. She dubbed him her "monkey," and made him her constant companion. Burghley, who took the projected marriage very seriously, gave lengthy consideration to its advantages and disadvantages. Feeling in London for the most part was strongly against it, and an effort was actually made to assassinate Simier, probably at the instigation of Hatton and Leicester. Simier, outraged at the attempt upon his life, took prompt vengeance upon Leicester by telling Elizabeth of the earl's recent marriage, with the inevitable result that Leicester had to remove himself from Elizabeth's sight.

So successful was Simier in preparing the queen for the coming of his master that, upon Alençon's arrival on August 16, she at once fell (or seemed to fall) deeply in love with her youthful suitor, and there was widespread belief that she really would at last take a husband. She promptly named him her "frog," and spent hours with him every day. Leicester, back again at court, was filled with jealousy over Elizabeth's infatuation. On August 27 affairs at home caused Alençon's departure, and a final decision as to the marriage remained in abeyance for some

[4] Wallace, *The Life of Sir Philip Sidney*, p. 197.

[5] Hume, *The Courtships of Queen Elizabeth*, pp. 199 ff.

[6] *Ibid.*, p. 159.

months. There was endless deliberation, the privy council debating the matter constantly from the 2nd to the 8th of October. The council on the whole inclined to disapprove. As for Englishmen generally, there could be no doubt of their strong opposition. Elizabeth was apparently eager to make Alençon her husband, but hesitated to outrage public opinion. Simier left on November 24. By January, 1580, Elizabeth's enthusiasm for the marriage had cooled, and though negotiations continued, the situation assumed a far less critical aspect. Leicester must have breathed more easily.

Philip Sidney was no less opposed than Leicester to the French marriage, but where Leicester's sentiments were motivated largely by self-interest, Sidney's were occasioned by his unselfish desire for the welfare of England and his devotion to the cause of European Protestantism. For him, as for Leicester, apprehension in regard to Elizabeth's marriage must have been constant during this period.

As Sidney had been born on November 30, 1554, he was probably some two years Spenser's junior, but the fact that he was not only Sir Henry's oldest son but also generally regarded as heir to the great fortunes of his two uncles, Leicester and Warwick, and that he had traveled widely, would have caused Spenser to look up to him even if Sidney had not been blessed with a character that won universal admiration. When Spenser referred to him as the pattern of "noblesse and of cheualree," and declared of him

> That all mens hearts with secret rauishment
> He stole away, and weetingly beguyld,[7]

he was speaking the literal truth. Men admired Sidney's high-mindedness, his courage, his gentlemanly accomplishments, such as his skill at tilting; but, more than that, they loved him. Although personal magnetism is not easily explained, Professor Wallace thinks that Sidney's instinctive and constant kindness accounts in large part for the extraordinary affection men felt for him.[8]

In the summer of 1575 Sidney had returned from three years of Continental travel. Since that time he had been much at court and had hoped for an opportunity to serve his country in some useful capacity, but with little success, though Elizabeth did send him on a mission of no great importance to the Emperor Rudolf at Prague. During these years he developed a strong interest in Ireland, where his father was lord deputy, and in the Netherlands, scene of Protestantism's most crucial struggle; and

[7] *Astrophel* 21-22.

[8] Pp. 287-288.

his imagination was so captivated by the possibilities of the New World that he found means, in spite of his slender income, to invest in all three of Frobisher's voyages. As yet he was known, not as an author, but as a patron to men of learning. Service to the state was his consuming ambition; authorship, an occupation for his idle hours—even his noble *Defense of Poesy*, he called " this ink-wasting toy of mine."

While the French marriage was being negotiated, in 1579, there occurred an event that Greville has made famous.[9] The young earl of Oxford quarreled with Sidney on a royal tennis court and ended by ordering him from the court and twice calling him a puppy. Sidney's irritation could hardly have been lessened by the fact that members of the French commission, friends of Oxford, were interested spectators from neighboring galleries. Before leaving the tennis court, Sidney gave the earl the lie, and the efforts of Elizabeth herself were required to bring peace. His opposition to the French marriage was so great that, soon after his quarrel with Oxford, he sent his famous letter of expostulation to the queen. Perhaps because of its directness and obvious sincerity, she was less affronted than might have been expected. After delivering this blast, Sidney retired to Wilton, the home of his sister, the countess of Pembroke, where he occupied himself with his *Arcadia*, but he was sometimes in London, staying as usual at Leicester House.

Closely bound in friendship to both Leicester[10] and Sidney was Edward Dyer, who is remembered today chiefly for his oft-quoted lyric " My mind to me a kingdom is." He was a wise, upright man, who won the deep regard of some of the finest spirits of the age. Harvey contemplated dedicating his virelays

> To the right worshipful gentleman
> And famous courtier
> Master Edward Dyer,
> In a manner our only English poet.
> In honour of his rare qualities
> And noble virtues.[11]

The warmth of Sidney's attachment to Dyer is indicated by the fact that Sidney bequeathed his books to Greville, the closest of all his friends, and to Dyer, and that Dyer, like Greville, was one of the four gentlemen chosen to hold the corners of Sidney's funeral pall. Dyer's imagination,

[9] *Life of Sir Philip Sidney*, pp. 63-69.
[10] Sargent, *At the Court of Queen Elizabeth*, p. 18.
[11] *Letter-Book*, p. 89.

like Sidney's, was fired by Frobisher's voyages, and he shared Sidney's hopes that England might maintain a strong foreign policy and aid the cause of European Protestantism, especially in the Netherlands. Also, like Sidney, he hoped in vain for a prominent post in the government, and struggled throughout his life against the debts that hung like millstones about the necks of so many who associated themselves with the glittering, costly life of the court.[12]

How Spenser formed his connection with these three courtiers is unknown. But so intimately were the three associated with one another that Spenser's contact with one would lead naturally to acquaintance with the other two. Sidney is thought to have studied briefly at Cambridge while Spenser was there, and might then have made the acquaintance of both Spenser and Harvey,[13] or a connection that Harvey had with Leicester as early as 1576—in 1578 Harvey expected to visit France and Italy on a mission for Leicester—may have opened for Spenser a pathway to the great lord.[14] Moreover, we should not forget that all three courtiers favored aspiring writers, so that some of Spenser's unpublished verse might have aroused their interest in him.

Still another courtier with whom we know Spenser had some association at this time was Daniel Rogers, son of that John Rogers who had had the distinction of being the first martyr during Mary's reign. Daniel Rogers' knowledge of languages enabled him to serve the English government in various useful ways abroad, and he had lately returned from some years of diplomatic service in the Netherlands and in Germany. He was an ardent Protestant and a trusted and devoted friend of Sidney's and Languet's. Harvey also regarded him as a good friend and once expressed a willingness that Spenser, if he especially desired, might share one of Harvey's letters with him.[15]

However the connection was formed, there can be no doubt that Spenser for a time served Leicester and was on a friendly footing with Sidney, Dyer, and Rogers, frequented Leicester House, and had the entrée of the court. This sudden rise in his fortunes is revealed by scattered sentences in the five Spenser-Harvey letters that were issued in a small volume in 1580.[16] Two of the five letters are by Spenser. They seem like the more or less casual products of a genuine correspondence, but Harvey's three

[12] Sargent, p. 89; for their common aspirations, see *ibid.*, pp. 41, 43, 46-47, 53.

[13] Wallace, p. 107.

[14] Smith in Harvey, *Marginalia*, pp. 18, 21; Harvey, *Works* 1. xxxvi.

[15] *DNB*; Sidney, *The Correspondence of Philip Sidney and Hubert Languet*, pp. 146, 164, 208; Harvey, *Works* 1. 107.

[16] *Ibid.*, pp. 3-107.

letters, especially two of them, are in the main extensive essays on the scientific aspects of a lately experienced earthquake and on "English versifying"; that is, composing verse in accordance with Latin quantitative principles. Any one who has dipped into the scribbled pages of Harvey's "paperbook," which reveal all too clearly the disingenuous schemes simmering in the brain of the ambitious scholar, will be inclined to believe Nashe's statement that Harvey published the letters without Spenser's knowledge,[17] or at any rate that the initiative was Harvey's. Question though we may the taste of the project, we must value highly the precious biographical information thus preserved.

The letters are in two groups, with separate title-pages. The second group, "more lately delivered unto the printer," contains the earlier letters, one by Spenser, written partly at Westminster, where he seems to have resided, and partly at Mistress Kerke's, on October 15 and 16, and including what is really another letter written on October 5 from Leicester House, but, owing to some one's negligence, not sent at the time; and one by Harvey from Cambridge, dated October 23, 1579. That part of Spenser's letter which should have been dispatched on October 5 is wholly concerned with a journey to France that Spenser hopes, fears, thinks he will make "the next week," if "my lord" (evidently Leicester) can send him. He will employ his time, his body, and his mind in Leicester's service, and will be "maintained mostwhat of him." Spenser is pleasantly excited over the thought of the journey and is extremely busy. Sidney has asked him to correspond, and he hopes Harvey will write, always sending his letters by Mistress Kerke. A part of this communication is a long Latin poem. In this he reveals why he fears as well as hopes to be sent abroad. He is in love, head over ears in love, and he does not fancy parting from his beloved. Many lines of the poem are devoted to Harvey's immoderate ambition, at which he pokes good-humored fun. Harvey, he is well aware, would never permit love to bar the way to fame and glory, but may it not be that too austere an avoidance of folly is the counsel of folly? An intermediate course is best. Spenser concludes with a wittily exaggerated picture of himself wearily ascending the Alps and even visiting the Pyrenees, the Caucasus, and Babylon.

But something must have interfered with the proposed trip, for that part of the letter written ten days later contains no mention of it. The plan previously made by Leicester for Spenser's journey may have been altered as a result of the deliberations over Elizabeth's marriage, which were then completely absorbing the attention of the privy council.[18] The

[17] Nashe, *Works* 1. 296; 3. 127.

[18] Hewlett, *PMLA* 42. 1061.

portion of the letter written on the 15th and 16th is mainly concerned with Spenser's anxiety over the publication and dedication of some of his works. He has succeeded in winning the favorable attention of men prominent at court and evidently hopes for handsome preferment from them, but the situation is critical, and he dreads taking a false step that will spoil everything. He is most eager for Harvey's counsel, and will, on his part, by every possible means, seek to advance his friend's interest at court. Spenser's problems are these. Shall he intermit the " uttering " of his works, lest by cloying " their noble ears " he win contempt or seem to be bent merely on gaining further benefits? The next sentence shows that he is really thinking of *The Shepheardes Calender* and Leicester. If he dedicate a certain work to " his excellent lordship," will the fact that it is made in honor of an unknown private person (obviously Rosalind), whose true worth some may not recognize as Spenser and Harvey do, or that its contents are not weighty enough, make its dedication to Leicester unfitting? Before concluding his letter, he alludes again to this topic. *The School of Abuse*, dedicated lately to Sidney, has been scorned, " if at least it be in the goodness of that nature to scorn." Dedicating books is ticklish business. Spenser fears, if he dedicate *My Slumber* and other pamphlets to Sidney, he may fare no better. " I meant them," he adds, " rather to Master Dyer."

Sidney and Dyer, the letter informs us, have him " in some use of familiarity," and Harvey may imagine what kindly remarks are made about him by the two gentlemen and by Spenser. Just now the reformation of English verse has become the hobby of his two court friends; indeed, they have proclaimed in their Areopagus " a general surceasing and silence of bald rhymers "—a humorous bit of figurative language that need not be construed to imply that the tribunal consisted of more than the two eager experimenters in the application of classical prosody to English verse. Spenser, who has been drawn to their faction, sends Harvey some verses of his own in the new style; and he promises to show some of Harvey's, which have just arrived by the carrier, to Sidney and Dyer on his next going to the court, for Harvey has long been a convert to the humanistic belief that classical quantitative principles might be adapted to English verse.[19]

Here and there the letter touches upon human relationships, experiences,

[19] Cf. G. Gregory Smith in *Elizabethan Critical Essays* 1. xlvi-lv. Spenser's association with Sidney in London may account for the *sestina*—Spenser's sole experiment in the form—tacked on to " August " of the *Calender* (Harrison, *PMLA* 45. 717).

and actions with tantalizing incompleteness. For instance, this cryptic sentence may imply either that Spenser has or that he has not had an interview with the queen: "Your desire to hear of my late being with her majesty must die in itself." And who is the Mistress Kerke at whose home he dispatches, receives, and writes letters? Is she a relative of the E. K. whose greetings Spenser in this letter conveys to Harvey, and who, according to Spenser, is composing "painful and dutiful verses" on Harvey?[20] And should we identify this E. K. with the editor of the *Calender*, and again with Edward Kirke of Pembroke Hall? And what should we make of the following remark apropos of the *Calender*? "The self former title still liketh me well enough, and your fine addition no less."[21] Have we here a hint of Harvey's cooperation in its editing?

Harvey's reply on October 23 to Spenser's communication of the 5th and 16th must have been slightly disappointing to Spenser. Harvey adopts a tone of good-natured banter, and refuses to believe that Spenser's affairs are in an extremely critical state. He is willing to wager that Spenser won't go abroad for several weeks. Spenser's English "Trimetra" he likes better than Spenser will perhaps easily believe, and yet he points out several metrical flaws. Spenser's eye must have lingered over that portion of the letter where Harvey, lapsing into the Latin that the friends found suitable for their more intimate confidences—an epistolary lowering of the voice—replies to Spenser's admission of love. Assuming a tone of half-serious raillery, he says: "Listen to me, my good wooer, great lover of the ladies, Pamphilus extraordinary, regard the end which awaits you, and all lovers, and the whole sect of women-worshippers. . . . Love is bitterness. . . . " And he concludes in English: "Credit me, I will never lin baiting at you till I have rid you quite of this younkerly and womanly humor."

But this chilling blast apparently had no effect, for there now seems little question that Spenser had married before he left with Lord Grey for Ireland. Odd indeed would it have been for an Elizabethan of Spenser's temperament to postpone marriage till the age of forty, and yet not till 1931 did Mr. Douglas Hamer demonstrate to the satisfaction of most that Spenser was married at about this time.[22] Sylvanus, Spenser's son, he pointed out, could not have conducted certain lawsuits till he was of

[20] Cf. Hamer, *NQ* 180. 223.

[21] Cf. Welply, *ibid.*, p. 458.

[22] *RES* 7. 271-286; cf. also Welply, *NQ* 180. 438. The argument for Spenser's earlier marriage based on *Daphnaïda* 64-67 seems questionable since the "like wofulnesse" of Spenser is not widowerhood but a sense of "this worlds vainnesse and lifes wretchedness" (34).

age, and hence must have been born not later than 1582. Moreover, Harvey, who on October 23 had expostulated so bitterly with Spenser for becoming involved in love, was sending friendly messages on April 23, 1580, to "Mistress Immerito" and "my most charming Lady Colin Clout."

Close on the heels of Mr. Hamer's argument came a letter to the London *Times* from Professor Mark Eccles, in which he called attention to a parish register entry concerning the marriage of "Edmounde Spenser to Machabyas [that is, Maccabaeus] Chylde" at St. Margaret's, Westminster, on October 27, 1579.[23] Her extraordinary name, he suspects, may be laid to a custom whereby the name for a child was sometimes chosen by opening the Bible at random. Machabyas had been christened at Westminster on September 8, 1560, so that she was evidently about twenty years old. In his Latin poem that should have gone to Harvey on October 5, 1579, Spenser had remarked that the truly wise man does not postpone marriage too long, and it may well be that he was contemplating this important step at the very moment Leicester proposed the foreign journey. If we are to believe that the Spenser who was married at St. Margaret's on October 27 was the poet, we may conjecture that Spenser felt free to proceed with his marriage after the journey abroad had been given up; unfortunately for the literary historian, there were several Edmund Spensers in England at this time,[24] so that we cannot be certain that it was the young Machabyas Chylde who became the charming Lady Colin Clout of Harvey's letter.

On December 5, *The Shepheardes Calender* was entered on the Stationers' Register by the printer Hugh Singleton, who but a month before had narrowly escaped having a hand chopped off for printing John Stubbe's notorious attack upon the French marriage.[25] The *Calender* must have been published between December 5 and March 24, since the title-page is dated 1579. Spenser would have been less than human if he had escaped agitation on taking this first irretraceable step in the realm of authorship. In his day a gentleman was chary of printing; witness, for example, Sidney's and Dyer's failure to publish their works, and Harvey's plan to tax Spenser with the issuing of his virelays. Moreover, Spenser knew only too well that his book contained dangerous matter. The conventional references in his address "To His Booke" to envy's barking and to Sidney's protecting wing were not idle words. Anonymous though the

[23] *TLS*, December 31, 1931, p. 1053.
[24] Hamer, *NQ* 180. 184.
[25] Byrom, *The Library* 14. 144.

publication was, he must have been aware that the authorities could, if they wished, easily discover the identity of "the new poet." He doubtless relied on the praise of his queen and on his friendship with great courtiers to save him from unpleasant complications. Hopefully he thus ends his address "To His Booke":

> And when thou art past ieopardee,
> Come tell me, what was sayd of mee:
> And I will send more after thee.

Finally, the thought of immortality through verse, so precious to the Renaissance mind, fortified his spirit:

> Loe I haue made a Calender for euery yeare,
> That steele in strength, and time in durance shall outweare. . . .

This concluding assertion was well justified. The *Calender* today is regarded as ushering in the great era of Elizabethan poetry. In its own day, if not greeted with the enthusiasm accorded to such rare best-sellers as Lyly's *Euphues*, it was very well received, for new editions appeared in 1581, 1586, 1591, and 1597. The most famous contemporary comment is that of Sidney, who, in his *Defense of Poesy*, named Chaucer, Surrey, Sackville, and the author of the *Calender* as the only English poets he could think of who had "poetical sinews in them." [26]

We turn now to the later group of Spenser-Harvey letters, which constituted, however, the first part of the little volume. The Preface, allegedly by a friend of the two young men, warns the reader not to judge of quality by quantity—sometimes a hare hides in a little field. The first letter—by Spenser—he considers good and sensible, but the other two—by Harvey—he has never seen surpassed among English letters. If Harvey was, as we guess, the author of this Preface, we must conclude that, having once chosen the role of duplicity, he decided to play the part wholeheartedly.

The first letter is dated "Quarto Nonas Aprilis" (April 2), "Nonas" being perhaps a slip for "Idus" (April 10), since Spenser's mention of an earthquake that occurred on April 6 makes the earlier date impossible.[27] Five months and a half have elapsed since Harvey's letter of October 23. Spenser does not now show the agitation over his prospects revealed by his previous letter, though he says nothing that indicates any change of relationship with his great courtier friends. "Little news is here stirred," he writes, "but that old great matter [presumably the French marriage] still depending. His honour [Leicester] never better." That Spenser still

[26] P. 47.

[27] Child in his ed. of Spenser 1. xvi.

feels his former great caution about dedicating anything to Leicester is suggested by this sentence: " Of my *Stemmata Dudleiana*, and especially of the sundry apostrophes therein, addressed you know to whom, must more advisement be had than so lightly to send them abroad. . . . " Sidney and Dyer are both mentioned in such a way as to show that his friendly intercourse with them continues. Nowhere is there any note of disappointment or disillusionment; on the contrary, the letter is vibrant with enthusiasm over various literary plans. Thus, after discussing " English versifying " at length, he speaks of hoping soon to issue a book in quantitative meter entitled *Epithalamion Thamesis.* In his brief allusion to this work, we have an early hint of his lifelong delight in rivers and streams. His *Dreames* and *Dying Pellicane* are finished and about to be printed. The former, with its gloss, in the manner of a paraphrase, in which are " some things excellently, and many things wittily discoursed of E. K.," will make a book as large as the *Calender*; and illustrations such as would suit Michelangelo have been provided. Of particular interest is the first mention of Spenser's masterpiece—a portion of *The Faerie Queene* has been sent to Harvey, and his criticisms are eagerly awaited. The letter contains two especially intimate passages. The first of these pictures Spenser translating verses *ex tempore* in bed for Harvey as the two friends lodge together in Westminster. The other, in Latin, says that Spenser's sweetheart wonders why Harvey has failed to answer her letter, and adds, in whimsical vein, that his continued failure to reply may prove fatal to both men.

The first of Harvey's two letters is dated April 7. Three quarters of the letter, or some 26 pages as printed by Grosart in *The Works of Gabriel Harvey*, is devoted to the earthquake of April 6 and to earthquakes in general, and furnishes Harvey a good opportunity to parade his learning. A few interesting personal remarks occur. At the beginning, Harvey sends greetings to Spenser and his sweetheart. The latter part of the letter, to which reference has been made in an earlier chapter, deals chiefly with highly spiced Cambridge gossip. It also includes references to several of Spenser's works: his *Dying Pellicane* and his *Dreames*, his nine English comedies and his Latin *Stemmata Dudleiana.* Harvey mentions some of his own literary ventures, which are still far from complete. A postscript warns Spenser that the letter may be shown only " to the two odd gentlemen you wot of," and adds: " Marry, I would have those two to see it, as soon as you may conveniently." Indeed the erudition and wit of this letter were possibly designed less for Spenser than for Sidney and Dyer.

The remaining letter, dated April 23, is a reply to Spenser's letter. Much of it is devoted to the subject of "English versifying" and to presenting specimens of verse composition, but there are passages of rare biographic interest. Several highly flattering references to Sidney and Dyer—for instance, as "the two very diamonds of her majesty's court"—and permission in a postscript to communicate this letter to "the two gentlemen," indicate not merely that Harvey continues to hope for their favor, but also that Spenser is still in close touch with them. Again Spenser's works are referred to. Jocularly Harvey mentions a "certain famous book, called the new *Shepheardes Calender*." He likes the delicate invention of Spenser's *Dreames*, and hopes they may have a place in England comparable to Petrarch's *Visions* in Italy, but he is apparently disappointed in *The Faerie Queene*. He feels sure that Spenser's *Nine Comoedies*, called, in imitation of Herodotus, the *Nine Muses*, more nearly approach Ariosto's comedies than does *The Faerie Queene* the *Orlando Furioso*, which Spenser in a recent letter had said he hoped to surpass. Of great significance are certain remarks which reveal Harvey's fear that Spenser's poetic efforts are not leading to any pecuniary profit. Turning ironical, Harvey remarks that Spenser is not everybody, and perhaps he may live by *Dying Pellicanes* and purchase great lands and lordships with the money from his *Calender* and *Dreames*. As for Harvey, he is going to turn his back on trifling love poetry and work at the law. So, he says, Cuddie argues in the tenth eclogue of the *Calender*. Evidently Harvey, from the first perhaps a little skeptical, is beginning to fear that Spenser's connections with the great may lead to nothing. Yet a reference to the "goodly Kentish garden" of Spenser's "old lord" (the bishop of Rochester) seems tacit assumption of a continued relationship with the new lord, Leicester. Both Rosalind and Spenser's new sweetheart are mentioned. Gentle Mistress Rosalind, says Harvey, once reported Spenser to have "all the intelligences" at commandment, and another time christened him her Signor Pegaso. Harvey will reply to the letter of Spenser's sweetheart as soon as he can, and meanwhile sends as many greetings as she has hairs on her little head. Through Spenser's love, she is another dear little Rosalind, but the same Hobbinol, with Spenser's permission, loves her deeply. Then he bids her farewell with those deeply significant words of address to which reference has already been made: "O mea Domina Immerito, mea bellissima Collina Clouta."

This last letter appears to reveal in Spenser a young man still in contact with his courtier friends, full of ambition, industriously occupied with many literary projects, deeply in love, but, at least in Harvey's judgment, in danger of missing material rewards for his efforts.

Spenser's allusions to Leicester, Sidney, and Dyer in his letters to Harvey, though guarded, permit us to infer something of his relation to these men. Toward Leicester his dominant feeling seems to have been awe; toward Sidney and Dyer, gratitude for their friendliness, and toward Sidney also admiration for his gentleness and goodness. In Spenser's poetry we may read still more clearly his opinion of Leicester and Sidney. In *The Ruines of Time*, composed after both men were dead, each stands forth cameo-like, and in sharp contrast to the other. It is Leicester's greatness that is stressed, his pre-eminence among the powerful, his closeness to Elizabeth. Naturally the patronage of so great and rich a man was prized. Spenser calls himself " his Colin " and speaks of the benefits received from him, a thought that he was to echo some years later in *Prothalamion*:

> Next whereunto there standes a stately place,
> Where oft I gayned giftes and goodly grace
> Of that great Lord, which therein wont to dwell,
> Whose want too well now feeles my freendles case. . . .

Along with Leicester's unparalleled eminence, Spenser portrays the utter and sudden collapse of his reputation at death. Scarcely is one found to close his eyes, and no one to sing his praises. The first of the two series of visions with which the poem ends, illustrating as it does the vanity of earthly greatness, sharply emphasizes what has been said of Leicester; and we are left with the strong impression that Elizabeth's great favorite could dazzle, yet was incapable of winning a secure place in men's affections.

With Sidney just the reverse was true. It is his radiant, lovable spirit, his valor as a soldier, his gifts as a poet that are emphasized. His death is described as a natural return to his own country, yet too early a departure " for all that did his loue embrace," and the second group of visions, of which he is clearly the subject, all typify his flight to heaven.

This year or more of close contact with Leicester's circle could hardly have failed to affect Spenser's views. His distrust of Burghley, his interest in exploration and colonization, and his eagerness that England should play a positive, efficient role in the support of European Protestantism, if they did not originate in his association with these men, must surely have been fostered by it. And it seems incredible that his desire for political preferment should not have been stimulated and directed by the similar ambitions of Sidney, Dyer, and Rogers. To Leicester's circle throughout this period the one topic of painful and engrossing interest was, of course, the French marriage. In these men, Spenser must frequently have encountered taut nerves and a state of unnatural excitement. Doubtless he entered heartily into their apprehensions, and it would have been strange indeed if the dramatic arrival of the Frenchman had left no traces in his writings. Possibly his whole career would have been different if he could have associated with Leicester and his friends under more normal conditions.

But fortunately for Spenser's state of mind, his creative impulse was strong at this time, and his literary interests, as his letters reveal, were absorbing much of his thought and energies. Of all the unpublished works mentioned in the letters, oddly enough, only *The Faerie Queene* later appeared under the title named. The most puzzling of the works alluded to are his nine comedies, which Harvey compares to those of Ariosto. Because Spenser's genius seems essentially undramatic, except as regards masque or pageant, it is hard to conceive of his having produced nine comedies at all comparable to the Plautus and Terence-like comedies of Ariosto. Yet, stimulated by the consciousness of his rapidly maturing powers, he may have experimented with more varied literary types than we suspect. Some of his works were perhaps merely tentative drafts, and others may have failed of publication at this time because of the sudden alteration in the course of his life caused by his departure for Ireland.

Among the productions mentioned in the letters, we look vainly for any allusion to *Prosopopoia: or Mother Hubberds Tale*, and yet it was completed, in all likelihood, during the period that now concerns us. Though not printed till 1591, it was, Spenser tells us, composed long before in the raw conceit of his youth. This racy beast fable is his one formal satire. The earlier part of it, in which his protagonists, a fox and an ape, play the part of laborers and then of churchmen, was probably written in the *Calender* period, for the treatment of ecclesiastical abuses sounds very like that in the *Calender*. The remainder, in which he takes his two beasts to court, gives us presumably his reaction to much that he was observing at Elizabeth's court—its frivolity, cynicism toward love, disdain of scholars and of the clergy, and greed. His first impression of the court seems to have persisted. In later works he often alludes to its vanity and falseness. Nor was his view distorted. "Elizabeth's court," writes Professor Edward P. Cheyney, "was not characterized by high-mindedness or appreciation of the more delicate sentiments of life, and if actual violence and disorder were repressed, and if there was less open immorality than in some of the other courts of Europe, it was nevertheless filled with petty jealousies, conflicts and intrigues." [28]

[28] *A History of England From the Defeat of the Armada to the Death of Elizabeth* 1. 50.

But Spenser was too honest to pretend that it contained only such villains as Reynold and the ape. If not in Leicester, at least in Sidney and Dyer and Rogers he had before his eyes men who were courtiers and yet gracious and good. And so our satirist interrupts his tirade to usher in "the brave courtier." Castiglione back in the earlier years of the century had roused men's concern for manners with his portrait of the versatile, high-minded gentleman, and Spenser was fortunate to be personally acquainted with at least one man who must have seemed a living embodiment of the best that such writers as Castiglione, della Casa, and Guazzo had been able to depict.

The final episode of the poem, in which the two scoundrels, after being banished, steal the crown, scepter, and hide of the sleeping lion, and return, the ape as king, the fox as his crafty prime minister, is somewhat different in spirit, as if written after an interval. Only animals people this second court, including a strange bodyguard of foreign beasts

> Bred of two kindes, as Griffons, Minotaures,
> Crocodiles, Dragons, Beauers, and Centaures,

which support the tyrannical ape. The fox and the ape, formerly types, now suggest individuals. Reynold is easily identified with Burghley. If the whole poem—barring minor revisions—was written, as seems likely, "in the raw conceit" of Spenser's youth, then the ape of this final adventure can be none other than Alençon, or a fusion of Alençon and Simier, and the foreign beasts are his French companions, presently to be transformed into hybrid creatures, neither French nor English.[29] In a word, we have here a prophecy of what will happen if the suit of Alençon succeeds. The Braggadocchio-Trompart-Belphoebe episode in *The Faerie Queene*, if its usual interpretation is correct, indicates how deeply the thought of Alençon's marrying Elizabeth offended Spenser. Furthermore, Spenser was always a warm-hearted partisan, full of loyalty to his friends and heedless of consequences. Strange would it be if the impending French marriage had not set his pen in motion. We may, then, suppose that he sent his knavish fox and ape back to court in order to express through them his feelings about Alençon and Burghley. Indeed, this brilliant little satire, a sort of appendix to the general satire that precedes, is, under the circumstances, just what we should expect from him. Since the only contempo-

[29] Greenlaw, *PMLA* 25. 548; Dr. Harold Stein and Professor Brice Harris, who believe that the final adventure was written in 1590, identify the ape, respectively, with James VI of Scotland and with Burghley's son Robert Cecil (*Studies in Spenser's Complaints*, pp. 92-95; *HLQ* 4. 191-203).

rary allusions to the poem, as Dr. Harold Stein has observed,[30] occur after its publication, the manuscript may not have passed beyond the small circle of Spenser's friends. The *Complaints* volume, in which it appeared in 1591, was " called in," that is, withdrawn from circulation by the authorities, but only after many copies had been sold. As we read today the trenchant attack on Burghley, we are filled with wonder, first at Spenser's temerity in publishing such a poem, and secondly at his having been visited with no severe penalties for so ruthless a handling of England's foremost statesman.

Did this poem, we may ask, have any bearing on Spenser's going to Ireland? The late Professor Greenlaw answered this question in the affirmative.[31] In a brilliant and influential study entitled " Spenser and the Earl of Leicester," he sought to demonstrate that Leicester, embarrassed by Spenser's well-meant but rash treatment of the Alençon suit, promptly shipped off his incautious young secretary to Ireland with Lord Grey. An essential link in Greenlaw's chain of reasoning is provided by the translation *Virgils Gnat* published by Spenser among his *Complaints*, in 1591, but " long since dedicated to the most noble and excellent lord, the earl of Leicester, late deceased." A dedicatory sonnet to his patron begins thus:

Wrong'd, yet not daring to expresse my paine,
To you (great Lord) the causer of my care,
In clowdie teares my case I thus complaine
Vnto your selfe, that onely priuie are . . . .

If any Oedipus guesses the riddle, continues Spenser, let him hold his peace. Yet evidently we are expected to view the poem as a personal allegory, for the sonnet concludes:

But what so by my selfe may not be showen,
May by this Gnatts complaint be easily knowen.

The gnat's complaint, of course, is that a shepherd whom he sought to warn of a threatening danger brushed the insect aside and killed him, thereby banishing him to the underworld as a reward for his altruistic endeavor. Greenlaw plays the part of Oedipus, and, in spite of Spenser's monition, divulges the answer. The gnat's warning of the shepherd, he maintains, represents Spenser's warning the earl of the misfortunes that will overtake him if Elizabeth wed Alençon, and the banishment of the gnat to the underworld depicts the banishment of Spenser to Ireland, almost as sorry a recompense as that of the poor gnat. Greenlaw seems to

[30] P. 79.

[31] *PMLA* 25. 554 ff.

have arrived at a reasonable solution of the riddle, and yet we should remember that not a few important pieces of the jigsaw puzzle of Spenser's life may have been lost. Indubitably Spenser made this poem an allegory of an overzealous but unappreciated act of his in behalf of his patron, but we should not be too positive that that act was the writing of *Mother Hubberds Tale*, which may have received no such manuscript publicity as Greenlaw supposes, may indeed never even have been seen by Leicester.

In view of all the circumstances, Spenser's going to Ireland in 1580 as Arthur Lord Grey's secretary seems natural, quite aside from any disruption of the good relations between Spenser and Leicester. By the spring of 1580, Harvey, we recall, believed that Spenser's court connections were leading him nowhere, and Spenser, because of his marriage, probably required money as never before. A post of responsibility in England he doubtless longed to secure; yet the almost futile efforts of even such prominent courtiers as Sidney and Dyer to hook and land anything satisfactory must have shown him how difficult were the waters in which he had elected to fish. Although Leicester is often assumed to have procured Spenser's appointment with Lord Grey, the Sidneys are more likely to have brought it about. Sir Henry Sidney, Philip's father, had spent much of his life in Ireland and had been its most successful governor. He had chosen to go to Ireland as a young man and had served there off and on during a period of twenty-two years. Though keenly aware of the tragic aspects of Irish life, he was willing, under certain conditions, to return as lord deputy in 1582, one condition being that his son Philip should accompany him and eventually succeed him as lord deputy. Evidently Sir Henry felt that service " in that unhappy country " was not without its compensations. Philip himself had some first-hand knowledge of Ireland; and one of his intimate friends, Lodowick Bryskett, who had accompanied him on his extensive European travels, had been in Dublin on government service for some years. Moreover, both Sir Henry and Philip were close friends of Lord Grey, deeply interested in his appointment, and anxious in every way to contribute to his success as governor. In a letter of September 17, 1580, to Lord Grey, Sir Henry Sidney lays great emphasis on the importance of employing honest, faithful men in his management of affairs, and names many on whom he himself had been able to rely.[32] It

[32] Grey, *A Commentary*, pp. 68-74. Dr. Friedland takes Spenser's sonnet to Lord Grey (see *infra*, p. 109) to indicate that Grey became Spenser's patron long before the appointment to this secretaryship (*Shakespeare Association Bulletin* 18. 45), but may not the words " Patrone of my Muses pupillage " be understood merely as " patron of the earlier years of Spenser's poetic career " (cf. *pupilage* in *NED*)?

seems extremely likely that Spenser was recommended to Grey by Sir Henry and Philip, and not less on Grey's account than on his own.

On June 29, Grey wrote to the earl of Sussex from London that he had been commanded to be ready to depart for Ireland in ten days.[33] Grey found the journey, when finally begun, disappointingly slow, for he was held by contrary winds at Beaumaris, on the island of Anglesey, for ten days. Then taking advantage of a very light wind, he crossed in two days and two nights, and arrived at Dublin on Friday morning, August 12.[34] With him, we suppose, went Spenser.[35]

[33] *Ibid.*, p. 67.
[34] *Ibid.*, p. 77.
[35] Ware, *De Scriptoribus Hiberniae*, p. 137.

IX

THE SAVAGE ISLAND

THOUGH ELIZABETHANS were wont to contrast the savagery of Ireland with the civility of their own land, they knew that there had been a time when no such contrast could have been made. Writes Spenser:

> Whylome, when *IRELAND* florished in fame
> Of wealths and goodnesse, far aboue the rest
> Of all that beare the *British* Islands name. . . .[1]

Spenser, of course, refers to the period of more than three hundred years that followed the conversion of the island by perhaps the most successful of all missionaries, St. Patrick. About the story of St. Patrick's life and missionary activity cluster many delightful legends, but it is no legend that for several hundred years after his death in 461 Ireland was the most lively center of Christian faith, of learning, and of the arts in northern Europe. During this time, her monasteries sheltered scholars from Britain and Gaul and Germany, and her missionaries, stirred by a mighty and persistent enthusiasm, moved out in ever widening circles to disseminate the gospel that they had so lately embraced.

The golden age of Ireland was brought to an end by the Norsemen, or Danes, as they were usually called. Toward the end of the eighth century, the slender prows of their strong, swift boats began to cut the Irish Sea. For centuries they came out of the north like flocks of rapacious birds. They built towns along the coast, from which they sallied forth to rob and burn the monasteries and waste the country. Different in blood from the Celtic Irish, they were less readily absorbed than in England, and long remained a distinct and hated race. Their presence, coupled with the tribal organization of the Irish, which precluded any unified national feeling, led to an almost constant state of confusion, turmoil, and petty warfare. Now and then the sunlight of better days glimmered through the dark clouds, as when Brian Boru made himself in 1003 king, in his own tribal way, of all Ireland, but such rifts in the clouds were few.

In 1169 came the mail-clad, castle-building Normans, with their concept of feudalism and their genius for organization. Now at last, one might imagine, Ireland would enjoy some peace and stability, without which

[1] *F. Q.* 7. 6. 38.

there could be little cultural growth. Great Anglo-Norman families acquired nominal possession of large areas; feudalism, in name at least, was established; and the English monarchs visited the country at intervals, in order to renew the fealty of chiefs and nobles. But the conquest was really never complete. The weakness, even unreality, of English rule became all too evident when the Scotch Edward Bruce, after being crowned king of Ireland at Dundalk in 1316, almost made himself, by means of fire and sword, king in fact. Though he was finally defeated by the English, faith in the efficacy of English rule declined, and in the course of time many great Norman families assumed Irish names and adopted the Irish mode of life. The English Pale grew ever narrower, and for a time Ireland seemed almost lost to the English crown.

Then appeared the Tudors. England, wearied by the fatuous and interminable Wars of the Roses, welcomed their vigorous, autocratic rule, which brought stability, prosperity, intellectual ferment. But to unhappy Ireland, Tudor rule was no such blessing. There Tudor policy varied from conciliation to stern repression. Henry VIII disestablished the Irish monasteries, which in that land were almost the sole custodians of learning. Edward VI introduced Protestantism officially among a people who had no understanding of it nor desire for it. Mary and Elizabeth founded English plantations, or settlements, with too little regard for the rights of those who then possessed the soil. For the first time in her history Ireland was being subjected to thoroughgoing conquest, but the process was so protracted, and conducted with so many changes in tempo, that the experience was peculiarly bitter. Such peace as Ireland enjoyed was largely the peace of exhaustion, not the tranquillity that fosters learning and the arts and political progress.

To this troubled country Spenser now came, and since he was destined to make it his home for the rest of his life, we shall be justified in pausing for a closer glance at both the land and its people.

Elizabethan writers compared the shape of Ireland to an egg, but its shores, chiseled, especially to the west, into many deep bays, are notably lacking in an egg-like smoothness. Its mountains, rising mainly about the coast, reach at their highest an elevation of 3,414 feet. Through its wide central plain move the tranquil waters of its largest river, the Shannon. The great bog of Allen, above which Spenser says the gnats were wont to rise at evening like a cloud,[2] extends across four southeastern counties. Then as now Ireland was an emerald isle, but its bogs and lakes were more

[2] *Ibid.* 2. 9. 16.

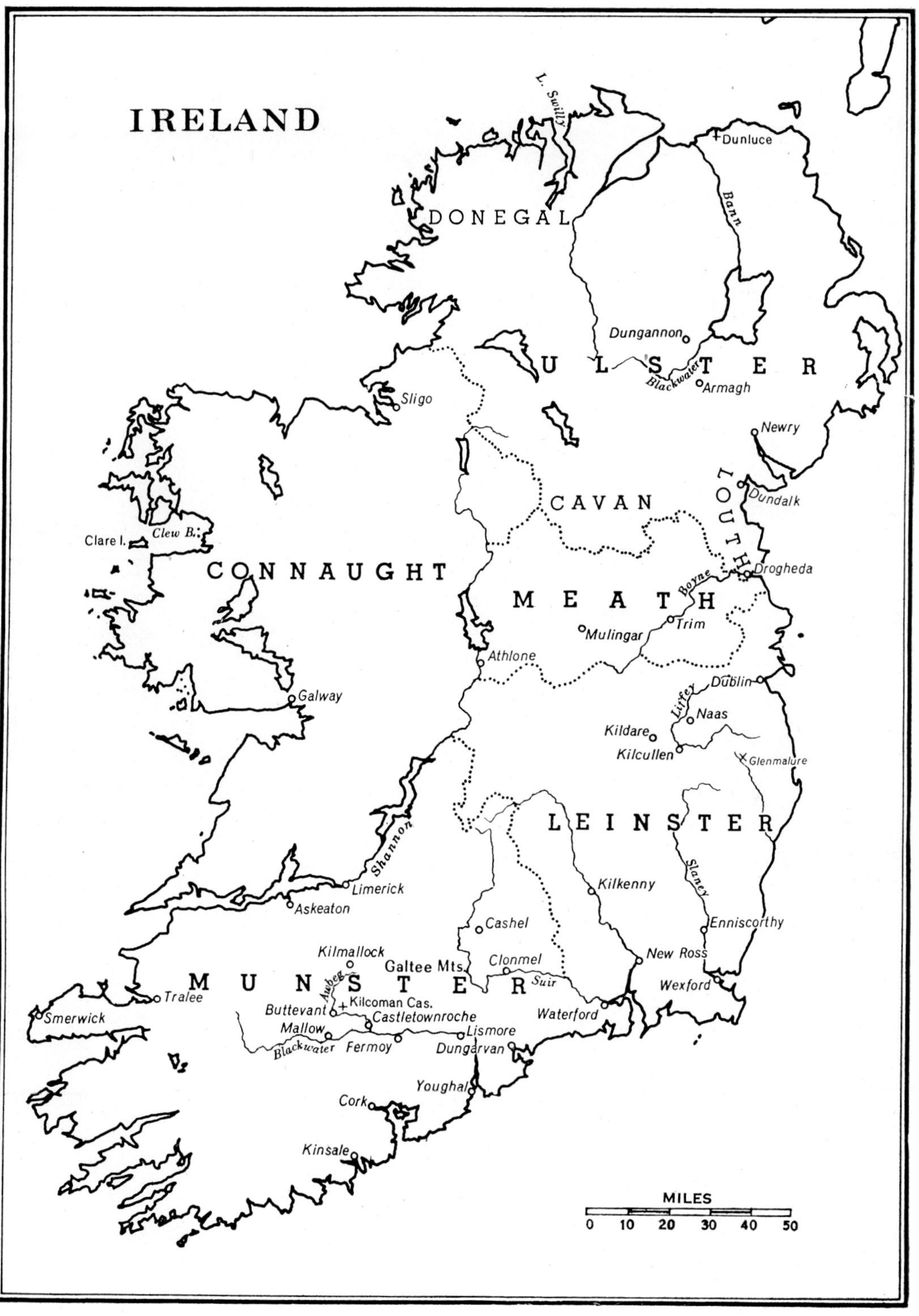
IRELAND
L. Swilly
Dunluce
Bann
DONEGAL
Dungannon
U L S T E R
Blackwater
Armagh
Sligo
Newry
CAVAN
LOUTH
Dundalk
Clew B.
Clare I.
CONNAUGHT
Drogheda
Boyne
MEATH
Trim
Mulingar
Athlone
Galway
Dublin
Liffey
Naas
Kildare
Kilcullen
Glenmalure
LEINSTER
Shannon
Slaney
Kilkenny
Limerick
Askeaton
Cashel
Enniscorthy
Kilmallock
Galtee Mts.
Clonmel
New Ross
MUNSTER
Awbeg
Suir
Wexford
Tralee
Smerwick
Buttevant
Kilcoman Cas.
Castletownroche
Waterford
Mallow
Fermoy
Lismore
Blackwater
Dungarvan
Youghal
Cork
Kinsale
MILES
0 10 20 30 40 50

extensive, and its woods, so scanty today, then covered large areas, and provided, within their dark recesses, a refuge for wolves and outlaws alike.

The political units of Ireland were much as they are now, except that from early times it had consisted of five instead of four main divisions, and that some of the counties, especially in Ulster, as yet existed only on the maps of the lord deputies. In addition to Ulster in the north, Connaught in the west, Munster in the south, and Leinster in the east, there was the small province of Meath. Wedged between Ulster and Leinster, it extended from the Shannon to the Irish Sea. It is now a part of Leinster.

In spite of mountains, fens, and forests, the natural productiveness of each of the great divisions of Ireland was recognized. Ulster was described by the traveler Fynes Moryson as "in some parts fertile, in other parts barren, but in all parts green and pleasant to behold, and exceedingly stored with cattle." Connaught he describes as "fruitful," but mentions its "many bogs and thick woods." Leinster, he says, "is fertile, and yields plenty of corn, and hath a most temperate, mild air."[3] Munster, in the words of Spenser, was normally "a most rich and plentiful country, full of corn and cattle." In *Pacata Hibernia* it is said to have been accounted "the key of the kingdom, both by reason of the cities and walled towns (which are more than in all the island besides), the fruitfulness of the country, being reputed the garden of Ireland, and the commodious harbours, lying open both to France and Spain."[4] Unfortunately, the Elizabethan wars, from which Ireland was suffering acutely when Spenser arrived, were gradually reducing the population and discouraging the cultivation of the soil.

Ireland was governed at this time by a lord deputy and council of state, resident at Dublin. Their duties were lightened by the fact that Connaught and Munster each had a lord president, or governor, and council of its own. During Grey's administration Munster was, however, temporarily without a president. Ulster was governed by Irish chieftains, who, when not in revolt, acknowledged the authority of the crown and were responsible to the lord deputy. A parliament, which was rarely summoned, met at Dublin.

Though we may speak of how Ireland was ruled, we must recognize that much of it was not greatly troubled by any sense of responsibility to the central government. Aside from the Pale, the towns, and certain districts mainly in the south and east, Ireland was still governed by her chiefs

[3] *An Itinerary* 4. 190, 189, 187.

[4] *View*, p. 135; *Pacata Hibernia* 1. 2.

and nobles, many of them nominally at least in cooperation with the English but actually doing very much as they pleased.[5] Rebellion on a large scale, moreover, broke out periodically, and all the resources of the government were required to put it down. Even in times of peace, large bodies of outlaws dwelt in the mountains and forests of such comparatively populous provinces as Munster and Leinster, subsisting largely on booty taken in their marauding expeditions. Smaller bands also infested the country, led sometimes by a dashing young man of family who had slipped heedlessly into such a life. To Spenser the situation resembled that in Saxon England, when the country was plagued by robbers and outlaws, every corner of the realm having its Robin Hood, who lived in the greenwood and preyed on travelers and country dwellers.[6] Many could have sympathized with John Derricke's wistful query as to why St. Patrick banished the serpents from Ireland but left the outlaws.[7]

To English eyes it must have seemed that man had done little to enhance the natural beauty and charm of Ireland. He had dotted the land with castles, to be sure, but had given more heed to their strength than to their beauty or comfort as residences. Some of these had been turned by the shock of war into ruins. Indeed, Ireland was already a land of ruins, for the monasteries and abbeys were falling into decay, and indifference to the established faith was such that most churches were either level with the ground or wretchedly thatched and repaired.[8] The custom of leasing land from year to year, instead of for longer terms, though approved by the landlord as well as by his restless tenant, encouraged few permanent improvements.[9] We cannot wonder that the tenant felt no interest in fertilizing the soil and planting garden and orchard if all might be abandoned shortly to another. The frequent wasting of the land by war was also a deterrent to improvements. The homes of the peasants were therefore hovels, the fields were largely unfenced, and the land yielded far less than it might have. Husbandry appealed less than cattle-raising, and the methods of some tillers of the soil were of the crudest. Barnabe Rich in his *New Description of Ireland* tells of farmers who were accustomed to attach the plow to a horse's tail, with the result that when the hair was worn short, the plow had to stand idle,[10] and in fact the practice had to be forbidden by law. Though horses, sheep, and hogs were raised, cattle

[5] O'Connor, *Elizabethan Ireland*, p. 150; Spenser, *View*, p. 8.
[6] *Ibid.*, pp. 131, 186-187. [7] *The Image of Irelande*, p. 43. [8] *View*, p. 210.
[9] *Ibid.*, p. 105; Dymmok, *A Treatice of Ireland*, p. 5; Plomer and Cross, *The Life and Correspondence of Lodowick Bryskett*, p. 38.
[10] "An Epistle" in praise of William Cokyne and p. 26.

absorbed the chief interest and constituted the main wealth of the country. During much of the year the herds were fed on mountains and waste lands far from human habitations, with the result that the incivility and wild love of liberty of the herdsmen were increased. Though accounts differ, their cattle were apparently smaller and less productive than those of the English. Moryson attributes their small size to the fact that they had to be penned up at night for fear of wolves and the ubiquitous cattle-thieves.[11] The roads were poor and unfenced, and the streams, being generally unbridged, were crossed at fords. There were no roadside or village inns.

In the towns English culture was able to maintain a much firmer footing than in the country, and during the Elizabethan wars the towns remained loyal to the crown. In all Ireland, there were, according to O'Connor, forty-three walled towns, most of them compactly built so as to be the more easily defended.[12] So largely did they manage their own affairs that they were virtually free cities. Of most consequence were the seaports. The principal city of Connaught was Galway, described by Campion as " a proper, neat city at the seaside," [13] but the province was administered from Athlone, far to the east, where, in a famous castle beside the Shannon, the governor resided. Limerick was the chief city of Munster. It was in reality two towns, each with its own walls, washed by the tidal waters of the Shannon. In 1589, Robert Payne told of visiting a grammar school in Limerick in which there were 160 scholars, " most of them speaking good and perfect English," because they were in the habit of translating Latin into English.[14] The president of Munster resided either at Limerick or at Cork. Cork, then consisting mostly of one long street, was a prosperous trading center, with a good harbor, but so surrounded by rebels that the citizens did not dare to marry their daughters into the country; and indeed there seems to have been nowhere much intermarriage, or even social intercourse, between town and country.[15] Waterford, with its excellent harbor, was a rich, populous city, second only to Dublin. Of inland towns, Kilkenny, on the River Nore, was the most important. It had reason to be proud of its gardens and orchards, and of its cathedral and castle, which rose on eminences at either end of the town. The castle was the principal Butler stronghold, residence of the earl of Ormonde, most powerful of Anglo-Irish nobles. In the country about Kilkenny was one of the most prosperous English settlements. In Galway, Limerick,

[11] *An Itinerary* 4. 193.

[12] P. 80.

[13] *A Historie of Ireland*, p. 2.

[14] *A Brief Description of Ireland*, p. 3.

[15] Camden, *Britain*, " Ireland," p. 78.

and Cork, best built of Irish cities, the houses were of stone, two stories high, and roofed with tile; in Dublin and Waterford, they were of timber, clay, and plaster.[16] Except in port towns, inns were lacking. Moryson, indeed, saw no public inns with signs hanging out, but says accommodations were available in private houses, including "featherbeds, soft and good, but most commonly lousy."[17] Though many of the townspeople must have been bilingual, there appears to have been a preference, except in Dublin, for the Irish speech.[18] In general we may think of the life that went on in the towns as not essentially very different from that in the provincial towns of England.

Dublin, of course, as the seat of government, surpassed all other Irish cities in importance. It was pleasantly situated on the river Liffey, with rolling hills to the south and level farming country to the west. Ancient Dublin Castle, official home of the lord deputy, had four massive towers and a gatehouse. Over the gate on poles were ranged the heads of notorious outlaws, hideous trophies of which the supply never ran low. According to Stanyhurst, writing in 1577, the castle had been "of late much beautified with sundry and gorgeous buildings."[19] In the pulpit of beautiful Christ Church Cathedral the most distinguished clergy preached their Protestant doctrines, in vain, to Irish ears. Outside the walls stood the more stately Cathedral of St. Patrick. In spite of a number of handsome buildings, if we may trust the opinion of Barnabe Rich, Dublin architecture, on the whole, deserved little praise, being "neither outwardly fair nor inwardly handsome." For him, the most notable feature of the city was the endless number of alehouses, for there was hardly a householder who could not find a corner of his house in which to set up a little bar.[20]

Dublin was the gateway to the English Pale, an area which varied in size at different times, but which, toward the close of Elizabeth's reign, extended through Leinster, Meath, and Louth.[21] Here, in general, English manners and customs prevailed, and in times of prosperity, the well-tilled fields and timbered houses must have suggested in some measure an English countryside. Many of its towns were walled or otherwise fortified, so that their gates could be closed at night against marauders, for the Pale

[16] Moryson, *An Itinerary* 3. 498.
[17] *Ibid.* 4. 198.
[18] Id. in Falkiner, *Illustrations of Irish History*, p. 262.
[19] Richard Stanyhurst in Holinshed, *Chronicles*, "Description of Ireland," p. 23.
[20] *A New Description of Ireland*, pp. 58, 70-72.
[21] Falkiner, p. 117.

was not free from outlaws and rebels. To most of the inhabitants, the depredations of the outlaws seemed no more injurious than the excessive taxation that the crown was in the habit of levying on the long-suffering inhabitants of the Pale.

The population of Elizabethan Ireland may be roughly divided into three groups. First there were the mere, or pure, Irish, the word " mere " conveying no suggestion of disparagement; secondly, the Anglo-Irish, or English-Irish, as Spenser called them, many of them descendants of the Anglo-Norman families who had settled in Ireland at the time of its conquest, but who, in the course of time, had intermarried with the Irish and become almost entirely Irish in manners and spirit; and, thirdly, the New English, consisting of adventurers, colonists, government officials, and others who had lately come to Ireland, and who, the English-Irish felt, were tending to dispossess them of their traditional rights and authority. The New English, in turn, heartily disliked the English-Irish, and believed that they furnished the most serious problem of the Irish government. Says Irenius in Spenser's *View of the Present State of Ireland*: " These do need a sharper reformation than the very Irish, for they are much more stubborn and disobedient to law and government than the Irish be, and more malicious against the English that daily are sent over." [22] The English were never reconciled to the assimilative powers of the Irish, which were continually ruining the English hopes of effectively leavening in time the Irish lump. Indeed it was a maxim that ten Englishmen would more readily turn Irish than one Irishman would turn English.

The antiquarians and travelers of Spenser's day have left us a number of brief descriptions of the Irish people. Broad generalizations regarding a whole nation are always dangerous, and especially so in the case of the Irish, among whom varying cultural levels and different modes of life prevailed. In general the writers on whom we must depend were thinking of the main body of the mere, or wild, Irish living outside the Pale and towns and beyond the influence of English garrisons and settlers. Almost all our authorities praise their strong, active, comely bodies. Even the lowest class, according to Payne, had a pure complexion and good physique.[23] Their loose living and their idleness are insisted upon. Those who could trace their descent from the head of a clan, and most of them by the aid of their bards could, scorned work, says Spenser, as fit only for churls; [24] and the soldiers were notorious for their idle, riotous lives. As for admirable traits, most accounts recognize their patient endurance of

[22] P. 195. [23] P. 4. [24] *View*, p. 187.

hardship, their bravery, their generosity, and their hospitality. Their simplicity of mind and their credulity also impressed the English. Camden lists many of their superstitions, of which the following is a sample: when they first saw the moon after its change, they commonly knelt and repeated the Lord's Prayer, addressing the moon with these words—" Leave us as whole and sound as thou hast found us." [25] Here evidently is a fusion of their ancient moon worship with Christianity.

Their diet, dress, and homes were generally of the simplest. They subsisted largely on milk, sour curds, and cheese, and on such herbs as shamrocks and watercresses, with sometimes a few oatcakes. Their favorite drink was ale or whisky. Feasts such as a nobleman and his tenants enjoyed are described by Stanyhurst. All sat about on straw pallets consuming flesh and whisky, and observing a respectful silence as the bard declaimed or the harper sang.[26] Two features of their dress seemed especially remarkable to the English—the wide, open sleeves hanging to the ground and the large, loose, warm mantle, which served a variety of uses. Also noteworthy was the glib, described by Spenser as "a thick curled bush of hair hanging down over their eyes." Camden says that the women were especially proud of their glibs if they were long and of golden color, and that they carefully curled them.[27] To Spenser both glib and mantle were devices of the devil, and he would have forbidden them by law; he describes many evil purposes served by each, as the ready disguise produced by pulling the glib over the eyes and the concealment of thefts under the mantle. Perhaps both seemed to him symbols of the Irish reluctance to adopt English ways. Their homes were constructed of clay or of boughs covered with turf. Tables and beds were lacking, and a great candle of reeds and butter set on the ground furnished light. At night they slept on the floor, covered with their mantles and perhaps warmed by a fire built in the center of the cabin.[28]

As with most Europeans who had reached the same evolutionary stage, war to the Irish—at least to a large element of the population—was a fascinating and glorious occupation. Their military forces consisted of horsemen, armed with spears; galloglasses, who were footmen carrying battle-axes; and kerns, or light-armed footmen, equipped with swords and bows. Already the musket was beginning to replace some of these more primitive weapons. Horseboys—actually men—cared for the horsemen's

[25] *Britain*, " Ireland," pp. 145-146.

[26] In Holinshed, *Chronicles*, " Description of Ireland," p. 45.

[27] Campion, p. 18; Spenser, *View*, pp. 65, 80; Camden, *Britain*, " Ireland," p. 145.

[28] Moryson, *An Itinerary* 4. 202.

mounts and did some fighting, and men bearing weapons and food attended the footsoldiers. English writers never tire of condemning the kerns and horseboys for their idleness, wastefulness, and cruelty. Spenser declares that the horseboys, brought up to knavery and villainy, are fit only for the halter, and that the welfare of Ireland demands that kerns, stokaghes (the kerns' assistants), and horseboys be driven to the plough.[29] Though hardy and courageous, the Irish were inferior to the English in arms and equipment, and so had to depend often on guerrilla warfare. Derricke, in his *Image of Irelande*, describes a lively engagement—the irregular battle formation of the Irish, their terrible battle-cry, their hurling of darts and brandishing of spears, the discharge of English bullets, the clash of swords, and then the retreat of the Irish, sounded by the bagpipe, and followed by a precipitous flight to bog and wood.[30] In the pacification of Ireland, many Irishmen served under the English; indeed, O'Grady thinks the Elizabethan conquest was really effected by the use of these seasoned and capable soldiers.[31]

In addition to the soldiers, Irish society included, at the top, the chieftains, nobles, and knights, together with those who immediately served them—physicians, bards, harpers, tale-tellers. "One office in the house of great men," writes Campion, "is a tale-teller, who bringeth his lord on sleep with tales vain and frivolous." [32] Then there were jesters—"loose fellows"—and professional card-players, who had access to gentlemen's houses and spent their time wandering up and down the land. These gamesters were so reckless that, when their money was gone, they would play away their "mantle and all to the bare skin" and then "pawn portions of their glib" and "the nails of their fingers and toes." [33] Serving the whole clan, from highest to lowest, were the judges and priests. From the farmers, the largest class of all, the soldiers were recruited. At the bottom were the cotters and laborers, who were known as churls. The constant unrest of the time, with frequent loss of corn and cattle, must have made agriculture a joyless occupation. Moreover, both freeholders and tenants suffered terribly from the tyranny of the soldiers, who, when billeted upon them, lorded it over their hosts and literally ate them out of house and home.

The Irish had a different cultural history from the English, and they naturally disliked relinquishing certain traditional institutions and practices that seemed well adapted to their needs. One of these was their so-

[29] *View*, pp. 93, 202.
[30] Pp. 62-67.
[31] In *Pacata Hibernia* 1. liii.
[32] P. 18.
[33] *Ibid.*, pp. 19-20.

called Brehon law, according to which justice was administered by judges known as brehons, and crimes of every sort were punished by fines nicely adjusted to the seriousness of the offense. The English were shocked that even the stain of murder could be wiped away by a fine.[34] Another and very important custom was the election of their chief and also the election of one who should succeed him on his death. This heir elect, called a tanist, was chosen from the relatives of the chief, a brother or some older man being generally preferred to the chief's son. Spenser tells of an interesting ceremony that followed the election. The chief, while standing on an elevated stone, often in the footprints of the tribe's first chief engraved thereon, swore a solemn oath to preserve the ancient customs of the country. He then received the wand of office and, descending, turned thrice forward and thrice backward. The tanist swore a similar oath with but one foot upon the stone.[35] To the English, accustomed to the right of primogeniture, this democratic mode of managing the succession was highly objectionable. They desired the stability that would spring from the chiefs' becoming titled nobles, responsible to the crown, with hereditary rights in the lands they controlled. But the mere Irish, who regarded the lands as belonging to the clan, wanted no such change, and the endeavor to force it upon them was a source of constant friction. Brehon law and tanistry, in spite of English efforts, persisted in many parts of Ireland.

The faith of Ireland was almost wholly Catholic. Even in Dublin, according to Barnabe Rich, writing in 1610, ten out of eleven were Catholics,[36] and in the north some of the monasteries remained in the possession of their inmates till the time of James I. Yet the main body of the Irish, in Spenser's opinion, were so blind and ignorant in their belief that they were hardly better than infidels: though they could perhaps say their *Pater Noster* and *Ave Maria*, they understood not one word of either. In the Irish districts, he says, the livings were many of them so poor as scarcely to provide the incumbent with a gown, and were held by those whose pastoral duties began and ended with baptizing after the Popish fashion.[37]

Apparently the Catholic faith had long been kept alive among the mass of the Irish mainly through the earnest yet feeble and ignorant efforts of the begging friars. About 1580 the Counter Reformation began to make itself felt in Ireland. The sons of well-to-do families journeyed to the universities of Reims, Douay, and Louvain, and from the Continent a

[34] *View*, pp. 7-8.
[35] *Ibid.*, pp. 10-11.
[36] *A New Description of Ireland*, p. 61.
[37] *View*, pp. 109, 115, 113.

stream of zealous Jesuit missionaries flowed steadily into the country. During Sir John Perrot's deputyship, from 1584 to 1588, recusancy gained great headway.[38] In 1596, William Lyon, bishop of Cork and Ross, who had had twenty-six years of service in Ireland, reported that, where he used to preach to a thousand, he now had a congregation of not five;[39] and Moryson, a few years later, asserted that when the people "were forced to go to church (as the Mayor and Aldermen of Dublin to attend the Lord Deputy)," they stopped "their ears with wool or some like matter, so as they could not hear a word the preacher spoke."[40]

Spenser, who had seen many abuses in the church at home, saw all these, and more, greatly magnified in Ireland. So long as Ireland was filled with unrest and war, he believed there was little chance of establishing the reformed faith. After peace had come, he thought it might be introduced, not by force and terror, but by gentleness, through the instruction and example of discreet ministers of the Irish nation.[41] But this hope was not to be realized. In the seventeenth century the Catholic faith of Ireland became sufficiently vital to draw the towns and the country districts to one another. The failure of the Reformation in Ireland was ultimately, more than anything else, what made impossible any real spiritual union with England.

[38] *C. S. P. Ir.* (1588-1592), pp. 365 (37), 517.

[39] *C. S. P. Ir.* (1596-1597), p. 14.

[40] In Falkiner, p. 264.

[41] *View*, pp. 111, 208.

X

WITH LORD GREY

SPENSER'S LIFE during his first two years in Ireland must have been closely bound up with that of his patron and employer. Our knowledge of Arthur Lord Grey de Wilton, as of so many prominent Elizabethans, is meagre. Perhaps we may read a fanciful account of his youth and young manhood in certain lines of Spenser's which describe the rearing of Artegall, hero of Book V of *The Faerie Queene.*

For *Artegall* in iustice was vpbrought
Euen from the cradle of his infancie,
And all the depth of rightfull doome was taught
By faire *Astraea,* with great industrie. . . .
And men admyr'd his ouerruling might;
Ne any liu'd on ground, that durst withstand
His dreadfull heast, much lesse him match in fight,
Or bide the horror of his wreakfull hand,
When so he list in wrath lift vp his steely brand.

Even as a boy, Grey had peculiar opportunities to learn the art both of government and of war from his father, whose military and administrative gifts were almost constantly employed by four sovereigns, beginning with Henry VIII, on a stage that extended all the way from Picardy to Scotland. Also from his father, a supporter of Lady Jane Grey, he may have derived his vigorous Protestantism. In 1557, when he was about twenty-one, Arthur Grey fought at the battle of St. Quentin, and again, in the following year, at the siege of Guisnes. Here, if not earlier, he came face to face with the horrors of war, for he tells us that, when sent out as a hostage during a truce, he had to cross a bulwark on naked and new slain bodies, some yet sprawling and groaning under his feet.[1] In 1560 he accompanied his father to Scotland and took part in the siege of Leith, where he was shot in the shoulder while courageously leading certain demilances in a charge. Records of his life do not indicate further military service till duty called him twenty years later to Ireland, but probably he maintained his interest in military science. Sir Henry Sidney in a letter to him in 1580 says that sending Grey instructions of a military nature would be like a certain scholar's offering to read *De Arte Militari* to Hannibal.[2]

[1] Grey, *A Commentary,* p. 33. [2] *Ibid.,* p. 68.

On his father's death in 1562, Arthur succeeded him as fourteenth Baron Grey de Wilton. He resided at Whaddon, Buckinghamshire, for the ancestral castle at Wilton-upon-Wye had previously been sold to pay a ransom for his father, who had been captured at Guisnes. As chief magistrate in the county, Grey had an opportunity to exercise the justice that he was later to administer in the larger theatre of Ireland. Grey was deeply religious, as many remarks in his letters indicate. Sir Henry Sidney recognized this side of his friend's character. " As I know you are religious," he writes, soon after Grey's departure for Ireland, " so I wish your lordship to frequent sermons and prayer in public places; it would comfort the few Protestants you have there. . . ." [3] To Elizabeth this trait caused some concern, and she privately warned Grey not to be overzealous in religious matters.[4] If, however, we may trust the language of her instructions drawn up in July, 1580, she had faith in his wisdom and judgment and in his integrity; [5] indeed she had considered him for the Irish post nine years before. Grey had long been eager to serve the state, but not in Ireland. Now reluctantly, but in obedience to the call of duty, he had consented to go.[6]

At dawn on Friday, August 12, 1580, the " Handmaid," on which Grey had sailed, arrived at the peninsula of Howth in the port of Dublin,[7] and we may imagine the excitement attending his reception, for the coming of a new deputy was always a great event. Did the fact that he reached Dublin on Friday increase the forebodings with which from the first he had viewed his mission to this unlucky land? We may assume that he took up his residence at once in the square northeast tower of Dublin Castle, known as Store-house Tower, for here the lord deputies seem to have had their private rooms. Within the massive, battlemented walls of the castle, the very heart of the Irish government beat. Here were held the courts of justice and the high court of parliament; here were the exchequer and treasury of Ireland; here the state records were preserved; and in the dungeons languished rebels who were fortunate enough to keep their heads on their shoulders.[8] Spenser, as Grey's secretary, must soon have become familiar with Dublin Castle, and he may also have resided there. Later Grey apparently lived for a time at Kilmainham Priory, west of

[3] *Ibid.*
[4] *C. S. P. Ir.* (1574-1585), p. 275 (25).
[5] Grey, pp. 74-76.
[6] *Ibid.*, p. 67.
[7] *Liber . . . Hiberniae* 1. 2. 4.
[8] Falkiner, *Illustrations of Irish History*, pp. 19, 20.

Dublin.[9] Kilmainham had been the principal house in Ireland of the Knights Hospitallers, but after the suppression of the monasteries, it had been used as a residence by some of the deputies, who preferred it to the castle.

It would be interesting to know whether Spenser's wife accompanied him to Ireland or went over later. Lord Grey's wife, we know, made preparations toward the end of August to join her husband, requiring, by the way, forty-two horses and ten carts for the journey to the seaside. She arrived at Dublin on October 12.[10]

Spenser shared his duties with at least one other secretary, Timothy Reynolds. The fact that each was allowed annually £15 for pens, ink, and paper implies many an hour devoted to driving a quill across paper or parchment in the writing of letters and copying of documents, unless this large sum represented in part the secretary's compensation. Spenser addressed numerous letters that he did not write, and during his two years as secretary paid out hundreds of pounds as " rewards " to messengers.[11] Fifty documents are extant in his neat secretary hand.[12] According to Professor Raymond Jenkins, who identified thirty-four of these, and made valuable inferences from them, Spenser must have been " perpetually at his chief's elbow, not only at Dublin but also on military expeditions," and was evidently " the one man upon whom Grey most relied to answer the complaints of Elizabeth and Burghley." [13] If, then, we are to think of Spenser as accompanying the lord deputy on his various journeys, we shall follow the destinies of Grey with deep interest.

Before the first crowded day in Ireland had passed, Grey had acquainted himself with recent developments and had written about them to the queen. The Pale, he told her, was " sore vexed " by the revolt of James Eustace, Viscount Baltinglas, who had spoilt and burnt her loyal subjects. The rebels of Munster were still holding out, and on that very day word had come that two of their leaders, Sir James of Desmond, a brother of the earl of Desmond, and Dr. Nicholas Sanders, the Papal nuncio, on the way to join the rebels of the Pale, had been attacked, and Sir James taken. Connaught, according to its governor, Sir Nicholas Malby, was being threatened from the north. Turlough Luineach O'Neill, the great Ulster

[9] Jenkins, *PMLA* 52. 349, note 50.

[10] *Acts of the Privy Council* (1580-1581), p. 181; *C. S. P. Ir.* (1574-1585), p. 260 (31).

[11] Book of Concordatums, quoted by Carpenter, *A Reference Guide*, pp. 47-48. On December 31, 1580, and again on June 26, 1581, Spenser was paid £10, sums intended apparently for his expense account.

[12] Plomer, *MP* 21. 201-207; Jenkins, *PMLA* 52. 338.

[13] *Ibid.*, pp. 338, 340, 341.

Gate of Dublin Castle and neighboring houses, with Sir Henry Sidney leaving on a state progress. From John Derricke's *The Image of Irelande*, 1581; reprinted, Edinburgh, 1883.

chief, in spite of all his pestilent Scotch wife could do, was still loyal. "Your majesty thus sees," he concluded, "what uncertain conditions this your realm standeth in." And then he added what was to be the burden of many of his letters, that the soldiers were murmuring over a lack of pay and victuals—a type of complaint that seems to have caused the economical queen very little distress.[14]

Conditions in Ireland had indeed been "uncertain" for some time. One of the greatest uprisings of Elizabeth's reign, that of the Desmonds of Munster, had really begun eleven years before when James Fitzmaurice, cousin of Gerald Fitzgerald, fifteenth earl of Desmond, had taken up arms. Though obliged to make peace, he had bided his time and had sought aid on the Continent. Family and tribal jealousies had motivated his actions, but religion had also played its part. Eventually he had given the rebellion a strong religious emphasis, and had received some encouragement in France and Spain, but more at the court of Gregory XIII. Finally he and the learned and zealous Dr. Sanders had sailed with a few troops from northern Spain and had dropped anchor on July 17, 1579, in the harbor of Dingle, on the southwestern coast of Ireland. A day or two later they had begun to construct near by at Smerwick the celebrated Fort del Oro, whose entrenchments are still visible. But within a month Fitzmaurice's years of planning had been suddenly terminated when he had been slain by members of the hostile clan of Burkes. The flame of rebellion that he had kindled was not, however, quenched by his death. Sir John and Sir James, brothers of the earl of Desmond, had joined the rebellion upon Fitzmaurice's arrival; and finally, on November 1, the earl himself, with reluctance, for he well knew how fateful was this move, had allowed himself to be proclaimed a traitor.

Soon the earl of Ormonde had taken the field against the insurgents, and Butler and Geraldine, as so often in the past, had again crossed swords. In March, 1580, Ormonde and the lord justice, Sir William Pelham, had begun a frightful wasting of the Desmond lands in Limerick and Kerry. The Irish chroniclers known as the Four Masters thus describe their operations: "It was not wonderful that they should kill men fit for action, but they killed blind and feeble men, women, boys, and girls, sick persons, idiots, and old people," and carried their cattle and other property to the English camp; "but great numbers of the English were slain by the plundered parties, who followed in pursuit of the preys."[15] To the

[14] Grey, pp. 77-78. For a sympathetic view of Elizabeth's frugality, see Neale, *Queen Elizabeth*, pp. 106, 284-286.

[15] Four Masters, *Annals of the Kingdom of Ireland* 5. 1731.

English, devastating the land and thus reducing the people to a state of famine seemed the only way to end a widespread rebellion. By the time Lord Grey set foot in Ireland, the rebels were in serious straits, with many ready to make peace; yet the rebellion continued.

Before turning his attention to Munster, Grey determined to attack Baltinglas and his associate Fiagh MacHugh O'Byrne, who, with their followers, were encamped to the west of the Wicklow Mountains. Depending largely on raw recruits from England, Grey marched south into County Wicklow. Baltinglas withdrew before him over the mountains into Glenmalure, a narrow, rocky, thickly wooded valley which cleaves the irregular mass of the Wicklow Mountains from the southeast like a deep sword thrust. Grey followed, and, unmoved by the advice of those experienced in Irish warfare, sent half his men down into the glen to drive out the rebels while he waited with the rest on the mountainside to attack them as soon as they should appear. The English troops, in their unserviceable blue and red coats, pushed along the glen over rocks and through bogs, and had frequently to cross the Avonbeg River. According to Sir William Stanley, an officer who brought up the rear, they exposed themselves dangerously when they clambered up a hillside out of the bottom of the glen. At this point, the Irish, lurking behind trees and rocks, fell upon them, killed thirty, and scattered the rest in desperate flight.[16] To Grey, and to Spenser, too, who was probably an eye-witness, this defeat surely seemed an ominous beginning of the new lord deputy's efforts at the pacification of Ireland. Years later Spenser referred to the stream of Glenmalure as "balefull Oure, late staind with English blood." [17] Those who knew the temper of Ireland at the moment were dismayed, for an English defeat, which occurred but rarely, was sure to raise the spirits of the disaffected and fan the smouldering embers of revolt.

Lord Grey had not been formally inducted into office on his arrival because of Lord Justice Pelham's absence in Munster with the sword of state. The ceremony was therefore postponed till September 7. In St. Patrick's Cathedral, before Lord Justice Pelham and the peers and councillors of the realm, Nicholas White, master of the rolls, read solemnly the queen's letters patent, and Lord Grey received the sword of state and took the oath of office.[18] Upon Spenser, who adored fine weapons and armor, Grey's ceremonious receiving of the sword amid almost regal

[16] Bagwell, *Ireland under the Tudors* 3. 61-62; John Hooker in Holinshed, *Chronicles*, "Chronicles of Ireland," p. 169; *C. S. P. Ir.* (1574-1585), p. 247 (83).

[17] *F. Q.* 4. 11. 44.

[18] *Liber . . . Hiberniae* 1. 2. 4.

pageantry probably made a deep impression; and this ceremony was no doubt recalled when Artegall in *The Faerie Queene* was represented as receiving Chrysaor, the sword of adamant and gold whose terrible strokes nothing on earth could resist.[19]

Two days after this ceremony, Grey left for Drogheda, thirty miles to the north, in order to confer with Turlough Luineach O'Neill, who had grown suddenly restive as a result of the defeat of the English at Glenmalure. If, as seems likely, Spenser was a member of Grey's party, his antiquarian tastes would have been pleased by this ancient town, with its towered walls and noble ecclesiastical buildings, and he would have enjoyed the quiet beauty of its setting on the " pleasant Boyne " four miles from the sea. Surely he would have been no less pleased at the opportunity to observe the powerful Irish chief of Tyrone, whose combination of diplomacy and armed force, and whose frequent changes of front, had made him a perennial problem for the English.

While Grey was at Drogheda, an important event took place far away in Kerry. For years the Munster rebels had awaited foreign aid. Now at last a force of some six hundred Spaniards and Italians, under the command of a colonel, Sebastiano di San Joseppi, arrived from Corunna in four vessels, and landed at Smerwick. There they proceeded at once to establish themselves in Fort del Oro, constructed a year before by James Fitzmaurice. The precipitous walls of stone that formed the seaward end of the fort, together with fourteen cannon mounted on the ramparts, gave such an impression of strength that Vice-admiral Bingham, of the English fleet, and the earl of Ormonde, who had crossed the mountains into Kerry with 1600 troops, both thought that the prudent course was not to attack it.[20]

On October 5 Grey set out for Smerwick with 800 men; and Spenser, presumably, was with him. The long journey, impeded by autumn rains, was broken at Kilkenny, Cork, and Limerick.[21]

At Kilkenny, the castle of Thomas Butler, tenth earl of Ormonde, must have sheltered Grey and Spenser, and we can imagine the satisfaction of both men in exchanging the hardships of the march for the comforts and amenities of the earl's splendid residence. In a dedicatory sonnet to Ormonde published with *The Faerie Queene*, Spenser praises the earl's " braue mansione " as a veritable oasis of learning and refinement in a beautiful yet barbarous land, and speaks of the generosity and " true

[19] 5. 1. 9-10. [20] Bagwell 3. 65 ff.

[21] *C. S. P. Ir.* (1574-1585), pp. 257 (12), 258 (13), 261 (43, 40).

honour" of its master; nor does he forget its mistress and her ladies in waiting. Elsewhere he calls Lady Ormonde the nymph of the River Suir and testifies to her grace and courtesy and to the love she awakes in the hearts of every rank.[22] It is not surprising that Spenser felt drawn to the earl and his wife. Reared at the English court with Edward VI, Ormonde had absorbed the culture of the Renaissance and had been the first of his family to embrace Protestantism. He had carried back to Ireland an understanding of the English and a sympathy with their aims which kept him, through his long life, loyal to the crown. Yet he had a thorough understanding of the Irish too, indeed felt himself one of them, and though he could on occasion be ruthless, he believed in conciliation and often insisted on a course of mercy toward those who had revolted. In 1559, he had become lord treasurer of Ireland and held that post during the remainder of his life. Elizabeth was warmly attached to handsome Black Tom, as he was called because of his swarthy complexion, and had frequently taken his part against his great rival and traditional foe, the earl of Desmond, for these two earls, who almost shared southern Ireland, had been often in more or less open conflict over some question involving their princely domains. Years later, when Ireland was trembling on the verge of the greatest of its Tudor rebellions, that of Hugh O'Neill, earl of Tyrone, Spenser was convinced that Ormonde alone held the south in leash "with the terror of his greatness and the assurance of his immovable loyalty."[23]

Late in October Grey reached his destination on the windy extremity of Kerry and pitched camp eight miles from Smerwick. There, on November 5, he learned of Admiral Winter's arrival, and on the 7th, with the cooperation of the admiral, he began the investment of the fort. That night trenches were dug, and cannon from the fleet were mounted, and on the 8th bombardment commenced. Before the end of the second day of bombardment, negotiations for surrender were in progress, and on November 10 the fort was turned over to the English.[24]

From a report promptly sent to Secretary Walsingham,[25] and from a letter of Grey's to the queen, written at Smerwick on November 12, we learn many interesting facts concerning the capture of the fort.[26] On November 7, a day spent by Grey in reconnoitering, its defenders appear

[22] *Colin Clouts Come Home Againe* 524-531. [23] *View*, p. 122.

[24] *C. S. P. Ir.* (1574-1585), pp. lxix ff.

[25] Hennessy, *Sir Walter Ralegh in Ireland*, pp. 207-211.

[26] See *supra*, note 24; according to Professor Jenkins (*PMLA* 52. 343, note 19), Grey's letter was probably penned by Spenser.

The site of Fort del Oro, on Smerwick Harbour. From a photograph by Professor Charles G. Osgood.

to have been in good spirits. They flew the Pope's banner and other ensigns, kept up a lively fire, and sent out thirty men to skirmish with the English. But the English artillery fire on the following day brought discouragement, and the banners of the previous day were replaced by two flags, one white and the other black, which were intended as a signal to the earl of Desmond to come to their rescue. On the day after, when no assistance appeared, they showed only the white flag, and then sought desperately by negotiation to secure the best possible terms of surrender. Their case was not improved when they told Grey they had been sent to Ireland by the Pope. He refused all terms, insisting that they turn over the fort to him and yield themselves " for life or death." About sunset, the colonel himself came forth, and finding Grey inflexible, put himself at his mercy and agreed to place all in Grey's hands the next morning.

Next day Grey drew up his troops in battle array before the fort, whereupon the colonel and ten or twelve of his chief gentlemen appeared " trailing their ensigns rolled up," and formally handed the fort over to the English. Grey then sent in certain gentlemen to guard the arms and stocks of provisions. These men were followed by bands who at once put the six hundred common soldiers to the sword, four hundred being " as gallant and goodly personages " as Grey ever beheld. They hanged some Irishmen and some women whom they found in the fort and reserved several persons for examination. The colonel and a few others were given to Grey's gentlemen and captains to be held for ransom. In the fort were found coin to the value of £329 and arms sufficient to equip four thousand men. There was also enough food—biscuit, bacon, oil, fish, rice, beans, peas, and barley—to have lasted the inmates six months, but water was lacking, and many were ill.[27] Amid the disorder and tumult, much of this booty was wasted by the soldiers. As a small finale to the massacre they broke the arms and legs of three men—an English servant to Dr. Sanders, an Irishman named Plunket, and a friar—and then hanged them on gallows set up on the wall of the fort.

This horrible slaughter of the foreigners at Smerwick was unhappily quite in accord with the practice of the time, and neither the report to Walsingham nor Grey's letter to Elizabeth contains the slightest apology for it. Elizabeth was delighted with what Grey had done, except that she doubted the wisdom of granting life to those spared by Grey. As time passed, though she began to feel that Grey's administration was too costly, her heart continued to be warmed at the thought of his exploit at

[27] *C. S. P. Ir.* (1574-1585), pp. lxxvi, 261 (42).

Smerwick.[28] Spenser, in the *View*, takes the trouble to explain why mercy was not shown. First, there was fear that, if the troops were spared, they might join with the Irish; and secondly, there was a desire to use their destruction as a warning to the Irish rebels, who had of late been greatly heartened by the thought of foreign assistance. To Spenser it seemed that " there was no other way but to make that short end of them which was made." [29]

Though the massacre in itself would not have seemed culpable to most men of Spenser's day, Grey would have been condemned if he had promised life and then failed to grant it. And that is exactly what the Spanish ambassador to England, Bernardino de Mendoza, accused him of a month later.[30] Spenser in his *View* passionately denies Grey's bad faith, adding weight to his denial by causing his mouthpiece, Irenius, to assert, " myself being as near then as any." [31] But because Spenser's account of the affair is inaccurate in certain respects, the value of his defense has been questioned.[32] When, however, we recall that sixteen years had passed, we are prepared for discrepancies. Moreover, our knowledge of Grey makes a different conclusion almost impossible. Stern he was, even at times pitiless, but shifty and dishonorable he surely was not.

The importance attached by Spenser to this event may perhaps be seen in his having made it the climax of the Fifth Book of *The Faerie Queene*. At first thought, the violent duel there presented between Grantorto—" Great Wrong "—a mail-clad giant, armed with huge, iron-studded battle axe, and Artegall, seems inappropriate as a representation of the invaders' brief engagement with the English, followed by their massacre. But Spenser was looking past the unsuccessful band of strangers to the haughty Catholic powers from whose shores they had come, and was brooding on the potential danger of such intervention, especially if backed by a considerable Irish revolt.

Full of gratitude for a victory that he modestly attributed more to " the providence and mighty power of God " than to his own efforts, Grey re-

[28] Hennessy, pp. 212-213, 215.

[29] *View*, p. 140.

[30] *C. S. P. Sp.* (1580-1586), p. 69.

[31] *View*, pp. 139-140; for Don Sebastian's own version of what happened, which confirms Grey's assertion that the surrender was unconditional, see Renwick's edition of the *View*, pp. 287-288; and for an argument that Grey made " terms which he afterwards violated," see O'Rahilly, *Journal of the Cork Historical and Archaeological Society*, 2nd Series, 42. 1-15, 65-83. Professor O'Rahilly puts no trust in Sebastian's account.

[32] Spenser's most important divergence from Grey's account is that the invaders declared they were mere " adventurers," commissioned by neither Pope nor king.

turned to Dublin by way of Limerick and Clonmel. Before leaving Limerick, he sent troops to Sir Nicholas Malby in Connaught and garrisoned some of his army at strategic points in Munster, hoping thereby to make life difficult for the traitor earl of Desmond.[33]

To Spenser the whole campaign must have been of intense interest. Probably he did not enjoy the long journeys over poor, muddy roads and the bad food, which even the queen solicitously took note of; but his antiquarian taste was surely engaged by the rude culture of a strange land, and his love of beauty touched by its mountains, rivers, and towns—the "spacious Shenan spreading like a sea," "the gentle Shure" flowing by "sweet Clonmell," and the marble city of Kilkenny amid its orchards. Already the landscape of Ireland, sprinkled with castles and possessing a rugged grandeur by virtue of its forests and "deserts" and mountains, must have begun to print itself sharply on his memory, ready to be drawn on later for subtle suggestions when he came to picture faeryland.

Of the great Anglo-Norman family of the Geraldines, there were two chief branches, one headed by the earl of Desmond, the other by the earl of Kildare. The family was supposed to have originated in Florence, as Surrey tells us in his famous sonnet on the Lady Geraldine, and its Irish founder had come from England with Strongbow. The earl of Desmond, as we have seen, was now being hunted through Munster by the forces of Grey. The other branch was at this time represented by Gerald Fitzgerald, eleventh earl of Kildare. His grandfather, the eighth earl, had been the most distinguished of the family, and as lord deputy had ruled Ireland for over thirty years. Their great castle at Maynooth, fifteen miles west of Dublin, though long a ruin, still seems an expression of the power and grandeur of the family.[34] The earls of Kildare had suffered an eclipse when Silken Thomas, grandson of the great earl, had been executed for treason, but their fortunes had been revived by Queen Mary, who had reestablished the earldom of Kildare and granted it to Gerald. As a young man Gerald had had interesting experiences on the Continent, including life in Rome as a protégé of Cardinal Pole, warfare against the Moors, and service with Cosimo de' Medici at Florence. Like Ormonde, he had become a Protestant. His small, slender body housed a valiant soul and a hot temper.

In the hands of this man Grey had placed the prosecution of the war against the rebels of the Pale when he had left for Smerwick. Upon his return he was informed that Kildare had not been carrying on the war

[33] Letter reproduced by Jenkins, *PMLA* 52, opposite p. 338.

[34] Bryan, *Gerald Fitzgerald*, pp. 6, ix, 2.

with vigor, and indeed that he and his son-in-law, Baron Delvin, had been in treasonous communication with Baltinglas. On December 23, at a meeting of Grey's council, the Lord Chancellor Gerard produced what must have been a scene of the utmost tenseness and excitement by openly charging the earl with disloyalty. Grey promptly confined Delvin and Kildare in Dublin Castle.[35] This action, taken against men of such prominence, must have been in the highest degree distasteful to Lord Grey. After having held them for a year and a half, he sent them to England, where both were detained for a time, but neither was convicted of treason.

Grey would have been fortunate if he could have devoted his energies exclusively to the insurgency that was rocking so much of Ireland, but unfortunately his own army must have been constantly on his mind. Today a military recruit has to meet certain physical and mental standards, but at that time the English levies for foreign service, especially for Ireland, where campaigning had no allurements, were frequently of miserable quality. When companies were to be raised, too often the town loafers and idiots and the inmates of the jails were "pressed" and bundled off to Ireland, going "with as good a will," says Barnabe Rich, "as a bear is brought to the stake." [36] Having arrived, the men deserted, bullied the people they were sent to protect, and easily sickened and died. Their morale was not improved by their poor and insufficient food nor by the fact that their pay was usually far in arrears. Moreover, the queen, who bitterly resented the cost of her armies, was always demanding their reduction below a limit thought safe by her military leaders. The dispatches to England during this winter refer often to the hunger, cold, and illness of the men, and to their desertion and death.[37] Spenser, who had once written of soldiering as the noblest profession, must have been appalled on observing at close range an English army containing so many rogues, drunkards, and vagabonds. Possibly his intimate contact with Grey's forces gave a still brighter glow to the days of chivalry, when the press gang and all that it implied were unknown.

In January or February of the year 1581, when Grey was on a journey toward the borders of Connaught, he was overtaken by a man bearing important letters from London.[38] The messenger was Lodowick Bryskett,

[35] *C. S. P. Ir.* (1574-1585), pp. 275 (26), 276 (31).

[36] *Acts of the Privy Council* (1580-1581), p. 141; *C. S. P. Ir.* (1574-1585), p. 287 (62); Rich, *The Fruites of long Experience*, pp. 61-62, 64, *passim.*

[37] *C. S. P. Ir.* (1574-1585), pp. 273 (5), 280 (4), 288 (75, 76), 290 (3), 292 (25).

[38] Plomer and Cross, *The Life and Correspondence of Lodowick Bryskett*, pp. 13, 18.

who has been mentioned as an official in the Irish government and a close friend of Philip Sidney's. Though Bryskett was clerk of the council at Dublin, he had been in England for a year and a half, partly because of the death of his mother, but also apparently because of his inability to turn his back resolutely on the charms of London society and the English court. The son of a Genoese merchant who had settled in London, he entered Cambridge in 1559, but did not graduate. Later he became a protégé of Sir Henry Sidney, and was with Philip on the latter's long European tour, to the pleasures of which he makes delightful allusion in one of his elegies on Sidney.[39]

Grey was at first inclined to blame Bryskett for his long absence, but the two were soon on a friendly footing, and Bryskett, as time passed, became one of Grey's most zealous supporters. To Spenser, the arrival of this gifted, traveled gentleman, with whom he was perhaps already acquainted, must have been highly gratifying. The two became warm friends, and each one later played a part, as we shall see, in the writings of the other.

In spite of a craving for the amenities of English life, and a tendency to complain about the laboriousness and poor pay of his clerkship, Bryskett was an energetic, capable official. Probably as a mark of esteem, in 1577, a year or two after becoming clerk of the council, he had been granted also the post of registrar or clerk in chancery for faculties.[40] The duties implied by this odd-sounding title were the making out and recording of "faculties"; that is, special ecclesiastical dispensations and licenses that had formerly been granted by Rome but were now issued by the archbishop of Dublin—for example, says Carpenter, a permit for the removal of a grave.[41] Bryskett was to hold the office during good behavior, with the fees belonging to it.

On March 14, 1581, Bryskett obtained the lucrative office of controller of customs on wines, and eight days later he surrendered to Spenser his clerkship for the faculties. Because of being secretary to the lord deputy, Spenser was permitted to assume this office without the payment of the usual fee.[42] As Professor Jenkins surmises, Grey probably arranged that Bryskett, if confirmed in the office of controller, should yield the other post to Spenser; thus Grey could make provision for two worthy officials.

[39] *A Pastorall Aeglogue vpon the Death of Sir Phillip Sidney, Knight, &c.* 84-92, printed with *Astrophel.*

[40] Fiant 3010, *Thirteenth Report,* p. 27.

[41] *MP* 19. 413.

[42] Fiant 3694, *Thirteenth Report,* p. 136.

Spenser retained the clerkship for over seven years.[43] Since he was allowed a deputy, we may assume that the post was regarded as a sinecure. The acquiring of it was probably a fateful move for Spenser: it meant putting down into the soil of Ireland a first small root which, followed by others, kept him in the savage island as long as he lived.

In April, Grey made a nine-day journey into West Meath to investigate charges of extortion brought against the troops operating there. At Mullingar he dispensed swift and impartial justice. Bryskett, who was with him, says Grey was deluged with complaints. The more important of these Grey disposed of himself; the rest he placed in the hands of others, and directed that the treasurer make restitution, deducting the necessary sums from the pay of the captain whose soldiers were concerned. The poor must have been amazed at this prompt relief from the tyranny of the soldiers. Grey also executed thirteen " notable malefactors," including a priest who had been adjudged a spy. Bryskett thought he had never seen so short a journey made to better purpose.[44]

In spite of Grey's conscientious efforts, the state of the country was not improving. In every province there was unrest or open rebellion. In Munster the earl of Desmond still eluded capture, and the combined activities of rebels and soldiers were rapidly transforming that province, except for its towns, into a wilderness. A number of Grey's associates believed that Ormonde was pursuing too mild a course, was indeed willing that the war should drag on. " This man," wrote Raleigh, " having been lord general of Munster now about two years, there are at this instant a thousand traitors more than there were the first day." [45]

On April 21, Bryskett drew for his patron Walsingham a startling picture of the critical state of Ireland. In both Connaught and the Pale, he said, the rebels were held in check only by the watchfulness of Malby and Mackworth. In Munster, Ormonde, for all his professions of " exceeding toil and travail," had achieved very little. In Ulster, Turlough Luineach O'Neill presented a friendly front while privately sowing the seeds of revolt over the whole realm. Never, declared Bryskett, since the Conquest, had Ireland been in so perilous a state, and unless the fire was

[43] After retaining the post for over seven years, Spenser was succeeded by Arland Ussher (father of the celebrated James Ussher) on June 22, 1588. Spenser seems to have shared the clerkship during part of this time with Roland Cowyk (*Liber . . . Hiberniae* 1. 2. 29), but whether he was Spenser's deputy, as Jenkins thinks (*PMLA* 47. 112), or a representative of the crown, provided by law, it would be hard to say.

[44] Plomer and Cross, pp. 22-23.

[45] Bagwell 3. 86.

extinguished, it was likely "to burst out into greater flames than ever before."[46]

Grey was fully aware of the critical state of affairs and pleaded for the means of suppressing rebellion with a stronger hand. But Elizabeth determined, instead, to try conciliation and directed that pardons be offered. Spenser was one with Grey in believing that temporizing would never cure the situation; often in *The Faerie Queene* he expresses his faith in resolute action, as in these lines:

> Who so vpon him selfe will take the skill
> True Iustice vnto people to diuide,
> Had neede haue mightie hands, for to fulfill
> That, which he doth with righteous doome decide. . . .[47]

We can imagine, therefore, how completely Spenser shared Grey's dismay when Elizabeth, instead of supporting more severe measures, sent over a general pardon. A passage in the *View* depicts clearly Spenser's indignation at this sudden and disconcerting shift in policy. When the land, says Spenser, had been prepared for reformation, complaint was made against Grey

> that he was a bloody man, and regarded not the life of her subjects, no more than dogs, but had wasted and consumed all, so as now she had almost nothing left but to reign in their ashes. Ear was soon lent thereunto, all suddenly turned topsy-turvy. He, noble lord, eftsoons was blamed, the wretched people pitied, and new counsels plotted, in which it was concluded that a general pardon should be sent over to all that would accept of it; upon which all former purposes were blanked, the governor at a bay, and not only all that great and long charge which she had before been at quite lost and cancelled, but also all that hope of good which was even at the door put back and clean frustrate. . . .[48]

We cannot wonder that Grey believed his usefulness as lord deputy was at an end. He had exerted himself to the utmost to do his duty as he saw it, and duty with him was a stern mistress; but he had not been able to please the queen. Moreover, he felt that she was adopting a policy fatal to the welfare of the country. He therefore asked for his recall, and thus began a series of appeals that were to continue for over a year.[49]

[46] Plomer and Cross, pp. 21-23.

[47] 5. 4. 1.

[48] P. 137; the pardons were sent April 19, 1581.

[49] Grey's first suggestion that he be recalled was on April 6, 1581—*C. S. P. Ir.* (1574-1585), p. 296 (6). Lack of funds and the general pardon caused him to appeal urgently for recall on April 24—*Ibid.*, p. 300 (48). The *Calendar of State Papers* reveals sixteen such appeals, illness during his second winter being offered as one reason.

In May he started south through the counties of Wicklow and Wexford to curb the rebellious activities of the O'Byrnes, O'Tooles, and Kavanaghs. For these tribes, nature had provided in the glens and woods of the Wicklow Mountains and other mountains extending farther south an almost impregnable stronghold from which they could issue forth to rob the farmers of the plains, and hence the task of controlling these hardy forest-dwellers offered endless difficulty. Grey's route skirted the eastern slopes of this range, so that he had on his right the fresh green of extensive forests and on his left at times the blue of the sea.[50] But perhaps the danger of meeting bands of unfriendly tribesmen distracted attention from the beauty of the spring scene. As his forces journeyed past Glenmalure, bitter thoughts must have visited both him and Spenser as well as others who had seen the defeat of the English there by Viscount Baltinglas and Fiagh MacHugh O'Byrne less than a year before. Grey repaired fortresses, executed a notorious rebel, burnt the country of another rebel, and visited garrisons.

The expedition went as far as the city of Wexford. Spenser, with his antiquarian enthusiasm, very likely appreciated the opportunity of inspecting this ancient town at the mouth of the "sandy Slane." Wexford was a Danish town taken at the beginning of the Norman conquest, and here the first English colony had been planted. Therefore, says Camden, "this whole territory is passing well peopled with English, who to this very day use the ancient Englishmen's apparel and their language," the latter, however, mixed with Irish.[51] Within a few months Spenser was to acquire property in this county, as was also Bryskett, who soon determined to exchange the ill-paid duties of clerk of the council for life on a farm near Enniscorthy, a few miles north of Wexford.

From Wexford, Grey wrote a letter to Walsingham and another to the privy council, in which he informed them that Ormonde had been relieved of his command of the Munster forces. Ormonde, said Grey, had accepted gracefully the queen's pleasure in this matter. The address on one of these letters is in Spenser's hand.[52]

On the return journey Grey devoted some days to a pursuit of Fiagh through his own Wicklow glens. Though unsuccessful, Grey pressed him so closely that Fiagh sued for peace, but with conditions that Grey thought too preposterous to consider—pardon for the earl of Desmond and all his followers and religious freedom for the rebels. Could Fiagh

[50] *C. S. P. Ir.* (1574-1585), p. 307 (45).
[51] *Britain*, "Ireland," p. 89.
[52] *C. S. P. Ir.* (1574-1585), pp. 306 (43), 307 (45); Jenkins, *PMLA* 52. 345, note 30.

have been serious? Spenser was, without doubt, bitterly disappointed by Grey's failure to take the chief of the O'Byrnes. He deplored the fact that this upstart—his rise to prominence had been rapid—should reside safely in his Wicklow fastness almost under the nose of Dublin and be able to match his power with that of the government.[53] His remarkable location was his strength but also his undoing. It permitted him to threaten and often pillage the most highly developed area of Ireland, but at the same time it made his ultimate capture a virtual necessity. Though he was clever as a fox in eluding his enemies, the pursuit continued at intervals until, sixteen years later, his head and quartered body went to adorn the gate of Dublin Castle.

Back in Dublin, Grey and his secretary were no doubt soon deeply immersed in matters of administrative detail. Yet ever present in Grey's mind was the thought that he must be freed from his deputyship. On July 1 he wrote to his friend and kinsman, Sir Christopher Hatton, asking his influence toward that end. Elizabethan gentlemen found it a thankless task to serve the great queen unless they were warmed by the sunlight of her good will, and Grey was no exception. Moreover, he felt that another might be more successful. "And yet," he writes, "my conscience, in the comfortless impression of this disfavour, will always bear me witness that I rest simply blameless herein towards her majesty, whose service, never forslowing, I have ever followed with all dutiful care and travail, as faithfully as the power of my body and mind would give me leave." [54]

Meanwhile, Turlough Luineach O'Neill, in disregard of peace terms arranged by Grey in September of the previous year, was causing trouble in Ulster. His sword was never idle long. Neither a body weakened by excesses nor a promise to keep the peace could make him permanently renounce the joys of warring against his neighbors. On July 4, he assisted Con O'Donnell in a fierce battle with Sir Hugh MacManus O'Donnell. Had Elizabeth been willing, Grey would no doubt have dropped peaceful efforts and attempted to quench once and for all this firebrand of the north. Instead he journeyed to the Ulster Blackwater and there renewed his pacific efforts.[55] Bryskett, who was of Grey's party, played an important role in the negotiations and acquitted himself well. Though we have no record of letters written by Spenser while Grey was on this trip, we suppose he went too. If so, he probably had his first sight of this northern province, whose beauties and natural advantages seem to have moved him

[53] *View*, pp. 150-152 .
[54] Grey, p. 79.
[55] *C. S. P. Ir.* (1574-1585), p. 314 (5).

profoundly. The following description of eastern Ulster, which, he reminds us, had formed in the time of Edward II the chief part of the English Pale, occurs in the *View*:

And sure it is yet a most beautiful and sweet country as any is under heaven, seamed throughout with many goodly rivers replenished with all sorts of fish most abundantly, sprinkled with very many sweet islands and goodly lakes like little inland seas, that will carry even ships upon their waters, adorned with goodly woods fit for building of houses and ships so commodiously as that, if some princes in the world had them, they would soon hope to be lords of all the seas, and ere long of all the world; also full of very good ports and havens opening upon England and Scotland, as inviting us to come unto them to see what excellent commodities that country can afford, besides the soil itself most fertile, fit to yield all kind of fruit that shall be committed thereinto, and lastly the heavens most mild and temperate, though somewhat more moist than the parts towards the west. . . .[56]

After Grey's return to Dublin, news of his successful negotiations with Turlough, coupled with rumors of energetic preparations for an expedition against the Leinster rebels, caused the submission of many of the O'Byrnes, including Fiagh MacHugh, and sent Viscount Baltinglas in flight to Spain.[57] Grey was thus sufficiently relieved of anxiety for the Pale so that he felt free to visit Munster, where the Desmond rebellion persisted. His purpose was to organize a more unified, energetic effort to suppress it. Four companies of foot and 200 horse that he took with him enabled him to do some fighting, and he inspected the various Munster garrisons. One of his most important acts was to put Captain John Zouche, whose courage and honesty and tireless energy he admired, in charge of all the forces in Munster.

He went by the way of Kilkenny, Waterford, and Youghal to Cork.[58] From Cork he wrote to Burghley that the queen's recent general pardon was prolonging the rebellion: the corn that had been spared had gone to the woods to support the rebels, who otherwise would have had to starve. Yet conditions in much of Munster were extremely bad. More than a year and a half before, Pelham and Ormonde had started a systematic wasting of the province, and what had been left by the armies had of necessity been taken in large part by the rebels. Even the towns were in a serious plight, which was being aggravated by the fact that they had to feed the garrisons left hungry by a lack of provisions from England. Many of the poor, on whom this burden tended to fall, were facing

[56] Pp. 25-26.

[57] Murdin, *A Collection of State Papers*, pp. 356-357.

[58] *Ibid.*, pp. 357 ff., 363 ff.; *C. S. P. Ir.* (1574-1585), pp. 323 (14 IV), 327 (51).

starvation. To us today, with our uniformly well-fed armies, it seems almost incredible that the lord deputy should have had to fill letter after letter with such a plea as: "Good my lord, help us, and that with some speed, to money and victuals." In many of the country districts famine had already produced shocking results. So profoundly was Spenser moved by what he saw on this journey that his memory years later gave to a description of it in the *View* a graphic quality and an eloquence that have made of the passage a classic:

> The end, I assure me, will be very short. . . . The proof whereof I saw sufficiently ensampled in those late wars in Munster, for notwithstanding that the same was a most rich and plentiful country, full of corn and cattle, that you would have thought they would have been able to stand long, yet ere one year and a half they were brought to such wretchedness as that any stony heart would have rued the same. Out of every corner of the woods and glens they came creeping forth upon their hands, for their legs could not bear them; they looked anatomies of death, they spake like ghosts crying out of their graves, they did eat of the dead carrions—happy where they could find them—yea, and one another soon after, insomuch as the very carcasses they spared not to scrape out of their graves, and if they found a plot of water-cresses or shamrocks, there they flocked as to a feast for the time; yet not able long to continue therewithal, that in short space there were none almost left, and a most populous and plentiful country suddenly left void of man or beast. Yet sure in all that war there perished not many by the sword, but all by the extremity of famine, which they themselves had wrought.[59]

From Cork, Grey went to Limerick. He was back in Dublin by November 6, having devoted less than two months to this journey. The distressing conditions in Munster naturally grew worse, so that by the following spring "griesly famine" was stalking everywhere.

A traditional privilege of the deputy was to reward his associates in the Irish government by favors in the form of leases and forfeited lands. The lord deputy, says Moryson, "may give the lands and goods of felons and traitors convicted to any of his servants or friends," as also "intrusions, alienations, fines, and like things of great moment." [60] Grey naturally exercised this privilege, and in fact so freely in the case of certain persons during the winter of 1581-1582 that a chorus of angry expostulation went straight across the water to Elizabeth's ears.[61] She was assured that revenue which should have been hers was being diverted to Grey's friends, and she promptly responded by curbing Grey's generosity. Against this action by the queen, Bryskett protested vigorously to Walsing-

[59] P. 135.

[60] In Falkiner, pp. 235, 236.

[61] *C. S. P. Ir.* (1574-1585), pp. 329 (71), 341 (29), 343 (39).

ham in a letter of May 10, 1582. In Bryskett's judgment, a governor would soon lose prestige if he lacked the means of rewarding those who served him, and he wondered whether the agitation had not risen from the desire of Grey's enemies to make him weary of his post.[62]

Spenser, who, like Shakespeare, combined the man of affairs with the poet, profited by Grey's good will toward him, though we are ignorant as to what part, if any, Grey had in helping him secure the first lease that he is known to have acquired. On December 6, 1581, Spenser was granted a lease far away in the southeastern corner of Ireland, at Enniscorthy, in County Wexford.[63] It included the site of a friary, with mill and orchard; a manor, ruined castle, and old weir; and farm lands. Three days after his grant had been passed, he conveyed this property to Richard Synnot, a gentleman of consequence residing near Wexford.[64] It is worth noting that Synnot had previously held this very property.[65] Perhaps his strong desire to repossess it accounts for Spenser's parting with it so quickly. It would be highly interesting to know more about this first recorded transaction by Spenser in Irish lands. In 1586 Vice Treasurer Wallop leased a portion of Synnot's holdings at Enniscorthy and rebuilt the thirteenth-century castle as his dwelling. This fine structure, restored and enlarged, is still in use.

The statement is often made that Spenser invested the funds derived from the sale of his lease of the Enniscorthy lands in a dissolved Augustinian monastery at New Ross, also in County Wexford. Actually there is no record of when he obtained the property at New Ross, or with what funds. We do know, however, that he bought the lease from Lord Mountgarret, of Ballyragget, Kilkenny, and that he sold it to Sir Anthony Colclough, of Tintern, Wexford, by 1584, for Colclough died in that year.[66] Evidently we have here another early business venture on Spenser's part.

To the rebellion of James Eustace, Viscount Baltinglas, Spenser owed the opportunity to secure several pieces of property, one of which at least gave him not merely an investment but a country home. Baltinglas, it will be recalled, when Grey arrived, was in revolt, having drawn his sword in the sincere but vain hope of re-establishing Catholicism in Ireland. Because he had ties of blood with many nobles of the Pale, and because, with the notable exception of Ormonde and Kildare, most of the

[62] Plomer and Cross, p. 38.

[63] Fiant 3785, *Thirteenth Report*, p. 149.

[64] Fiant 5963, *Sixteenth Report*, p. 276.

[65] Fiant 2663, *Twelfth Report*, p. 157.

[66] Ferguson, *The Gentleman's Magazine*, 1855, 2. 606; Lewis, *A Topographical Dictionary of Ireland* 2. 581.

Anglo-Irish nobles were Catholics, he had won a considerable following. When further resistance seemed futile, he escaped in 1581 to Spain, where he was kindly received by Philip II. A plan of his to raise troops in Spain for the invasion of Ireland came to nothing. He remained there till his death in 1585, at which time he was formally attainted, but his estates were lost to him when he went overseas.

In January, 1582, Grey was required to furnish the authorities in England with a list of "lands and goods of the rebels" given away by him. From this list we learn that Spenser had received the lease of a house in Dublin that had belonged to Baltinglas and the custodiam of an estate in County Kildare called the Newland, which had belonged to John Eustace, presumably a relative of Baltinglas involved in his rebellion. There is some reason to believe that the owner of the Newland was soon pardoned, so that Spenser may not have profited by his estate.[67]

Of much more interest is the fact that on August 24, 1582, Spenser leased "the site of the house of friars called the New Abbey, co. Kildare, with appurtenances; also an old waste town adjoining, and its appurtenances, in the queen's disposition by the rebellion of James Eustace." Spenser had the right to hold this property for twenty-one years, at an annual rental of £3. And as usual in such cases, he was forbidden to transfer it to anyone but an Englishman or a native of the Pale, or to charge "coynye and livery,"—that is, to exact food and shelter for man and horse from his tenants, after an ancient practice which the English were doing their best to stamp out.

The abbey was a Franciscan friary founded by Roland Eustace, baron of Portlester, in 1486, and dissolved fifty-three years later, being in ruins at the time of its suppression. We can imagine Spenser's wandering through the desolate choir, with its stone effigies of the founder and his wife, and through the confessional chapel and the refectory, all of which were still intact long after Spenser's day, and observing with admiration the beautiful central steeple of the decaying pile. In connection with the abbey were a burial ground, an orchard and garden, and eight acres of pasture.[68] This property was situated near Kilcullen, twenty-five miles from Dublin, on a bank of the Liffey where the river winds through rolling farm land. Close by lay a portion of the great bog of Allen, to whose insect life Spenser refers in *The Faerie Queene*.

[67] *C. S. P. Ir.* (1574-1585), pp. 344-345 (40 III); Covington, *MP* 22. 63-65.

[68] Fiant 3969, *Thirteenth Report*, p. 174; Fitzgerald, *Journal of the Co. Kildare Archaeological Society* 3. 301-317; Ronan, *The Reformation in Dublin*, p. 232. Spenser was destined to hold this property for but seven and a half years, for, his rent not being paid during that period, "the lease became forfeited, and was annulled" (Ferguson, *The Gentleman's Magazine*, 1855, 2. 605).

That Spenser lived at New Abbey is to be presumed from the fact that he appears as " of New Abay " in the list of commissioners of musters for County Kildare in 1583. He was appointed again in 1584.[69] The commissioners of musters were required to summon the subjects of each barony, or county division, and record the arms and men available in that area. In 1583 he was one of twenty-seven such commissioners for Kildare. The small rent charged for New Abbey does not suggest a property in which the lessee would take great pride, but to Spenser the alteration of his status from that of even a lord deputy's secretary to that of a gentleman—he is thus designated in his leases—resident on a country estate may have seemed an elevation of no small consequence.

In describing Spenser's acquisition of New Abbey, we have passed over certain events of the winter and early spring of 1581-1582. To these we must now return. As Grey and Spenser looked back upon this period, the chill season must have seemed appropriate to the grim work that absorbed their attention. In spite of Elizabeth's general pardon, certain persons connected with Baltinglas' rebellion had to be brought to trial, and also others concerned in the later uprising of William Nugent; and a number were executed.

The most sensational case was that of Sir Nicholas Nugent, chief justice of the common pleas. Of the prominent Anglo-Norman family of the Nugents, two nephews of the chief justice had given the government much cause for anxiety. These were Christopher Nugent, fourteenth Baron Delvin, who, it will be remembered, was confined by Grey in Dublin Castle with his father-in-law, the earl of Kildare, in the winter of 1580, and Lord Delvin's brother, William Nugent, also suspect in connection with Baltinglas' rebellion. William had sought refuge with Turlough Luineach O'Neill, but after failing in an effort to head a revolt against the government, had escaped, in January, 1582, to Scotland. One of the charges brought against the chief justice was that he was privy to William Nugent's rebellion. As we now view the charges, his guilt seems doubtful, and it may be that the conduct of his two troublesome nephews weighed unjustly against him. The trial was held at Trim, in East Meath, not far from Dublin, on April 4. Grey was present and probably Spenser. If so, Spenser, though absorbed in the trial, may have allowed himself a few glances at the many antiquities of one of the most interesting of Irish towns. Here today we may view the stately ruins of the Abbey of St. Peter and St. Paul, the great towers of King John's Castle, and, dominating these and other ancient buildings, the Norman watchtower known as Yellow

[69] Fiant 4150, *Thirteenth Report*, p. 205; Fiant 4464, *Fifteenth Report*, p. 49.

The village of Kilcullen, County Kildare, near which was New Abbey, leased by Spenser in 1582. From Thomas Cromwell's *Excursions through Ireland*, London, 1820.

Steeple, rising on what is said to have been the site of an abbey founded by St. Patrick. On April 6 Nugent was hanged. He met his death with patience and resolution but to the end protested his innocence.

By executing prominent residents of the Pale, of whom Sir Nicholas Nugent was the most conspicuous, Grey, according to Camden, "incurred great displeasure with the queen." [70] Grey's forthright, uncompromising methods could hardly appeal to one who herself practiced the most circuitous and temporizing diplomacy, and who was a master of compromise. Spenser in the *View* clearly describes Grey's mode of procedure:

> . . . his course indeed was this, that he spared not the heads and principals of any mischievous practice or rebellion but showed sharp judgment on them, chiefly for ensample sake, that all the meaner sort, which also were then generally infected with that evil, might by terror thereof be reclaimed and saved, if it were possible, for in that last conspiracy of the English Pale, think you not that there were many more guilty than that felt the punishment. . . ? [71]

Within Grey's own official family, as well as in England, were those who disapproved his practices, and during his last year in Ireland they were constantly sending complaints of him to their friends and patrons at the English court. Certainly such complaints, made behind his back and therefore the more disquieting, intensified his desire to be rid of the whole thankless task.

The duties required of a governor's private secretary, including many long, dangerous journeys with his chief, seem not entirely to have excluded social and literary pursuits from Spenser's life. Yet had it not been for a book entitled *A Discourse of Ciuill Life*, published by Lodowick Bryskett in 1606, this more humane side of Spenser's first two years in Ireland would be quite unknown to us. Bryskett's book is, in the main,[72] translated from a work by Giovanni Battista Giraldi Cintio, and deals with that subject of never-failing interest to the Renaissance mind—the education of a gentleman. Like his model, Bryskett's discussion is cast into the form of three dialogues, but for each he has written an original introduction, and for Giraldi's speakers he has substituted a group of Dublin friends; namely, John Long, archbishop of Armagh; Sir Robert Dillon, successor to Sir Nicholas Nugent as chief justice of the common pleas; George Dormer, the queen's solicitor; Captains Christopher Carleill, Thomas Norris, Warham St. Leger, and Nicholas Dawtrey; Thomas Smith, a popular Dublin apothecary; and Edmund Spenser.

[70] *The Historie of the . . . Princesse Elizabeth*, Book II, p. 118.

[71] P. 138.

[72] Plomer and Cross, pp. 72-82, and Erskine, *PMLA* 30. 837-842 (Erskine points out that the questions asked by Spenser on the third day are all in the original).

The conversations, according to Bryskett, were occasioned by the coming of these men to visit him at a little cottage he had recently built "somewhat more than a mile" from Dublin, where he was taking physic for a few days in the spring, not because of illness, but to prevent it. The talk soon turned on Bryskett's having lately resigned as clerk of the council. His friends wondered at his relinquishing such an office, but he assured them that he had had more satisfaction in this short period of leisure with his books than in all his years of service to the state. The study that most appealed to him was moral philosophy, and he was delighted once more to have freedom for it. When his friends quoted the proverb *Virtutis laus, actio*, he replied that he still had his post as controller of the customs on wines, and moreover held himself ready to serve the lord deputy and council on special assignments. Because he had never been capable of the exacting study demanded by Plato and Aristotle, he had depended, he said, on the Italians for an exposition of Greek philosophy. "Yet is there a gentleman in this company," he went on,

> whom I have had often a purpose to entreat that, as his leisure might serve him, he would vouchsafe to spend some time with me to instruct me in some hard points which I cannot of myself understand, knowing him to be not only perfect in the Greek tongue but also very well read in philosophy, both moral and natural. Nevertheless, such is my bashfulness as I never yet durst open my mouth to disclose this my desire unto him, though I have not wanted some heartening thereunto from himself. For, of his love and kindness to me, he encouraged me long sithens to follow the reading of the Greek tongue, and offered me his help to make me understand it.[73]

And now Bryskett hopes that this gentleman, who is none other than Spenser, will consent to give the company an exposition of moral philosophy; but Spenser declines, with the following explanation:

> For sure I am that it is not unknown unto you that I have already undertaken a work tending to the same effect, which is in heroical verse, under the title of a Faerie Queene, to represent all the moral virtues, assigning to every virtue a knight to be the patron and defender of the same; in whose actions and feats of arms and chivalry the operations of that virtue whereof he is the protector are to be expressed, and the vices and unruly appetites that oppose themselves against the same to be beaten down and overcome. Which work, as I have already well entered into, if God shall please to spare me life that I may finish it according to my mind, your wish, Master Bryskett, will be in some sort accomplished. . . .

As a counter proposal he tells of a translation by Bryskett from Giraldi, and suggests that Bryskett present its contents to them. Pressed by the others, Bryskett consents, and the discussion promptly begins.

[73] P. 25.

On the second day, which was fair and clear, before turning to philosophy, the company, led by Bryskett, took a pleasant green path to a little hill above his cottage, from which they had a delightful view of the city, sea, and harbor. Here they talked till they were called by a servant to dinner, after which they resumed their philosophical discussion.

On the third day, they again climbed the little hill. Before turning philosophers, they spoke of the quiet that Ireland was then enjoying. Lord Grey had "plowed and harrowed the rough ground," to the profit of the present deputy.

Though the conversations are represented as occurring on consecutive days, at least two years would seem to have elapsed between the first and third days. When the conversations began, Bryskett had but lately relinquished his clerkship of the council; hence the most interesting portion for us, the long introduction to the first day, appears to belong to the spring of 1582. But on the third day we learn that Grey's successor is now governor of Ireland.

Obviously just such a series of meetings as is here described did not take place, but just as obviously similar meetings might have occurred and almost certainly did. There is enough of known fact in the introductions by Bryskett to give us faith in the general veracity of these original portions. So far as Spenser is concerned, we need not doubt that he was one of Bryskett's circle of friends, that the talk of this group sometimes dwelt on philosophy and literature, that Spenser had made considerable progress with his *Faerie Queene* and had shown "some parcels" of it to certain of his Dublin friends, that he was respected for his command of Greek and his knowledge of moral and natural philosophy, and that he had encouraged Bryskett to read Greek and had offered to help him with it. Evidently the sharp alteration in Spenser's environment and mode of life had not even temporarily destroyed his interest in what was to be his greatest achievement.

Although other literary men besides Bryskett found their way to Ireland and seem to have resided at Dublin while Spenser was there, we cannot be sure that he was intimate with any of them. Barnabe Rich, soldier, romance-writer, and prolix critic of his age, Spenser must have known, as also Barnabe Googe, whose eclogues and translation of Palingenius' *Zodiake of Life* are believed to have had some influence on Spenser's writings.[74] Another man, Geoffrey Fenton, remembered for various translations, including his monumental rendering, from the French, of Guicciardini's history of Italy, went to Ireland, like Spenser, in 1580, and a few

[74] Greenlaw, *PMLA* 26. 425-427; Tuve, *JEGP* 34. 1-19; Covington, *MP* 22. 65.

weeks before Spenser's arrival became, through Burghley's influence, a secretary in the Irish government. Spenser's biographers are fond of imagining a delightful association between these two literary men, marooned together so far from the centers of Renaissance culture, but in reality there were very likely barriers to a warm friendship: Fenton shared neither Spenser's faith in a rigorous attitude toward the Irish nor his enthusiasm for Lord Grey.

Except for a short journey to Offaly to avenge the death of Captain Mackworth, who had been captured and flayed alive by the O'Connors, Grey seems to have remained in Dublin till his departure on August 31. These last months were a trying time for the lord deputy. His forces had been so reduced that he was unable to give Sir Nicholas Malby the aid necessary to suppress a foray into Connaught led by Con O'Donnell. And the earl of Desmond still eluded capture. To be sure, in January the head of Desmond's brother, Sir John, had been sent to Dublin by Colonel Zouche and fixed by chains on a tower of the Castle, the ring that was on Sir John being at the same time sent by Zouche as a present to Elizabeth; and in June the earl's wife had surrendered (conditionally) to Grey. But the earl himself, accompanied by a large army, continued to pillage and waste the country, with a savagery born of desperation. To the survivors in Munster, it must have seemed that a malign fate was presiding over their land. "At this period," remark the Four Masters, "it was commonly said that the lowing of a cow, or the voice of the ploughman, could scarcely be heard from Dun-Caoin [Dunquin, near Smerwick] to Cashel in Munster."[75] In *The Faerie Queene*, Artegall is accompanied by Talus, an iron man, "immoueable, resistlesse, without end," who never permits his master to fail in any enterprise. In what sharp contrast was Grey's situation. He sat in Dublin impotent to establish the peace and order for which he had been struggling ever since his arrival. It is therefore not surprising that he continued his earnest appeals for recall.[76]

To some, Grey seemed a failure. Burghley and Elizabeth in England, and Geoffrey Fenton, secretary of state, and Nicholas White, master of the rolls, in Ireland, were content to see an end of his rule.[77] But others warmly commended him, feeling that he had done as well as possible amid circumstances of intolerable difficulty. Wrote Bryskett: "Her majesty had never here a more willing, a more zealous, nor a more sufficient minister

[75] 5. 1785.

[76] Between April 8 and July 10, the *Calendar of State Papers* shows him to have made seven appeals for recall.

[77] For Burghley, see *C. S. P. Ir.* (1574-1585), pp. 343 (40), 383 (4); for Fenton, pp. 328 (60), 330 (82); for White, p. 336 (55).

for such an enterprise. . . ."; and Spenser described him as "a most wise pilot," who steered his ship amidst roaring billows and brought her safely through. If it be objected that both these men were warm personal friends of Grey, take the verdict of Fynes Moryson: "Such was the Lord Grey, in the late Queen's reign Lord Deputy of Ireland, who knew best of all his predecessors to bridle their fierce and clamorous nation." [78] His associates Loftus, Wallop, and Malby also regarded him highly.[79] Perhaps the question of Grey's success or failure can never be settled—unless to win the hearty approval of a man like Spenser can in itself be viewed as a kind of success, especially when it results in identification, if only in a few stanzas, with a hero of one of the world's greatest poems.

The last canto of the Fifth Book of *The Faerie Queene* may be read as an idealized narrative of Grey's deputyship. Yet if so read, we must conclude that the poet has given us rather a dream of what might have been than a sober picture of what was. In the account of Grey's leaving Ireland, however, there is no departure from fact:

> But ere he could reforme it thoroughly,
> He through occasion called was away,
> To Faerie Court, that of necessity
> His course of Iustice he was forst to stay. . . . [80]

Upon his arrival, two hags, Envy and Detraction, rave at him, while their dog of a hundred tongues, the Blatant Beast, adds his hideous baying to their clamor. But Artegall passes quietly on, paying no heed even when pelted by the hags with stones and a poisonous serpent. Into these closing seventeen stanzas of Book V Spenser has poured the passion of a heart that knows no caution when a slandered friend needs a defense.

Spenser felt that Grey had given him his real start in life. Without patronage in the form of his clerkship and leases, he might never have found leisure for great poetical achievement. His gratitude is expressed with characteristic warmth in a dedicatory sonnet to Grey published with *The Faerie Queene*:

> Most Noble Lord the pillor of my life,
> And Patrone of my Muses pupillage,
> Through whose large bountie poured on me rife,
> In the first season of my feeble age,
> I now doe liue, bound yours by vassalage. . . .

[78] Plomer and Cross, p. 23; Spenser, *View*, p. 27; Moryson in Falkiner, p. 308.

[79] For Loftus, see *C. S. P. Ir.* (1574-1585), p. 360 (27); for Wallop, pp. 275 (17), 356 (56); for Malby, *Cal. Carew MSS.* (1575-1588), p. 331.

[80] 5. 12. 27.

XI

EXILE SELF-IMPOSED

THE SUMMER months of 1582, preceding Grey's departure, must have been an anxious period for Spenser. Would his patron really be called home? And if so, would he return to take again the sword of state and finish what he had commenced, or would another fill his place? On July 12, Elizabeth wrote Grey from Nonsuch, asking him to come to England, the government meanwhile to be administered by Archbishop Loftus and Vice Treasurer Wallop; [1] but communication was slow, and the longed-for letter probably did not reach Grey for several weeks, so that it was August 31 before he left for England.

For Grey and for men like Spenser, Bryskett, and Malby, who loved him, the separation must have been painful. In addition to the ordinary grief of parting, there was for Grey a sense of deep dissatisfaction over his stay in Ireland. None knew better than Spenser how trying these two years had been for Grey. Elizabeth's accusations of harshness and extravagance had been hard to bear, but still harder perhaps the knowledge that some of his most intimate associates had failed to give him loyal support and had even seemed pleased at his loss of the queen's favor.[2] During the second winter he had suffered much from ill health, and had found the exertions demanded by his position almost beyond his strength. One of his sons had died in Dublin during the previous spring, and his soldiers had suffered a terrible mortality from inadequate food and clothing. But the bitterest draught from his cup of sorrow was probably his sense of frustration—so much blood and treasure spent, but his end not yet attained. On November 5 the bishop of Meath wrote of the departure of Grey's wife for England, a sure sign to Grey's friends in Ireland that there would be no reinstatement.[3]

Fortunately for Spenser, a week before Grey left, the lease of New Abbey was granted him, and when, in November, the chance of continuing as the lord deputy's secretary faded completely, his thoughts must have turned to a quite different mode of life on this property. While he was with Grey, there had been continual change, excitement, a sense of being in the confidence of one who was virtual dictator of Ireland. Moreover,

[1] *C. S. P. Ir.* (1574-1585), p. 385 (17). [2] *Ibid.*, p. 343 (40). [3] *Ibid.*, p. 410 (19).

NEW ABBEY, IN AUGUST, 1782.
From a sketch by Austin Cooper.

A sketch of New Abbey in 1782, with choir, refectory, and confessional chapel still standing. From the *Journal of the County Kildare Archaeological Society*, Vol. III.

he had found in Dublin an environment not wholly different from that of London, and had enjoyed there the society of congenial spirits. But twenty-five miles away near Kilcullen, on the borders of the Pale, there would be compensations. He would be one of the landed gentry. His ingenuity would be pleasantly exercised in making something of the monastic properties and the "old waste town adjoining." Best of all, he would have leisure for his pen. Leisure is needed by a poet; yet in spite of occasional relaxation with such friends as Bryskett, how little quiet he had thus far enjoyed! Finally, a day of riding would bring him to Dublin, so that he would not be completely divorced from his former life, and the walled towns of Kildare and Naas were but six or seven miles distant. Even if his estate yielded him small financial return, he had other sources of income, thanks to Lord Grey. Such considerations may have passed through Spenser's mind, but his purpose in residing at New Abbey, and the details of his two years there, must remain almost entirely conjectural.

Luckily the experience of his friend Bryskett at this time offers a curiously close parallel to Spenser's, and of Bryskett's experience we know a good deal. Bryskett's retirement followed a career in Dublin more extended but otherwise similar to Spenser's. He too had independent sources of income, he also elected to occupy monastic lands on the border of an English settlement, and like Spenser he had literary tastes to which retirement would give larger scope.

By the fall of 1581 Bryskett's failure to secure the position of secretary of state had caused him to determine on "a quieter kind of life, the better to attend my studies and to serve God." On January 15 he writes Walsingham more fully of his plans.[4] He intends to see whether by industry and toil he can "pick out of the soil a living," which, though modest, will be free from the discontent he has felt as clerk of the council at Dublin. "I mean," he continues, "to make proof (God willing) whether the life of a borderer in this land be alike perilous unto all men, and to see if a just and honest simple life may not, even among the most barbarous people of the world, breed security to him that shall live near them or among them." To this end he has secured from Nicholas White, master of the rolls, lands near Enniscorthy, County Wexford, formerly in the possession of the Priory of St. John's, a house of Augustinian Canons of St. Victor.[5]

[4] Plomer and Cross, *The Life and Correspondence of Lodowick Bryskett*, pp. 31, 32-34.

[5] Cf. Judson, *MLQ* 5. 144.

There I mean to confine myself for a time, till God shall please to make my planet favorably to shine, having armed my mind aforehand to take any toil, any hazard, and any other inconvenience that this confused state shall breed, and being fully resolved to esteem the coarse and hard, temperate fare of a plowman void of indignities far sweeter than all the dainty dishes of princes' courts, where (with humility and duty I speak it) I think it easy for a man to fill his belly, and to be puffed up with vanities and never accomplished hopes and expectations, but very hard for an honest man to purchase the due reward of his service.

Evidently he is contemplating an ambitious establishment, since he asks that twenty men be provided him, which he will match at his own expense, for protection against depredations that he fears from the neighboring Kavanaghs. Incidentally he expects to pay a rental ten times Spenser's. These men were not granted, as Elizabeth was bent on reducing her armed forces in Ireland, and so Bryskett resigned himself to "a more quiet kind of life" in the country.[6]

Is it fanciful to imagine that Bryskett's determination to try the life of a "borderer" influenced Spenser, who might conceivably, in spite of his Irish investments, have returned to England with Grey? Whatever induced Spenser to lease New Abbey and settle there, we can hardly question the value of this new manner of life to his poetic career. Seclusion and an opportunity for reflection have been needed for the creation of most of the world's great poetry, and it may be that here first in Ireland Spenser enjoyed favorable conditions for work on his epic. Indeed, considering his official duties both before and after the New Abbey period, it seems probable that a considerable portion of the first three books of *The Faerie Queene* was composed during his two years on the banks of the Liffey, with the pretty rolling county of Kildare about him and the Wicklow Mountains rising blue against the horizon to the east.

Though Spenser may have led a relatively quiet life at New Abbey, we cannot easily think of him as indifferent to political developments in Ireland. He had been too long in the very maelstrom of Irish affairs not to watch with fascination its confused and dangerous currents. For two years, Loftus and Wallop governed Ireland jointly. In Spenser's judgment, they were an ill-matched team: Loftus, as was natural to a churchman, favored a mild policy; Wallop preferred the forceful methods of Lord Grey.[7] But though they sometimes pulled against each other, their administration was made notable by one accomplishment—the ending of the Desmond rebellion. On December 3, 1582, Ormonde had been reap-

[6] Plomer and Cross, p. 37. [7] *View*, p. 141.

pointed lord general of Munster; and, while offering pardons to all except the earl of Desmond, he hunted the latter steadily for eleven months. Desmond's large army gradually melted away, and finally on a moonlight November night in 1583, the earl was tracked to a wooded glen near Tralee by Owen O'Moriarty, a neighboring landowner, with a few soldiers, and slain the next day.[8] Thus ended a pursuit that had lasted for nearly four years. On June 21, 1584, a new lord deputy was sworn in at Dublin, Sir John Perrot, a big, courageous, hot-tempered man who bore a suspiciously close resemblance to Henry VIII. He was experienced in Irish affairs, since he had been for six years president of Munster, and he now attempted to win the Irish by conciliation. Spenser, as one might expect, distrusted his policy, and indeed, twelve years later, expressed the conviction that Perrot's conduct of affairs, so contrary to Grey's and Wallop's, had contributed to a dangerous reaction. To Perrot's methods and those of his successor Spenser attributed the fact that Ireland was then "more dangerously sick than ever before."[9]

Bryskett, as his letter to Walsingham makes clear, went to Wexford, not with the thought of ending his days there, but to wait until his planet, shining favorably, should give him something more to his taste. And Spenser, too, with his unquenchable ambition, certainly thought of New Abbey as a wayside stop on his journey toward something better. Bryskett had been of use to Spenser at Dublin in passing on to him the clerkship of faculties, and now he was to do Spenser another good turn.

While Bryskett had been clerk of the council at Dublin, he had envied the clerk of the Munster council, who, illogically, was paid £20 sterling, nearly three times what Bryskett received.[10] On October 17, 1583, Thomas Burgate, clerk of the council of Munster, died, and Bryskett was appointed to this long-desired post, having been granted its reversion by the privy council, through Lord Grey's influence, in the previous March. But Bryskett was too busy at Enniscorthy to take up his new duties, and the clerkship was administered temporarily by an appointee of Ormonde's.[11] That Spenser was Bryskett's deputy on March 31, 1588, has long been known, and the conclusion now seems inescapable, thanks to the researches of Messrs. Plomer, Cross, and Jenkins, that Spenser became his deputy not long after Bryskett received the clerkship, probably in the summer of 1584.[12] Among various bits of evidence, the best is to be found

[8] Bagwell, *Ireland under the Tudors* 3. 113.

[9] *View*, pp. 141-142.

[10] Plomer and Cross, p. 9.

[11] *Ibid.*, p. 43.

[12] *Ibid.*, pp. 44-46; Jenkins, *PMLA* 47. 109-121. The presence of Spenser in Munster

in Spenser's penmanship, which has been traced in letters written for the president of Munster as early as March 7, 1585.

Bryskett as clerk of the council at Dublin had accompanied the lord deputy on his journeys, and Richard Boyle, who succeeded Spenser in the Munster clerkship, said that he attended the lord president "in all his employments."[13] Spenser, we may infer, maintained a similar close association with the brothers John and Thomas Norris, who successively ruled Munster throughout Spenser's connection with the clerkship. He must also have kept the minutes of the council meetings, written letters, and attested the correctness of documents copied by clerks attached to his office. Until recently the period of four or five years between Spenser's residence as a country gentleman at New Abbey and his resumption of that life at Kilcolman in County Cork had been almost a blank. Now because of the investigations mentioned above, and especially the careful study of these years made by Professor Jenkins,[14] the mists have happily receded, and by examining the careers of the Norris brothers we can form at least a fair notion of how Spenser was occupied.

Before turning to John Norris, let us glance for a moment at his family. His grandfather was the courtier Henry Norris, who, in a cool, manly fashion, had parted with his head as one of the alleged lovers of Anne Boleyn. His father and mother, partly because of his grandfather's loyalty to Anne, enjoyed the warm esteem of Elizabeth, who knighted his father and later made him Baron Norris of Rycote, and, with her odd weakness for nicknames, dubbed his mother "my black crow." These two possessed meek, mild natures in sharp contrast to the temperament of their six war-loving sons. It was as if a pair of doves had reared a brood of eagles. England proved too small for them: all saw military service abroad; four died in Ireland and a fifth in Brittany.

John Norris, the second son, had schooled himself in sixteenth-century warfare first in France, then in Ireland, and finally in the Netherlands before being summoned to the presidency of Munster. In these countries he had been associated with some of the most famous men of his time. In France he had served under Admiral Coligny, the great Huguenot leader, and in Ireland he had assisted Walter Devereux, first earl of Essex, in his vain, ambitious effort to establish a colony in Ulster. Here Norris was in contact also for a time with Francis Drake just back from

as early as February 1, 1585, is probably indicated by his loan (or advance of wages) to Captain Edward Barkley, constable of Askeaton, noted by Heffner, *MLN* 50. 194.

[13] Townshend, *The Life and Letters of the Great Earl of Cork*, p. 20.

[14] *PMLA* 53. 350-362.

his first successful freebooting expedition to the West Indies. Norris's experiences in Ulster converted him to the faith that Ireland was not "to be brought to obedience but by force." [15] His reputation as a soldier mounted steadily, and on his return from the Low Countries he was regarded as one of the ablest commanders of his time. This is the side of the man stressed by Spenser in a sonnet to Norris published with *The Faerie Queene.* He calls him a "Precedent of all that armes ensue," but rightly says that his courage and prowess are tempered with reason. When a president was needed for Munster, it is not surprising that the eyes of the privy council should have fallen on this skilful, wise soldier, at the moment back in England enjoying a respite from what had been his almost incessant military activity.

In July, 1584, Norris arrived and went at once to Munster. But in less than a month he was required by the Lord Deputy Perrot to assist him in a campaign against Sorley Boy MacDonnell, the old Scoto-Irish chief of northeastern Ulster, who had plagued the Irish government through most of his life. Since the beginning of the Tudor period, Scottish settlers had been filtering into Ulster. They now occupied the beautiful wooded glens of Antrim, whose proximity to Scotland gave their leaders a convenient asylum if pressed too vigorously by the English, and also a useful recruiting ground for the redshanks, or tan-legged Highlanders, who frequently and without warning appeared in northern Ireland in disconcerting numbers. Sometimes the English made peace with Sorley Boy and sometimes drove him across the sea, but he always soon reappeared, like a persistent hornet. Now Perrot, deeply concerned at reports of the arrival of large numbers of Scots, decided that there was immediate need of his presence in the north. On the journey to Ulster, which occupied much of the autumn, Norris so acquitted himself as to win the warm approval of Perrot. The deputy's forces went all the way to Dunluce, Sorley Boy's picturesque castle rising from the sea on its great pedestal of stone just off the northern coast not far from the Giant's Causeway. Most of the Scots disappeared before Perrot's arrival, but Dunluce was captured, and much booty was taken.[16] By October 16, Norris was back in Dublin. Whether Spenser accompanied him on this campaign or remained with Sir William Stanley, who was left in charge of Munster, we do not know. If he remained with Stanley, his life was not dull, for on September 17 Stanley wrote Walsingham that he had legally executed more than three hundred persons and thus rendered the whole province safe for travelers.[17]

[15] Bagwell 3. 131. [16] *Cal. Carew MSS.* (1575-1588), pp. 378, 380, 383.
[17] *C. S. P. Ir.* (1574-1585), p. 528 (92).

The northern campaign over, Norris had leisure to inspect his province. What he saw did not please him. Having been lately in the busy, populous Low Countries, he must have found the desolation of Munster especially terrible. On March 7, 1585, he wrote the privy council from Dublin that both cattle and people had largely disappeared, and that many of the remaining inhabitants, because of the extremity of their want, could hardly live without stealing. And again, three weeks later, he wrote Burghley from Clonmel—this letter and that of March 7 were penned by Spenser—that the province had suffered such a huge and universal wasting that it would be long before the inhabitants could gain the means of livelihood.[18] Evidently he felt that he had been appointed to rule over something very like a graveyard. Resettlement was clearly the only solution, and indeed plans were already on foot. An inspection of the forfeited lands, which had been started in September, 1584, was then in progress.[19] Throughout Spenser's years of service as deputy clerk, the colonization of Munster was the big task facing the officials of that province, so that Spenser's mind was turned perforce to the thought of land. Every detail of the huge resettlement project was known to him as it unfolded, including its intricate legal aspects, and hence his final acquisition of thousands of acres of forfeited lands was entirely natural.

By the end of March, 1585, Norris began to feel homesick for the Low Countries. He saw no immediate chance of exercising his military gifts in Ireland but abundant opportunity in the Netherlands. Instead of rusting forgotten in a desolate corner of Ireland, he would like to be saving Antwerp from the Spaniards.[20] The queen was willing he should go. Since some weeks of the two months before his departure were occupied with parliament, it is to be presumed that his restless energies found a satisfactory outlet. On April 26 parliament convened, and Norris attended as a representative of Cork. Spenser must have enjoyed being back in Dublin, and he undoubtedly watched the parliamentary proceedings with intense interest, and was gratified by the forceful, eloquent speaking of Norris. Perrot made a stately appearance at the opening of parliament, but his tactless dealing with the members prevented the passage of most of the legislation on which he had set his heart. Spenser in the *View* appears to express his personal interest in this legislation and to regret its failure.[21]

[18] *Ibid.*, pp. 554 (13), 556 (41).

[19] *Ibid.*, pp. 525 (74), 527 (90); the inspection was not completed till October, 1585—*ibid.*, p. 583 (9).

[20] *Ibid.*, p. 557 (43).

[21] Pp. 35-36.

Parliament met again during the following spring but not thereafter during Spenser's life. Shortly after parliament was prorogued, Norris left for England, taking with him letters of commendation written by his associates in Ireland, and in December his brother Thomas was appointed vice president of Munster.

Thomas Norris, though but twenty-nine years old, was already experienced in Irish affairs. A graduate of Oxford at twenty, he had come to Ireland as captain of a troop of horse at twenty-three, and had become familiar with Munster by sharing for many months the pursuit of the elusive earl of Desmond. In Connaught and Ulster he had also seen service. He was sensible and modest, and he knew how to get on with his companions. Like Spenser, he made Ireland his home for the rest of his life. Though we most readily think of him booted and spurred at the head of his troop of horse, we should remember that he was one of the visitors at Bryskett's Dublin cottage and perhaps liked a discussion of moral philosophy quite as well as a brush with Irish rebels. We cannot doubt that Spenser thoroughly enjoyed his close association with this capable, popular man.

During Thomas Norris's first year as vice president, the fear of Spanish invasion was constant. To the English, Spain seemed to cast a dark shadow across the island, but to many of the Irish this shadow looked like a band of light. Some of the chief men of the province, as the seneschal of Imokilly and Garret MacThomas, maintained an ambiguous attitude. To Vice Treasurer Wallop, they seemed to be looking expectantly toward a certain day, but he hoped it would be the day of their hanging, for good and true he thought they would never be.[22] The presence of this covertly disaffected element must have caused Norris uneasiness. Because the coast of Munster was vulnerable, sporadic efforts were made to increase the garrisons and strengthen the defenses. But how much there was to be done! Elizabeth had not a citadel or fort in all the cities of Munster except the Castle of Limerick, warned Norris, and even that was unmanned and decaying.[23]

Norris could not permit the disturbing rumors from Spain to absorb too much of his thought, for the province had to be resettled as soon as possible, and the surveys must be hastened. A commission, of which he and Wallop were members, worked steadily through the autumn of 1586, measuring and dividing the Munster lands into seignories of 12,000 acres each. The party stayed at Dungarvan for eight days while they surveyed

[22] *C. S. P. Ir.* (1586-1588), p. 46. [23] *Ibid.*, p. 181.

half the lands of Sir Christopher Hatton, who had literally danced his way into Elizabeth's favor. They spent eight more at Lismore and Youghal, while they plotted Raleigh's extensive lands. It was a wearisome task, for the neglected fields were overgrown with long grass, and often with heath, brambles, and furze, while the autumn rains and the shortening days further hindered their progress. Moreover, claimants to some of the lands had begun to appear, men who, though loyal, had sought an asylum elsewhere in Ireland during the Desmond rebellion, and their rights had to be weighed. The undertakers—those who "undertook" to hold the Desmond lands and provide them with English settlers—because of the slowness of the survey, returned to England for the winter, feeling that they had lost a year.[24] It was during this autumn and winter that the lands of Kilcolman were measured.[25] Spenser, presumably, was with Norris, and he may have inspected the very lands which were later to be his, without dreaming of the good fortune awaiting him.

Spenser, if closely attendant upon Norris, must have been often in the saddle, journeying here and there in Munster as Norris listened to grievances and settled disputes, and sometimes visiting Dublin on government business. The presidents of Munster had no official residence but leased one at either Limerick or Cork. Norris evidently preferred Cork, as his letters were more often written there, or at Shandon,[26] a castle of the Barrys that stood just across the northern branch of

> The spreading Lee, that like an Island fayre
> Encloseth Corke with his deuided flood. . . .[27]

One reason why Norris may have preferred Cork to Limerick was that he temporarily held Desmond property at Mallow, eighteen miles north of Cork. In 1587 this property, including the Old Castle of the Desmonds beside the Blackwater, was assigned to him.[28] If Norris resided at Cork, Spenser could hardly have failed to establish himself there, and doubtless for the rest of his life maintained especially close connections with this important southern town.

Spenser may have been in Dublin several times in 1586. Norris, we know, was there on February 27, and again, as a representative of Lim-

[24] *Ibid.*, pp. 148 (4), 168 (52), xx-xxi, 249 (22).

[25] *Ibid.*, p. 261 (44).

[26] *Ibid.*, p. 438 (19); between December 30, 1585, and June 23, 1589, the State Papers, Ireland, contain eleven letters written by Norris from Cork, only four from Limerick.

[27] *F. Q.* 4. 11. 44.

[28] *C. S. P. Ir.* (1586-1588). pp. 278 (83), 450 (39).

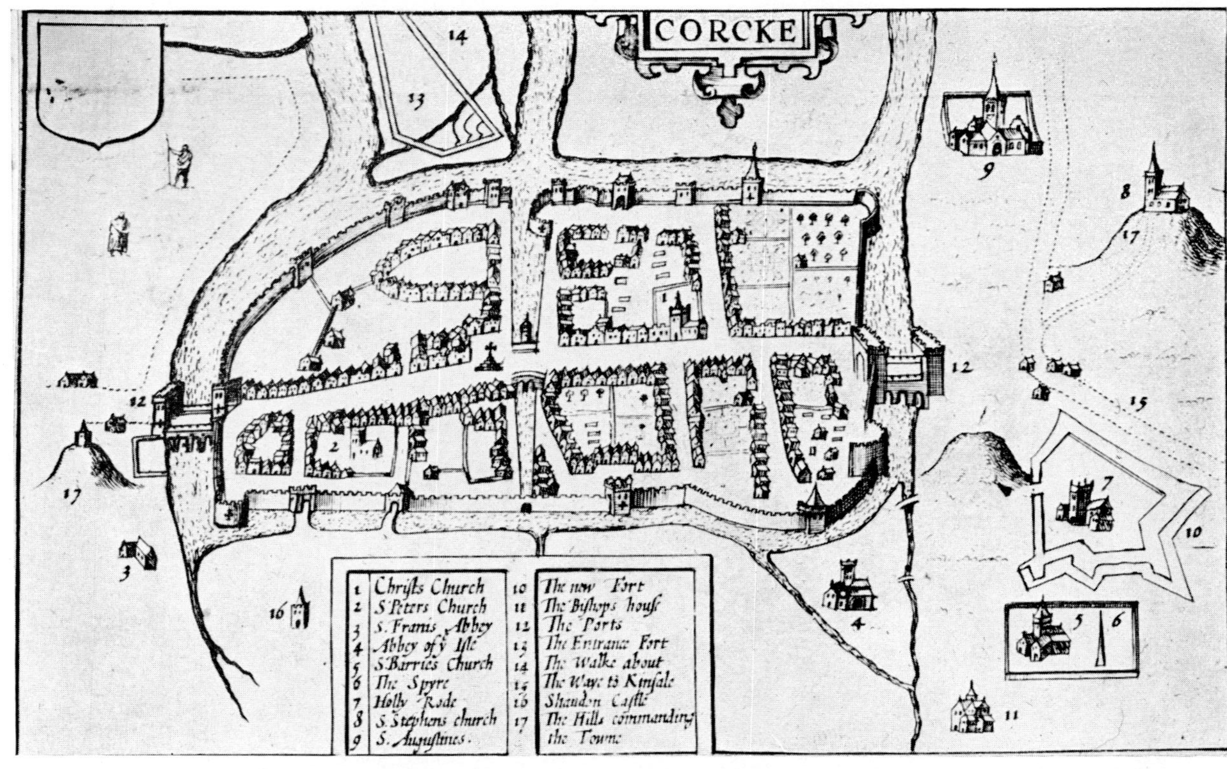

Plan of Cork executed by John Speed in 1610. The city, with Shandon Castle in left foreground, is viewed from the north. From *Pacata Hibernia*, London, 1633.

erick, at the session of parliament that met from April 26 to May 14. Its main business was passing a bill of attainder against the earl of Desmond and other rebels. Because of a practice among the rebels of conveying their lands to others before going into rebellion, so as to prevent their reverting to the crown, the bill invalidated all transfers made for twelve years prior to the Desmond rebellion. Though this provision was strenuously opposed, it was finally passed. Those hopeful of the success of the resettlement in Munster watched its passage with deepest concern. Spenser, no doubt a spectator, causes Irenius to say of this act: ". . . how hardly that act of parliament was wrung out of them, I can witness, and were it to be passed again, I dare undertake would never be compassed." [29] On July 18, Spenser was certainly in Dublin, for on that day he wrote there a sonnet to Harvey, which Harvey printed six years later in his volume entitled *Foure Letters, and certaine Sonnets.* This sonnet, called by Professor G. C. Moore Smith " the finest tribute ever paid " to Harvey's character and powers,[30] praises his old friend as a critic and congratulates him on his position of independence and detachment, from which in his " doomefull writing," he can lift up the good and damn the evil. Merely, it would seem, a small epistle in verse, it is signed " Your devoted friend, during life, Edmund Spencer." It was intended, perhaps, to console Harvey for his disappointments, since the preceding six years had contained little but frustration of his ambitious schemes for a public career; or it may have been merely the expression of a mood—composed at a moment when Spenser coveted his friend's leisure for literary work and freedom from the uncertainty and tyrannous demands of Irish life. Could Pegasus be blamed for now and then growing restive at the plow?

The most interesting and at the same time puzzling disclosure of Spenser's activities during the year 1586 is preserved in a document among the state papers which lists " Edmondus Spencer," prebendary of Effin, as delinquent, on December 8, 1586, in payment of his first fruits, or first year's income, required to be paid to the crown by the holder of a benefice. Effin is a parish near Kilmallock twenty miles south of Limerick, and a prebendary there was attached to Limerick Cathedral. Ordinarily a prebendary was a clergyman in active service, but stipends known as prebends were sometimes granted to laymen. For example, Sir Philip Sidney's income was in part derived from several prebends that he held. Professor Jenkins, mindful of Spenser's condemnation of unworthy seekers after church livings, supposes that Spenser served the parish actively.[31] But is

[29] *View*, p. 37.
[30] In Harvey, *Marginalia*, p. 57.
[31] Carpenter, *A Reference Guide*, p. 32, and *MP* 19. 406-410; Jenkins, *PMLA* 47. 119.

it not difficult to believe that a clerk of the Munster council, whose duties we know to have been many and exacting, should have undertaken "to minister to the illiterate Irish in this remote parish?" Since the considerations that induced him to accept this benefice at Effin are unknown to us, we can do no more than record the curious fact.

During 1587 the specter of invasion from Spain haunted the English. Rumors, like flocks of ill-omened birds, kept flying out of the south. Philip II had reason enough to make deadly war on England in view of the activities of British armies in the Netherlands and the havoc wrought by Drake on the Spanish main. No wonder the perennial hope of Spanish aid grew strong among certain of the Irish. In March, Norris took a step that he had long meditated, and arrested John Fitzedmund Fitzgerald, seneschal of Imokilly; Patrick Condon; and other leading gentlemen of the province whose loyalty he distrusted. This was a delicate move, for if the arrest of one had become known, the others could easily have eluded capture.[32] The experience of the seneschal of Imokilly illustrates the tragic quality of Irish life during this period. In addition to Imokilly, a Fitzgerald castle not far from Youghal, he possessed 36,000 acres of land in the province. He had been one of the first to associate himself with James Fitzmaurice's rebellion, and eventually his bravery and intelligence had made him more feared than the earl of Desmond himself. Ormonde, though long his foe in the field, greatly admired him, and had persuaded Elizabeth to pardon him. But he was now believed to be a dangerous person, fully cognizant of Spanish plans, and not averse to welcoming the invaders. After his arrest, Norris sent him to Dublin Castle for confinement. Two years later, just as the government had determined to free him, he died.

The year 1587 was important as initiating the actual resettlement of Munster. By spring the chief undertakers had decided among themselves which lands they would take, their assignments were approved by the English government, and the commission engaged in surveying was directed to content itself with less accurate surveys in order that the impatient undertakers might occupy their lands as soon as possible.[33] On April 26 two commissions were issued by Elizabeth, one to expedite the formal passing of their grants, and another to settle controversies among them.[34] The second commission was addressed to Norris, Wallop, and others, and included an undertaker by the name of Andrew Reade. He

[32] *C. S. P. Ir.* (1586-1588), pp. 278 (83), 288.
[33] *Ibid.*, pp. 271-272 (64).
[34] *Ibid.*, pp. 299 (23), 300 (26).

was a gentleman of means from Faccombe, Hampshire,[35] and to judge by his appointment on the above-mentioned board of arbitration, was held in esteem by the government. On March 14, Kilcolman had been assigned to him.[36]

With better weather, ships began to arrive bearing undertakers, or their agents, and settlers, who proceeded to establish themselves on their lands without waiting for letters patent to be passed.[37] Though the country lay sad and desolate under the bright spring sunshine, it was no longer devoid of human beings. During the four years since the Desmond rebellion had ended, the Irish had been drifting in until, as Sir Edward Fitton, one of the undertakers, wrote in June: "The country is generally wasted, but yet not a pile or castle in any place but what is full of the poorest creatures that ever I saw, so lean for want of food as wonderful, and yet so idle that they will not work, because they are descended either of kerne, horseman, or galloglas, all three the very subversion of this land." [38] But not all the natives were of this sort: satisfactory tenants were available, and the undertakers, being far short of their quotas of English families, yielded to necessity and accepted Irish tenants,[39] perhaps with the expectation of later replacing them with English. Thus at the very start, a crucial feature of the resettlement scheme became partially inoperative, and no later pressure by the English government could make the communities thoroughly English.

Our clearest glimpse of the resettlement project at this stage is to be had from the letters and tracts of Sir William Herbert, who acquired 12,000 acres in Kerry. In planting this colony, he seems to have been prompted by moral and patriotic motives more than were most of his fellow undertakers. Yet in many respects he was typical of his time. Who but a man of the Renaissance would have conceived the triple ambition to make himself remembered by writing a volume, planting a colony, and erecting a college? The following is from a letter of his to Burghley written four days after reaching his estate:

I came hither to the Castle of the Island the 26th of April. . . . Touching this place and seignory I find here divers inhabitants, some upon title, some upon sufferance; much heath ground, much barren ground, and much bog, and interlaced with them reasonable fruitful land. . . . Touching the estate of religion in

[35] *A History of Hampshire* 4. 316, 325, 363, 507.

[36] *Cal. Carew MSS.* (1575-1588), p. 449.

[37] *C. S. P. Ir.* (1586-1588), p. 367.

[38] *Ibid.*, p. xvi.

[39] *Ibid.*, pp. 405-406 (13), 427 (62); Dunlop, *The English Historical Review* 3. 266-267.

these parts, here is neither public prayers in any church nor private prayers that any of them doth understand, whereby it seemeth God is altogether unserved. I have taken order that public prayers shall be said in their own tongue, and that they shall assemble themselves at their churches on the Sundays. I have caused the Lord's Prayer and the Ten Commandments, and the Articles of the Belief, to be translated into Irish, and this day the ministers of these parts repair unto me to have it in writing. They have undertaken to instruct their parishioners in it. I find them very tractable and willing to learn the truth. I hope to do some good therein with them.[40]

Sir Edward Fitton was also appalled at the neglect of religion. According to him, though the clergy did not preach once in seven years, they were rigorous in gathering their tithes.[41] But for many, the welfare of the Irish on their estates was of small concern; most of their energy apparently was given to disputes with their fellow undertakers.[42]

Absorbed though Spenser surely was in the great plans for the transformation of Munster, he was no less interested in events outside Ireland, if we may judge by his later treatment of them in his poetry. In some of them, men whom he had served as secretary and whose activities he could not fail to follow with deep interest were involved. Leicester and Norris had both gone to the Netherlands in 1585. Their accomplishments were disappointing, though at least the reputation of Norris as a soldier did not suffer. Late in 1586, the news of Sidney's death at Zutphen found its way to Ireland. Spenser shared, we may be sure, in the general sorrow even if he did not till years later embody his grief in elegiac verse. On February 8, 1587, Mary Stuart was beheaded in Fotheringhay Castle. Of all the contemporary events treated in *The Faerie Queene*, none is portrayed with less disguise than her trial. Elizabeth is represented as deeply reluctant to take vengeance on her beautiful, false cousin. Prince Arthur, though at first moved to pity, is finally convinced of the justice of Mary's execution; but Artegall, as befits a knight of justice, never wavers.

The execution of Mary increased Philip's desire to invade England, since, if successful, he could now take the land for the Infanta Isabel. By the spring of 1588, he had assembled his great fleet—130 vessels, 80 of them over 300 tons. Though his objective in this case was not Ireland, fate caused a sixth of his ships to end their voyage on her rugged northern and western coasts, so that Ireland no less than England shared in the excitement caused by Philip's tremendous undertaking. The story of the

[40] *C. S. P. Ir.* (1586-1588), p. 331 (42)—a verbatim reproduction of Herbert's letter.
[41] *Ibid.*, p. 392 (55).
[42] *C. S. P. Ir.* (1588-1592), pp. 51 (2), 62 (31).

disasters that befell Medina-Sidonia's "Felicísima Armada" need not be repeated here in detail. From July 21 to July 30, it battled in the Channel and North Sea the lower, better maneuvered English ships, with their superior gun power and advanced fighting methods.[43] The victory was decisive. Northward past the east coast of England the damaged, scattered vessels ran before their pursuers. There was nothing they could do but attempt to return to Spain by circumnavigating the British Isles. The great storm, often described as an ally of the English, did not arise till a week after the Spaniards had been thoroughly defeated off Gravelines in the North Sea.

The losses on the Irish coasts were severe. Twenty vessels or more were wrecked at intervals all the way from the River Bann in the north to Desmond in the southwest. Large numbers of men were drowned. Geoffrey Fenton, when at Sligo, counted eleven hundred corpses washed up on less than five miles of shore. Many who reached land alive were either robbed or slaughtered by the natives or executed by the government. At the island of Clare, off Clew Bay, Connaught, of one hundred who landed, bringing with them a large amount of treasure, all except two were slain by the O'Malleys. Some were treated more humanely, but the hard existence of the natives left little surplus food for the half-famished refugees.[44] Toward the end of October, some 3,000 Spaniards were thought to be alive in Donegal. Fenton estimated that those drowned, killed, and captured on the Irish coasts exceeded 5,000. When we recall that half the Spanish fleet was lost without the destruction of a single English ship, we comprehend more easily the inclination, in Spain as well as in England, to attribute so astounding an outcome to the power of God.

To this colossal battle, Spenser in *The Faerie Queene* devotes eighteen stanzas of curious allegory.[45] Philip and his armada are portrayed by the Souldan riding in a lofty chariot, while Arthur on his horse—"More in his causes truth he trusted then in might"—typifies the English fleet. To equate the tall galleons with a Roman chariot is ingenious, yet the complexity and sustained effort of a nine-day battle involving more than two hundred ships is but feebly suggested. The defeat is represented as due entirely to the effect produced by the dazzling shield of divine truth on the

[43] Corbett, *Drake and the Tudor Navy* 2. 197, 200; J. K. Laughton in *The Cambridge Modern History* 3. 312.

[44] *C. S. P. Ir.* (1588-1592), pp. 68 (49), xxviii, 54 (10 X); cf. also Bagwell 3. 182-188 (Captain Francisco de Cuellar's interesting account of his experiences as a castaway in Ireland).

[45] 5. 8. 28-45.

Souldan's horses—that is, to the heaven-sent storm. In emphasizing the importance of the storm, Spenser is in accord with the view of his day, which tended to minimize what we now know to have been the extraordinary efficiency of the English navy.

At the moment when Philip's great fleet, poised for its descent on England, had been filling English minds everywhere with apprehension, a young Irish heiress succeeded in producing in her own small world of southwestern Munster a very respectable sensation. She was Ellen, sole heiress of Donal MacCarthy Mor, earl of Clancar. By suddenly marrying her cousin Florence MacCarthy Reagh—the ceremony was quietly performed "in an old broken church"[46]—she brought about a union of the two main branches of the MacCarthys, so that there was centered in one house a potential power far greater than English policy could view with satisfaction. Florence MacCarthy, to be sure, had remained loyal through the Desmond rebellion, and soon thereafter at the English court had won the favor of Elizabeth, which was expressed by a royal gift of 1,000 marks and an annuity of 200 marks. To a rival, in fact, he resembled "a damned counterfeit Englishman." But now this man of immense bulk, benign face, and scholarly, antiquarian tastes, this friend of Elizabeth, had suddenly become a menace, partly because of his prospective power in Munster, but also because of a rumor that he had been in communication with Spain. He possessed indeed the divided interests and wavering sympathies natural among prominent Irishmen in a land that lived under a peculiar unstable fusion of English and Irish control. Norris on June 29 took MacCarthy into custody and later his wife; Norris's feelings must have been oddly mingled on becoming the guardian of these two inasmuch as he himself had seriously considered wedding the wealthy Ellen a short time before. MacCarthy six months later was sent to Dublin and thence to the Tower of London, but Ellen, slipping out of Cork in disguise, went into hiding provided by her husband's friends. This affair was well known to Spenser; indeed there is extant a long letter written by Spenser for Norris, on July 1, 1588, in which the many dangerous implications of the marriage are fully set forth.[47]

During the autumn and winter of 1588-1589, Norris had to divide his attention between the Spaniards and the Munster undertakers. With thousands of Spaniards in the north and west of Ireland, Sir Richard Bingham, who had succeeded Sir Nicholas Malby as governor of Connaught,

[46] MacCarthy, *The Life and Letters of Florence MacCarthy Reagh*, p. 41.

[47] *C. S. P. Ir.* (1586-1588), p. 548 (66); the letter is quoted by Daniel MacCarthy in his life of Florence MacCarthy Reagh, pp. 38-43.

feared revolt. As a result of orders issued by him, seven or eight hundred Spaniards were put to death, and any one who harbored a refugee for as much as four hours was deemed a traitor. For fear of serious consequences should the Spaniards aid a native uprising, Norris, at the end of September, went into Connaught with a large part of the troops available in Munster.[48] It would be interesting to know whether Spenser accompanied him on this purely military expedition into a neighboring province. Early in 1587, Sir William Stanley, who was then fighting in the Netherlands, had transferred his allegiance to Philip, an action prompted by his lifelong sympathy with Roman Catholicism and his conviction that his many years of able military service had not been justly rewarded. Rumor now had it that he contemplated an invasion of Munster, and during the winter Norris was busy with preparations for his repulse. On January 22 at Shandon Castle Norris wrote a significant letter to the privy council, which Spenser penned for him. Doubt now existed, said Norris, about Stanley's coming. On returning from Connaught, he had found the province generally tranquil, except that some undertakers were causing trouble by seizing lands and castles to which they had not a shadow of title. Norris thought it would be wholesome if they were informed by the privy council that there were laws to be obeyed in Ireland as well as in England.[49] Even if the air was charged with rumblings of Spanish supported revolt and with protests of those who were suffering from the acts of lawless undertakers, this period had its compensations for Norris. His grant at Mallow of six thousand acres to which he had grown attached was passed, and he was knighted in December, 1588, by the new lord deputy, Sir William Fitzwilliam.[50]

It was also in 1588, or soon thereafter, that Spenser reached, in a material sense, the climax of his career. He had watched the long first act of the drama of the Munster plantation, with its painful delays, its defects in design, its clumsiness in execution. He knew as few in England could know the possibilities of failure, but also the chances of success. He had probably read with close attention the first government prospectus entitled "A note of the benefit that may grow in short time, to the younger houses of gentlemen, by this course," [51] in which were set forth the advantages to those who should become undertakers—to be chief lord of so great an estate, to have the homage of so many families and the disposition of so

[48] *C. S. P. Ir.* (1588-1592), pp. 49 (1 I), xxx, 45 (56).
[49] *Ibid.*, p. 112 (37).
[50] Fiant 5219, *Sixteenth Report*, p. 76; *DNB*.
[51] *Desiderata Curiosa Hibernica* 1. 57 ff.

many good holdings, and to enjoy the financial returns such as royalties and perquisites of courts, revenues from tenants, and profits from his own demesne. He had further, no doubt, familiarized himself with the detailed plans that specified just how a seignory, or fraction thereof, should be "planted." Each seignory was to be a more or less self-sufficient community, with a pyramidal design. In the case of an inferior seignory of 4,000 acres, the gentleman at the top would possess 800 acres, farmers and freeholders each 300, householders each 100, and cottagers, forming the base, each about 18. Each seignory, moreover, was to include a gardener, smith, mason, carpenter, thatcher, tailor, shoemaker, butcher, and miller. He had perhaps sighed at the thought of how difficult it would be to bring all these families from England and wondered whether this requirement would be so strictly enforced as to exclude the substitution of a few easily obtainable Irish tenants.

Just what steps led him to participate actively in the plantation we shall probably never know. His experience at New Abbey, the thought of his growing family, his natural ambition to get on financially and to found a house, the agreeable experience of Sir Thomas Norris with Mallow—probably all these as well as other considerations induced him to take advantage of an opportunity that came through Andrew Reade. As we have seen, Kilcolman was assigned to Reade in the spring of 1587, but what he did there toward fulfilling his obligations as an undertaker we do not know. This, however, we do know, that sometime between the autumn of 1588 and the spring of 1589, Spenser, through an agreement with Reade, occupied Kilcolman with the understanding that he would yield it to Reade or his representatives should they appear before Whitsuntide (May 22), 1589.[52] Their failure to appear seems to have put Spenser in possession of the estate on that date, though his patent was not passed till October 26, 1590.[53]

To Professor Ray Heffner, who first ferreted out the details connected with Spenser's acquisition of Kilcolman, it seemed probable that Reade let the estate go because it was claimed by a neighboring Anglo-Irish noble, Lord Roche. If not the whole estate, it seems clear that Roche claimed a considerable part of it. Spenser, in view of his connection with the government of Munster, was well fitted to contest Lord Roche's claims. These facts very likely account for the transfer, though other considerations may well have had a part in causing Reade to relinquish the difficult task

[52] Heffner, *MLN* 46. 493-498.

[53] Fiant 5473, *Sixteenth Report*, p. 137.

of planting Kilcolman. The year 1588 saw some cooling of enthusiasm on the part of the undertakers. To Roger Wilbraham, the Irish solicitor-general, whose inspection of the forfeited lands and hearing of Irish claims had given him a firm grasp of the whole situation, it was apparent by autumn that all things were growing faint in the enterprise. He saw no prospect that the undertakers could persuade the required number of honest English families to dwell in so unstable a country; and indeed some of the greatest undertakers were themselves becoming discouraged.[54] By March of this year sixteen undertakers, largely because of delays in the surveys, had felt compelled to withdraw from the project.[55] Spenser at least had the advantage of knowing what chance he was taking: he was in small danger of disillusionment.

At about the time Spenser took up his residence at Kilcolman, an event occurred in England that is of much interest to the poet's biographers; English readers were given their first opportunity to see a stanza of *The Faerie Queene* in print. The book in which it appeared, Abraham Fraunce's *Arcadian Rhetorike*, was entered in the Stationers' Register on June 11, 1588. Fraunce quotes 2. 4. 35, naming book and canto as well as author and work: evidently a portion of the poem was circulating in manuscript in London. Perhaps Bryskett, as Dr. Bennett suggests, took the manuscript with him on a visit to England, where we find him in the summer of 1587. He had been deeply interested in the inception of the poem, and was later to reproach Spenser for lagging in his great enterprise. Certainly Bryskett would have keenly enjoyed showing Spenser's masterpiece to Sidney's friends.[56] By whatever means Spenser's manuscript got to England, we may be sure that it advanced a reputation already launched among the initiated by the *Calender*. From the *Calender*, Fraunce also quoted, attaching Spenser's name to it in print for the first time.[57] Clearly the New Poet, even in advance of his real bid for fame, was beginning to win renown.

[54] *C. S. P. Ir.* (1588-1592), pp. 51 (2), 52 (8).

[55] *C. S. P. Ir.* (1586-1588), p. 508 (49).

[56] Koller, *ELH* 7. 109-113; Bennett, *The Evolution of "The Faerie Queene,"* p. 239. Marlowe, it would seem, had a look at Spenser's manuscript; see Bakeless, *The Tragicall History of Christopher Marlowe* 1. 205-209, but also Baldwin, *ELH* 9. 157-187.

[57] In 1586, William Webbe, in his *Discourse of English Poetrie*, p. 52, had referred to the author of the *Calender* as "Master Sp."

XII

KILCOLMAN

IF A BIRD were to fly south the fifty miles that separate the cities of Limerick and Cork, it would find itself, midway in its journey, above the Ballyhoura Hills. At that point there would extend before it a fertile plain ten miles in width from north to south and twenty in length from east to west. Below, where the hills melt into the plain, would lie the northern boundary of what was Spenser's estate, its western and southern limits being roughly indicated by the Awbeg River, which flows at first south, and then turns suddenly east near Buttevant, reaching, as it were, a protecting arm, with elbow bent at right angles, about Spenser's lands. Another smaller stream, the Bregoge, flows straight south across Spenser's one-time estate to its juncture with the Awbeg. On a clear day the mountains that enclose the plain would be visible; the loftiest are the Galtees, to the east of the Ballyhoura Hills, virtually a continuation of that range. At the southern edge of the plain, the course of still another river, the Blackwater, might be faintly distinguishable against the base of pale blue hills, which rise into the Boggeragh and Nagles Mountains.

From the wording of his grant, we learn a few interesting facts about the "manor, castle, and lands of Kylcolman" which passed formally on October 26, 1590, into the possession of "Edmund Spenser, gentleman."[1] The various ploughlands, not all of which can be certainly identified today,[2] are enumerated, and we are informed that he is to hold the estate "for ever, in fee farm, by the name of 'Hap Hazard.'" Though a tract of 4,000 acres was contemplated, it amounts by measure to only 3,028 acres. His rent from 1594 is to be £17 17*s.* 6 2/3*d.*, and half as much during the previous three years, and in addition 33*s.* 4*d.* "for the services of the free tenants." Twenty-four families, including his own, are to be provided with homes; of the settlers, two are to be farmers with 400 acres, two freeholders with 300, and eleven copyholders with 100 each. He is permitted to impark 151 acres for horses and deer. From a survey of the seignory made years later, we learn that it contained a "great quantity of

[1] Fiant 5473, *Sixteenth Report*, p. 137. For a fuller list of townlands, see Copinger, *Journal of the Cork Historical and Archaeological Society*, 1st Series, 2. 345.

[2] Henley, *Spenser in Ireland*, pp. 60-61 (including a useful map); on an ordnance map of 1937 appear the following townlands named as in Spenser's grant:—Kilcolman (West, Middle, and East), Rossagh (West and East), Ballyellis, Carrigeen, and Ardadam.

mountain," not capable of improvement, but "little bog," so that we may conclude that it crept well up the slopes of the Ballyhoura Hills.[3]

Although the estate passed from Reade to Spenser on May 22, 1589, the "planting" of English settlers had perhaps begun during 1588. At any rate, when Spenser answered a questionnaire sent out by the English government on May 12, 1589, he reported that six English families were then on the estate, and that others had promised to come over. To the query as to Irish on the estate, he was discreetly silent.[4] One sighs at the magnitude of his task. Bringing in and feeding his English tenants, providing them with habitations, turning the long-neglected soil under the plow, and establishing himself and his family on his own demesne—it seems an immense undertaking, especially for one whose resources were limited and whose time was not altogether his own, for he was still deputy clerk of the council of Munster. Nor should we forget that he was also a poet. On his desk, or more likely tucked away in his chest, was the manuscript of his *Faerie Queene*, and how passionately he must have longed for time to get at it; for he never forgot, we take it, that being a poet was the primary business of his life.

Suppose we now permit our hypothetical bird, which we left suspended over the southern edge of the Ballyhoura Hills, to swoop down to a small gray ruined castle near the middle of Spenser's one-time estate. Built on a little knoll, its walls rise at one corner into a tower three or four stories in height pierced by several windows. Murray's guidebook describes the castle as "a small peel tower about 40 ft. high clad with ivy, with cramped and dark rooms, a form which every gentleman's house assumed in those turbulent times," and states that its walls were about eight feet thick. Its windows command an extensive view, which in Spenser's day was perhaps restricted by the forests that were then a feature of Ireland. In the foreground is a little crescent-shaped lake, with marshy peat beds beyond, where sea gulls breed; then pleasant broken farming country; finally, if the atmosphere permit, the mountainous horizon.[5] As Spenser established himself here, did his thoughts ever revert to the previous owner, Sir John of Desmond, whom he had known only as a head impaled above the entrance to Dublin Castle and a limp body dangling for years on the North Gate of Cork until a strong wind blew it one night into the river?[6]

[3] Dunlop, *The Journal of . . . Antiquaries* 54. 144.
[4] *C. S. P. Ir.* (1588-1592), p. 198 (70).
[5] Henley, *Spenser in Ireland*, pp. 71 ff.; Judson, *Spenser in Southern Ireland*, pp. 7-48.
[6] Carpenter, *A Reference Guide*, p. 35; Gray, *RES* 6. 417-418.

Whether Spenser ever actually resided in the picturesque castle above the lake, we do not know. When the Desmond lands were surveyed in 1586, the castle was described as large—can it be that significant portions have vanished?—old, and in ruins, and then useful only for the protection of beasts at night.[7] Yet its powerful walls and some of its chambers are still intact, and perhaps no great amount of restoration was needed to make it at least temporarily habitable. Eventually he built, we know, "a fair stone house," [8] but it is not easy to believe that he would have had leisure or funds to erect this new structure at once. Some have supposed that his dating of *Colin Clouts Come Home Againe* " From my house of Kilcolman " on December 27, 1591, implies that he was then residing, not in the castle, but in a mansion house of his own building, but the word " house " was often used of even the largest Irish castles, as " the house of Askeaton " or " the house of Athlone." If not within the castle, he doubtless resided near by so that the protection of its sturdy walls might be available in time of need. Says Fynes Moryson, in writing of Ireland:

> Many gentlemen have castles built of freestone unpolished, and of flints, or little stones, and they are built strong for defense in times of rebellion, for which cause they have narrow stairs and little windows, and commonly they have a spacious hall joining to the castle and built of timber and clay, wherein they eat with their family.[9]

In addition to providing shelter for himself and his family, he must have turned his attention to other building operations, for the undertakers were required by Michaelmas, 1594, to erect, or at least renew, habitations for all on their estates, and the late wars could not have been kind to the thatched dwellings already there. But it is human to procrastinate, and in 1592 the queen's commissioners found that the undertakers had as yet done very little of the required building.[10]

The bustle and novelty of these first months at Kilcolman must have remained always a stirring memory to Spenser, to his wife, if she was still living, and especially to his son Sylvanus, now old enough to enjoy keenly the shift from life in a little walled town to that on a spacious estate, and probably also to his daughter Katherine.[11] The poet's sister Sarah, who married John Travers, registrar of the diocese of Cork, Cloyne, and Ross,

[7] Heffner, *MLQ* 3. 508.

[8] Dunlop, *The Journal of . . . Antiquaries* 54. 143.

[9] *An Itinerary* 3. 498.

[10] *C. S. P. Ir.* (1586-1588), p. 305; *C. S. P. Ir.* (1592-1596), p. 58 (44 V).

[11] Hamer, *RES* 7. 274; Welply, *NQ* 162. 182; according to Welply, the assertion that Lawrence " was a son of the poet is wholly untenable " (*ibid.*, p. 187).

Kilcolman Castle. From a photograph by the author.

is often placed by Spenser's biographers at Kilcolman. But according to the Travers records, in which, to be sure, some obvious errors occur, she was married in 1587 or 1588. If these records date her marriage correctly, she would presumably have shared the hospitality of Kilcolman only as a guest.[12]

The developments taking place on Spenser's lands were being duplicated all about him, so that he had the satisfaction of feeling himself part of a large cooperative movement. To the northwest, Hugh Cuffe, Esq., with twenty-one English settlers, was established on 11,000 acres, called Cuffe's Wood. The Awbeg River, which bordered Spenser's estate, formed the eastern boundary of Cuffe's large seignory. Gratifying to Spenser must have been the occasional presence of Sir Thomas Norris on his 6,000 acres at Mallow, less than eight miles away. Still nearer, at Carrigleamleary, on the Blackwater, was Roger Keate, with whom was associated a Mr. Piers; of both of these men, we shall hear more later. To the southeast of Kilcolman was Arthur Hyde, with his wife and children and fifty English persons, on an estate of almost 12,000 acres.[13] And farther down the valley of the Blackwater, where, turning suddenly south, the river moves, broad and stately, toward the sea at Youghal, was Sir Walter Raleigh's 42,000 acre estate of Inchiquin, already settled with 120 English, many of them with their families. Raleigh's estate was three and a half times as large as it should have been, through an odd mistake of Perrot's. Though in June, 1589, Elizabeth directed that it be reduced to 12,000 acres, her orders were apparently never carried out.[14] In 1589 Raleigh was rebuilding, or repairing, Lismore Castle, his Irish seat, which rises on a cliff beside the Blackwater at Lismore, just thirty miles from Kilcolman. This had been transferred to him two years before by the archbishop of Cashel, but the lands of his grant were farther east along the Blackwater toward Youghal; in Youghal he had a manor house at which he sometimes stayed, the pretty Elizabethan structure now known as Myrtle Grove.[15]

[12] Id., *NQ* 179. 74-78, 92-93, 95. The Travers records state that Spenser presented his sister with a dowry consisting of two ploughlands from his grant, but that, because this assignment of a part of the estate proved illegal, his grandson, Edmund Spenser, gave bond for a sum covering the value of these lands (*ibid.*, p. 95).

[13] Cf. Dunlop, *The English Historical Review* 3. 266-268; *C. S. P. Ir.* (1588-1592), p. 131 (10); and, for Hugh Cuffe's seignory, Fiant 5066, *Sixteenth Report*, pp. 44-45. Carrigleamleary was assigned to John Ryves, who died while on his way from England. Roger Keate then took it, "but could not rest quiet in it in respect of the Lord Roche." On April 21, 1589, it was formally granted to Thomas Saye (Fiant 5323, *Sixteenth Report*, p. 98).

[14] Dunlop, *The Journal of . . . Antiquaries* 54. 142 and note.

[15] Edwards, *The Life of Sir Walter Ralegh* 1. 96.

Many of the homely circumstances of a Munster settler's existence are faithfully depicted in a small tract written in 1589 by a Cork county undertaker named Robert Payne. As resident manager for a group of English partners, his object was to set forth the advantages of life in Ireland. He was evidently an expert farmer, and his account of crops, of wild and domestic animals, and of the economic side of an undertaker's life is pleasantly detailed.

> There be great store of wild swans, cranes, pheasants, partridges, heathcocks . . . and all other fowls much more plentiful than in England. You may buy a dozen of quails for 3*d*., a dozen of woodcocks for 4*d*., and all other fowls ratably. . . . You may buy the best heifers there with calves at their feet for 20*s*. apiece, which are nothing inferior to the better sort of Lincolnshire breed. Their chief horses are of as great price as in England, but cart horses, mares, and little hackneys are of a very small price. . . . You may keep a better house in Ireland for £50 a year than in England for £200 a year. . . .
>
> One hundred pounds will buy 60 milch kine, 300 ewes, 20 swine, and a good team. The ground to keep these cattle and use this team on will be 400 acres at £10 rent. . . .
>
> To husband this farm, your tenant must keep eight persons, which may be well done with the profit of the swine, winter milk, calves, and the crop which he should get upon your land with your team. . . .
>
> There is not that place in Ireland where any venomous thing will live. There is neither mole, pie, nor carrion crow; there is neither sheep dieth on the rot nor beast on the murrain.[16]

Payne's treatise may have been insensibly colored by a hope to attract solid, industrious settlers to Ireland. But Spenser too called Ireland a "sweet land." Both felt that nature at least would not hinder the success of the Munster colony.

Though nature may have smiled on the undertakers, certain men greeted them with sullen, frowning faces. Prominent gentlemen and nobles of Munster deeply resented the arrival of persons who, they felt, were encroaching on areas to which they themselves had rightful claims. Patrick Condon, Lord Barry, and Lord Roche, whose ancestral lands were near those assigned to Spenser and his English neighbors, quickly appealed to the law; and Lord Roche, as we have seen, demanded most if not all of Spenser's estate.

Because Maurice, Lord Roche, Viscount Fermoy, has so long been famous as Spenser's bad angel, we may be justified in looking briefly at his past. His Anglo-Norman ancestors came to Ireland soon after the Con-

[16] *A Brief Description of Ireland*, pp. 7-9, 14.

quest and established themselves about Castletownroche and Fermoy [17] in a district that includes the confluence of the Awbeg and Blackwater Rivers and lies to the southeast of what was Spenser's estate. The family's ancestral seat at Castletownroche, now incorporated in Castle Widenham, was built on a rock above the Awbeg River, where it flows between high banks through a picturesque glen, at a point but eight miles from Kilcolman Castle. In 1580, Maurice Roche infuriated his father by joining in the Desmond rebellion, but through the efforts of Lord Justice Pelham was won back to loyalty and reconciled to his father. Headstrong and impulsive, in the following year he was one of a group of youths accused of combining to become Robin Hoods. Though generally faithful to the English regime, he sometimes skirted the perilous brink of disloyalty and had committed several acts for which he had had to be pardoned.[18] The fact is that he was probably guided less by principle than by a sense of the superior strength of the English and by a conviction that his interests could best be served by adhering to their regime.

In 1587, Maurice Roche, now possessed of his father's titles, began laying claim to lands that were being occupied by the undertakers, and in that year insisted on his right to thousands of acres assigned to Roger Keate, Hugh Cuffe, and Arthur Hyde.[19] In order to fortify his demands, he went to England that winter for a conference with Elizabeth, though the lord deputy had forbidden him to visit the court. The queen gave him an audience at Somerset House and dismissed him hopeful that his grievances would be redressed.[20] Because the titles to Irish lands were in a tangle that nobody seemed able to straighten out, she sent over in 1588 Lord Chief Justice Anderson and others to apply their expert legal knowledge to the settlement of claims. To this commission, in the fall of 1588, Lord Roche carried his claims, the first having to do with Carrigleamleary, then in the hands of Roger Keate. But the commissioners did not dispose even of his first claim, for on being informed that the witnesses had been "sinisterly seduced" by Lord Roche, they declined to hear it; whereupon he refused to attend the hearing of any of his other causes. On October 15, this proud, high-spirited man wrote to Walsingham that the shameful treatment accorded him by the commissioners had cut him to the quick. They had ended, he said, by clapping him into the common marshalsea at Cork,

[17] Bagwell, *Ireland under the Tudors* 1. 76.

[18] *Cal. Carew MSS.* (1575-1588), pp. 256-257; *C. S. P. Ir.* (1574-1585), p. 287 (65); *C. S. P. Ir.* (1586-1588), p. 3.

[19] *Ibid.*, pp. 385 (40), 450 (39).

[20] *Ibid.*, p. 466 (9); *C. S. P. Ir.* (1588-1592), p. 123 (26).

where no nobleman had ever before been imprisoned, and had kept him there six days, all because he had said he would complain to her majesty of what they had done![21]

During 1589 he continued to send accounts of his misfortunes to Ormonde, to Elizabeth, and to Walsingham. Writing to Ormonde on February 16, he declares that the undertakers so vex him and intrude upon the little land remaining to him that it would have been better if he had never been born to inherit a foot of land. They took a hundred marks' worth of corn from him during the last harvest, and are even seeking his life. A servant of Piers and Keate at Carrigleamleary shot an arrow at him and admitted that he desired his death. Roche dares not venture from his house and longs for a temporary refuge near the River Suir in Ormonde's country.[22]

As the months passed, friction between the undertakers and Lord Roche increased. Ill feeling seems to have reached a climax on October 12, for on that day, Lord Roche, sitting in his castle beside the Awbeg, penned new statements of his grievances to both Elizabeth and Walsingham, while Spenser and some of his neighbors and their tenants, on the very same day, prepared a bill of complaints against Lord Roche.

Enclosed in the letter to Walsingham are particulars of certain injuries done to Lord Roche. Here first we learn of Roche's claim to Kilcolman. His accusations of Spenser are phrased thus:

> Further, one Edmund Spenser, clerk of the council in Munster, by color of his office, and by making of corrupt bargains with certain persons pretending falsely title to parcel of the Lord Roche's lands disposs[ess]ed the said Lord Roche of certain castles and sixteen ploughlands.
>
> Also the said Spenser, by threatening and menacing of the said Lord Roche's tenants, and by taking their cattle pasturing upon his lordship's own inheritance, and by refusing and beating of his lordship's servants and bailiffs, hath made waste six other ploughlands of his lordship's lawful inheritance to his no small undoing.[23]

The bill prepared by Spenser and his friends, which consists of a series of allegations each testified to by one or more persons, and which is signed by Spenser, may be thus summarized:

[21] *Ibid.*, pp. 14, 19, 23, 24, 59-60 (20).
[22] *Ibid.*, pp. 123-124 (26).
[23] Quoted by Heffner, *MLN* 46. 496.

BILL AGAINST THE LORD ROCHE

The Lord Roche in July, 1586, and at sundry times before and after, relieved and maintained one Keadagh O'Kelly, his foster brother, a proclaimed traitor. Secretly, upon the first report of the coming of the Spaniards, he caused powder and munition to be made in his house. He speaketh ill of the government and hath uttered words of contempt of her majesty's laws, calling them unjust. He hath imprisoned in his house sundry persons, viz., a man of Mr. Verdon's, a man of Mr. Spenser's, and others of the freeholders of this country. He apprehended one Ullig O'Keif for stealing nine cows, and later freed him, so the said Ullig would make feoffment to him of his land. He made proclamation in his country that none of his people should have any trade or conference with Mr. Spenser or Mr. Piers or any of their tenants. He killed a fat beef of Teig O'Lyne's because Mr. Spenser lay in his house one night as he came from the sessions at Limerick. He killed a beef of his smith's for mending Mr. Peeres's plough-iron. He hath concealed from her majesty the manor of Crogh, the freehold of one who was a rebel, and has lately entered into the said rebel's other land, which he gave him in recompense thereof, as he allegeth.[24]

The merits of the controversy between Lord Roche and the undertakers cannot be easily weighed today. We may, however, note that Lord Roche and Lord Barry recovered certain chief rents from Hugh Cuffe, that David Condon, the heir of Patrick Condon, recovered two seignories from the undertakers, and that Nicholas Shynan, in 1592, recovered two ploughlands that had been granted to Spenser.[25] Evidently claims against the undertakers received consideration. Lord Roche's failure to deprive Spenser of any of his lands[26] argues that Roche's claims were ill founded, and that the clashes with Roche's servants and bailiffs resulted from more or less justifiable efforts by Spenser to rid his lands of trespassers.

For Spenser, the fateful event of this first year at Kilcolman was a visit from Sir Walter Raleigh. Spenser had known him for a long time, having probably first met him at court in 1579, where both were members of Sidney's circle,[27] but certainly in 1580 and 1581, when Raleigh was serving as captain and in other capacities in Munster. It was on Raleigh's return from Ireland in December, 1581, that he had first won the regard of Elizabeth, who had swiftly transformed the poor and almost unknown soldier and courtier into one of the great men of her kingdom. Did

[24] S. P. 63. 247. 16 (the summary is based on a transcript made by Professor Ray Heffner).

[25] Dunlop, *The Journal of . . . Antiquaries* 54. 139, 140-141; Carpenter, *A Reference Guide*, p. 35.

[26] Dunlop, *The Journal of . . . Antiquaries* 54. 143; in 1622 the seignory was unimpaired except for the loss of Shynan's two ploughlands.

[27] S. P. Dom. Eliz. 151. 45 (reference furnished by Professor Helen E. Sandison).

Spenser in those early days share the feelings toward Raleigh of Lord Grey, who liked neither his carriage nor his company? [28] Now, though still hot-tempered, daring, and adventurous, Raleigh had undergone some mellowing from his varied experiences and responsibilities. His interest in letters, coupled with his love of action, and his belief in England's great destiny must have appealed to Spenser. Moreover, since both were undertakers, their common trials and hopes would have drawn them together. It is pleasant to visualize this tall, handsome knight, his native assurance enhanced by the sense of being Elizabeth's chief favorite (for Essex was only beginning to challenge his place at court), riding with his attendants past autumn fields up to the castle beside the lake.

With the arrival of Raleigh at Kilcolman, we enter upon a well-documented period of Spenser's life, for this famous visit, and the subsequent journey of the two men to England, are faithfully portrayed in *Colin Clouts Come Home Againe*. Whether rumors of Spenser's literary achievements or mere chance drew Raleigh to his estate, the two poets were soon discussing their writings, and Spenser gratified his guest by reading him a sample of his art. The selection chosen was a pretty love story of Spenser's own Awbeg and Bregoge Rivers. They are represented as lovers whom a stern father (the Ballyhoura Hills) forbids to wed, but Bregoge, cunningly slipping underground, rises later to mingle his waters with those of his love. And that, as Raleigh may have seen with his own eyes, is just what happened. The porous limestone bed of the Bregoge, except when freshets fill it, is dry for several miles before its juncture with the Awbeg, and the rocks which jut from it, says Spenser, were thrown there by a father wrathful at being outwitted by his daughter's lover. Only a poet who had grown truly attached to his surroundings would have been likely to recount this appealing little narrative.

Raleigh, in turn, read from his much admired eulogy of Elizabeth entitled *Cynthia.* The first ten books of this poem are unhappily lost, but Spenser describes them in Book III of *The Faerie Queene* as a true and lively picture of Elizabeth, in verse of melting sweetness. When Spenser published *Colin Clouts Come Home Againe*, in 1595, Raleigh had suffered imprisonment on acount of his affair with Elizabeth Throckmorton, the queen's maid of honor, and, as Professor Koller has pointed out,[29] Spenser, in the course of revising his poem for publication, appears to have substituted for a passage descriptive of the first ten books lines aptly characterizing the melancholy eleventh and twelfth books, written in 1592 when Raleigh was in deepest disgrace:

[28] *C. S. P. Ir.* (1574-1585), p. 364 (10).

[29] *ELH* 1. 53.

His song was all a lamentable lay,
Of great vnkindnesse, and of vsage hard,
Of *Cynthia* the Ladie of the sea,
Which from her presence faultlesse him debard.

The two poets continued the pleasant diversion of reading each other their verses until both were weary; and we cannot doubt that, before they finished, a bulky manuscript entitled *The Faerie Queene* had been thoroughly examined by Raleigh. Perhaps the account in Book III of wounded Timias in love with Belphoebe, who is nursing him back to health by means of such drugs as " divine tobacco," had been already composed; if so, we can imagine Raleigh's pleasure in this whimsical picture of his devotion to his queen. At all events, Raleigh was convinced that Spenser should not bury himself any longer in this remote spot, and prevailed upon his friend to go back with him to Cynthia's court, where approbation and reward surely awaited him. We receive the impression that Spenser was readily persuaded, and that, taking little with him besides his manuscripts, he soon accompanied Raleigh to the seacoast. Richard Chichester, a gentleman who had devotedly served the Lord Deputy William Fitzwilliam from Fitzwilliam's first connection with Ireland, and who had recently been made constable of the Castle of Limerick, was left by Spenser as substitute in his clerkship.[30] It would be interesting to know who assumed the heavy responsibility of managing his estate. Various considerations may have prompted this first recorded journey to England, such as obtaining more English settlers and confirming his title to Kilcolman. But the primary aim, we can hardly doubt, was, as Spenser implies, the presentation to his queen of the great work that had absorbed his creative energies for ten long years.

[30] *C. S. P. Ir.* (1588-1592), pp. 140 (59), 341 (15); *C. S. P. Ir.* (1592-1596), p. 243 (47); see also Fiants listed in Index of *Twenty-second Report.* Spenser's substitute, though referred to merely as " one Chichester," was, we may assume, the Richard Chichester who had been granted the constableship of the Castle of Limerick on September 16, 1588 (Fiant 5261, *Sixteenth Report*, p. 86).

XIII

AT CYNTHIA'S COURT

SPENSER AND RALEIGH probably sailed for England from a southern port, such as Cork, Youghal, or Waterford. After the shore had faded from view, the two friends fell naturally into a discussion of the sea as Elizabeth's domain; and who but a Devonshire sailor like Raleigh, commander of the "Falcon" at twenty-six or younger, builder of the "Bark Raleigh" four years later, colonizer of Virginia, and vice admiral of Cornwall and Devon, could more appropriately dream of England's imperial greatness? He ended the conversation with an assertion to which Philip II would scarcely have agreed:

For land and sea my *Cynthia* doth deserue
To haue in her commandement at hand.

Though Spenser fully shared Raleigh's hopes of England's naval destiny, he did not love the sea, and to him the voyage seemed long; but eventually they sighted the island of Lundy, so that their course had presumably been southeast. Soon they descried more land, which they knew was England, a white-walled refuge of fertile green plains set in a cruel sea. From Lundy they ran southwest along the rocky coast of Cornwall, rounded Land's End, entered Mount's Bay, and, passing St. Michael's Mount, came to anchor at Penzance. Even then an overland journey of more than 250 miles separated them from London.

The landing at Penzance instead of a port farther east may perhaps be accounted for by Raleigh's interests in Cornwall, where he was lord warden of the Stannaries, or tin mines, and lieutenant of the county. In Devonshire too his interests were many, so that the long journey to Cynthia's court was sure to be pleasantly broken. In *Colin Clouts Come Home Againe* Spenser mentions certain contrasts between Ireland and England, which must have impressed him most forcibly during his first days in England. It is therefore safe to say that as he passed overland with Raleigh his eyes lingered happily on the fruitful English fields and well-cared-for pastures and woods, but especially on the evidences everywhere of tranquillity. There was no lack of inns where he and Raleigh could lodge at night certain that their sleep would not be broken by howling wolves or hue and cry after cattle thieves. And by day, instead of the disease and famine that still cursed Munster, they were able to observe contentment bred of peace and plenty.

The travelers proceeded at once toward London, and Spenser soon found himself amid the dazzling splendors of the court. Raleigh's sponsorship must have been invaluable. To arrive as the friend and companion of the queen's first favorite would insure a sympathetic reception, an opportunity to present his *Faerie Queene* under the best of auspices. Indeed Spenser later acknowledged " the infinite debt " he owed Raleigh for his " singular favours and sundry good turns " in England,[1] of which the initial introduction to the queen was surely one of the chief. It is interesting to imagine the first meeting. Did Spenser play a part in a scene similar to one described by the German traveler Lupold von Wedel on a visit to the court five years before? On a December evening Wedel had taken boat down the Thames to the palace at Greenwich. There he had watched the queen, surrounded by her chief nobles, sit down alone to a dinner of forty dishes, after which, assisted by three " counts," she had washed her hands in a silver bowl—she dined thus in public only on festival days.

> Then she took the son of a count by his mantle and stepped with him to a bow window, where he knelt before her and held a long conversation with her. When he had left her, she took a cushion and sat down on the floor, called another young gentleman, who also knelt down on his knees and spoke with her. . . . Now dancing began. . . . The queen, as long as the dance lasted, had ordered old and young persons to come and converse with her, who, as I have mentioned, were all obliged to kneel on their knees before her. She talked to them in a very friendly manner, making jokes, and to a captain named Ral[eigh] she pointed with her finger in his face, saying he had some uncleanness there, which she even intended to wipe off with her handkerchief. He, however, prevented her and took it away himself. It was said that she loved this gentleman now in preference to all others; and that may be well believed, for two years ago he was scarcely able to keep a single servant, and now she has bestowed so much upon him, that he is able to keep five hundred servants.[2]

Whatever occurred at Spenser's and Raleigh's first meeting with Elizabeth, we know that Raleigh aroused her interest in *The Faerie Queene.* She was delighted with it,

> And it desir'd at timely houres to heare.

If the queen approved, why delay publication? The book was entered in the Stationers' Register by Ponsonby on December 1, 1589, with the

[1] Dedication, *Colin Clouts Come Home Againe.*

[2] *Transactions of the Royal Historical Society*, New Series, 9. 262-265.

authorization of John Whitgift, archbishop of Canterbury; and we may assume that the following weeks were fully occupied by Spenser in seeing it through the press.[3] On January 13, 1590, he finished a short preface in the form of a letter to Raleigh, which he placed at the end of the volume, a useful adjunct, since his story, in accord with classical theory, plunged *in medias res*, leaving the reader ignorant of the antecedent action and also somewhat in doubt as to the intent of the poem. This prefatory letter, written, he says, at Raleigh's command, curiously enough, misrepresents the genesis of the quests in Books II and III. Dr. Bennett believes that the twelve-day feast, during which the queen assigned to each knight his mission, was an afterthought. *The Faerie Queene,* in fact, shows many evidences of alterations, of imperfect fusings of parts, even apparently of changes in general plan. No wonder efforts to uncover the secrets of its evolution are multiplying.[4]

To Spenser, passionate book-lover and voracious reader, these days of contact with William Ponsonby, the publisher of his book, and John Wolfe, the printer of it, probably gave much pleasure. Long starved for a sight of the richly stored bookshops of St. Paul's Churchyard, he surely enjoyed many a stroll around the great cathedral past their tantalizing displays. Here William Ponsonby dwelt and sold books at the sign of the Bishop's Head. Though Hugh Singleton, who had published the first edition of *The Shepheardes Calender*, was still active, his business had not flourished, and Spenser would naturally have entrusted this ambitious undertaking to another. Perhaps the fact that Ponsonby had been licensed to publish Sidney's *Arcadia*, which, like *The Faerie Queene*, made its first appearance in 1590, may have recommended him to Spenser. At any rate, the connection turned out to be satisfactory, for Ponsonby from this time on was his regular publisher, and the nine volumes he issued for Spenser helped to make Ponsonby "the most important publisher of the Elizabethan period."[5]

Spenser surely visited often the presses of John Wolfe, for the correcting of proofs would be a considerable task. His visits probably continued after the printing had begun, since, as with other Elizabethan books, minor corrections were made during the actual printing off. Did he, we wonder, smile at the inadequacy of the full-page woodcut of St. George and the dragon placed at the end of Book I? This creature, no larger

[3] The work of the printer may, of course, have begun before December 1.

[4] Spens, *Spenser's Faerie Queene*; Walter, *MLR* 36. 37-58; and especially Bennett, *The Evolution of "The Faerie Queene."* For the twelve-day feast, see Dr. Bennett's discussion, pp. 35 ff.

[5] McKerrow, *A Dictionary of Printers*, p. 217.

than a mastiff, feebly struggling under the hoofs of St. George's charger, is no kin to the fire-breathing colossus of Spenser's imagination. Indeed this cut was not executed for *The Faerie Queene*, since it had been used two years before in a volume published by Francis Coldock.[6] In view of the fact that Coldock was (or became) Ponsonby's father-in-law, and that John Wolfe printed both works, the reappearance of the cut in *The Faerie Queene* is not hard to explain. Professor Francis R. Johnson thinks that all four of Wolfe's presses (we know he had four in 1587) may possibly have been simultaneously at work on the book. "In any case," he concludes, "it seems highly probable that in 1590 the second largest printing-house in London was devoting at least half its resources to the rapid printing of Spenser's *Faerie Queene*."[7]

John Wolfe had had an interesting career. After an apprenticeship of ten years with the distinguished printer John Day, he had acquainted himself, through travel, with the superior state of Continental printing. While abroad, Wolfe had perhaps worked for a time in the famous printing-house of the Giunti, whose fleur-de-lis device he adopted, and used often, as on the title-page of *The Faerie Queene*.[8] At a later time he had led a spirited revolt against the issue of royal patents, or monopolies, for the printing of certain classes of books. Subsequently he had, however, bowed to authority, and thereafter advanced rapidly in his profession. In 1586 he had printed the third edition of *The Shepheardes Calender,* and was now engaged by Ponsonby to print Books I to III of *The Faerie Queene*.

In addition to correcting proofs and providing a preface, Spenser had to give his attention to another weighty matter. A dedication to the queen and dedicatory sonnets to certain distinguished subjects were required, for the young poet who ten years before could not quite summon courage to inscribe his *Calender* to Leicester was now prepared to dedicate this new work to Elizabeth herself and also to eight prominent courtiers and all the fine ladies of the court. The whole book being in a sense a celebration of the virtue and grandeur of his queen, no lengthy inscription to her was needed, and so he contented himself with the words: "To the most mighty and magnificent empress Elizabeth, by the grace of God queen of England, France and Ireland, defender of the faith, &c. Her most humble servant: Ed. Spenser." For the others he composed ten sonnets.

Both Spenser's choice of these others, and, to a less degree, the order of precedence he gives them, furnish a glimpse of his mental processes in

[6] In *A Briefe Discouerie of Doctor Allens seditious drifts*, 1588 (the earlier use of this woodcut was called to my attention by Professors Lily B. Campbell and Merritt Y. Hughes).

[7] *A Critical Bibliography*, p. 17.

[8] Gerber, *MLN* 22. 131.

the winter of 1589-1590. The first sonnet is addressed to Sir Christopher Hatton, the lord chancellor, highest in rank of Elizabeth's ministers, a man of great wealth and influence and long a favorite of the queen. The next is to Robert Devereux, earl of Essex, the queen's newest favorite. Though only twenty-three, he was rapidly making a name for himself: he had exhibited courage in Flanders and in Spain and the graces of courtiership at home. Already it seemed to some that the mantle of Sir Philip Sidney hung upon his shoulders. Did Raleigh feel a jealous twinge when he noticed that this youth had been given a place of honor after Hatton? The third sonnet is to Edward de Vere, seventeenth earl of Oxford. Though arrogant and eccentric, he represented an illustrious family, and he was moreover famed as a poet and a patron of poets. The fourth sonnet is addressed to Henry Percy, ninth earl of Northumberland, a man of intellectual and literary tastes and a friend of Raleigh's. Natural is Spenser's inclusion of the four persons next honored—the earl of Ormonde; Lord Charles Howard, hero of the defeat of the Armada; Grey; and Raleigh. His ninth sonnet, to Elizabeth Carey, was very likely inspired by his desire to secure the patronage of the noble family to which he was related; this sonnet becomes a truly notable indication of esteem when we recall that all the other ladies at court had to content themselves with the anonymity conferred by his tenth sonnet. While an urgent desire for patronage no doubt prompted the choice of some of these persons, it seems certain that gratitude and affection were chiefly responsible for the selection of others.

But the writing of dedicatory sonnets was not finished. We can imagine the amazement and concern of Spenser's friends when they discovered that Lord Burghley, most influential of Elizabeth's ministers, had been omitted: clearly Spenser was no politician. The fact that at least eight extant copies of the book contain only the ten sonnets just mentioned shows that not until the binding had been well started did Spenser see the wisdom of making good the serious omission of Burghley and others.[9] His second installment of sonnets gives recognition to seven additional persons.

The new names include three men especially prominent in Elizabeth's government—Burghley, Walsingham, and Buckhurst; three men famous as sailors or soldiers—Cumberland, Hunsdon, and Norris; and a noble lady who as Sidney's sister and as patroness of poets found an entirely fitting place in this brilliant company—Mary Herbert, countess of Pembroke. Burghley as lord treasurer and virtual prime minister, and Walsingham as chief secretary and next to Burghley in the practical

[9] Johnson, pp. 15-16.

administration of state affairs both at home and abroad, were certainly to be reckoned with when government patronage was in question. The inclusion of Thomas Sackville, Lord Buckhurst, a relative of Elizabeth's, highly regarded by the queen, and serviceable to the state in many ways, seems an almost inevitable choice when his place in the world of letters is also recalled. Spenser's style no doubt owes something to his fine *Induction* in *The Mirror for Magistrates*, and it is pleasant to read Spenser's praise of his "golden verse." George Clifford, earl of Cumberland, a sea dog like Raleigh and Drake, was just back from his third voyage, a semi-piratical expedition that had involved a remarkable series of exploits. Henry Carey, Lord Hunsdon, was Elizabeth's cousin and the chamberlain of her household, and at the same time an honest, able soldier, whose military duties kept him much of the time on the Scotch border as protector of England's northern frontier. He is remembered today by many for his founding of a celebrated company of players. The choice of Sir John Norris and the countess of Pembroke is too obvious to call for comment. Whether on grounds of their own prominence or of their ability to advance his interests, Spenser could hardly have supplemented his first selections more wisely.

The additional seven sonnets must have been written by April 6, 1590, for on that day Walsingham, after a brief illness, died. Evidently the copies of the book containing the first series of sonnets were being distributed some days or even weeks earlier. While we do not know just when the printer began his work, we may be sure that the book was produced with unusual rapidity; and that Spenser's energies, during his first three or four months in England, were much preoccupied with the presses of John Wolfe.

Unless Spenser differed from most authors, he was both exalted and depressed as he saw the labor of so many years acquiring a permanent form under the flying fingers of Wolfe's journeymen. At such a time he must have valued the proximity of good friends. Several of them provided commendatory poems, a conventional addition without which a book of this character could hardly be ushered decently into the world. Raleigh furnished two sonnets which warmly praise Spenser's poem and at the same time seize the opportunity to laud Elizabeth with his usual enthusiasm; and Harvey contributed a poem that contrasts Spenser's pastoral verses of the *Calender* with the elevated plane of this epic. Probably none watched the progress of the book with more interest than these two.

The task of the binder in inserting the supplementary sonnets was bungled. In some cases the full seventeen appear as Spenser intended, but more often there is either repetition or omission. The observant eye of the poet was apparently no longer on his book. Indeed there is reason to believe that he returned to Ireland in the spring of 1590, and it may well be that he hurried away as soon as he had completed the additional sonnets. At any rate, the accounts of Vice Treasurer Wallop point to his presence in Ireland on May 30, 1590.[10] Considering the brief time he had been in possession of Kilcolman, and the anxieties created by Lord Roche, it is entirely natural that he should wish to make at least a hasty visit to Munster and then return to reap the benefits his book might be expected to yield.

During his absence, we may assume that his poem became rapidly known to the aristocratic circle for whom it was primarily intended. Ponsonby speaks in a foreword to the *Complaints* of its favorable reception. We cannot in fact conceive of anything but immediate success for a book so rich and varied.

The casual reader perhaps would not look far beyond the narrative. The multitude of the characters, the intricacies of the action, and the medievalism of the whole were thoroughly in accord with contemporary taste, had been encountered, for example, in Ariosto's magnificent epic, and were being enjoyed in Sidney's *Arcadia.* As a story, or collection of stories, the adventures of Una and the Red Cross Knight, of Sir Guyon, and of Britomart were bound to delight the essentially romantic Elizabethan.

For more earnest readers there was also the moral allegory. The Elizabethan age took its ethics seriously; and, in theory, at least, neither Spenser nor Sidney would admit into the company of true poets men who did not try to improve their fellows. Wrote Sidney: " . . . it is not riming and versing that maketh a poet . . . but it is that feigning notable images of virtues, vices, or what else, with that delightful teaching, which must be the right describing note to know a poet by"; [11] and Spenser's most explicit statement of his aims in *The Faerie Queene* concerns ethic teaching: " The general end therefore of all the book is to fashion a gentleman or noble person in virtuous and gentle discipline. . . ." That Spenser really thought of the moral influence of his book in connection with particular individuals is shown by his dedicatory sonnet to the young earl of Cumberland:

> To you this humble present I prepare,
> For loue of vertue and of Martiall praise,

[10] Wilson, *RES* 2. 456.

[11] *Defense of Poesy*, p. 11.

To which though nobly ye inclined are,
As goodlie well ye shew'd in late assaies,
Yet braue ensample of long passed daies,
In which trew honor yee may fashiond see,
To like desire of honor may ye raise,
And fill your mind with magnanimitee.

For statesmen, historians, and patriots there was other matter, in some cases, to be sure, slightly concealed through allegory, yet easily discerned by the thoughtful. To Burghley he says:

Vnfitly I these ydle rimes present,
The labor of lost time, and wit vnstayd:
Yet if their deeper sence be inly wayd,
And the dim vele, with which from comune vew
Their fairer parts are hid, aside be layd,
Perhaps not vaine they may appeare to you.

Burghley, if he had cared to read Book I with attention, would certainly have seen a record of the Reformation in England, not portrayed in the clear, hard lines of Dutch art, but with soft, impressionistic brush strokes, which leave some scope to individual interpretation. Though in Books II and III he would have looked in vain for any consistent historical allegory, he might have discovered in the adventures of the Knight of Temperance the advocacy of a wisely cautious political course very like that which his sober temperament approved; and in the person of Belphoebe, the virgin huntress, he would have recognized a depiction of Queen Elizabeth, though possibly in a style too rich and fanciful for his taste. Moreover, to see in the British and Elfin chronicles and in the prominent role assigned to Arthur a glorification of his sovereign would have required no clairvoyance: the hearts of few Englishmen failed to glow over the popular notion that the Tudors, by virtue of their Welsh blood, were destined to realize again the greatness of their predecessor King Arthur, were indeed realizing it in their growing might.

No beauty-loving Elizabethan could have been indifferent to the stylistic splendors of *The Faerie Queene*—to its magnificent new stanza, to its epic similes, to its graceful adaptations of the classics, of Chaucer, of Ariosto and Tasso, to its descriptions, often done in the bright primary colors of a saint's missal, to its remarkable lucidity in spite of a fondness for old words, to its melody that continues through canto after canto like the song of some miraculous, tireless bird. Its artistic excellence they doubtless felt even when they could not analyze it, as, for example, the relieving of an excess of sweetness and beauty by a sudden turn toward the violent, the grotesque, even the ugly.

Did they often think of the part Ireland had played in the poetry as well as the life of this new arrival at court? Did they realize that the mountains and forests, the clay cottages, the lonely castles, the crudely armed mobs, even perhaps the blood and crime and famine owed often a vague yet undoubted obligation to Ireland; [12] that, as Spenser himself says, we do indeed taste in *The Faerie Queene*

> Of the wilde fruit, which saluage soyl hath bred? [13]

Back in England after what one may surmise was a hurried visit to Ireland, Spenser would surely feel that his interests demanded the devotion of at least a portion of his time to attendance upon the queen, and we may think of him as following the court from one royal residence to another and mingling with the great company of officials and other courtiers whom Elizabeth chose to keep about her. Probably never before had he had so good an opportunity for an intimate scrutiny of the court. In *Colin Clouts Come Home Againe* and also, apparently, in a few lines added to *Mother Hubberds Tale*, the vivid, complex reactions to this experience have been preserved.

In some respects it was undoubtedly an agreeable experience. There were poets at court with whom he could discuss artistic theories and exchange unpublished verses. Not one, he says in *Colin Clouts Come Home Againe*, is the equal of Sidney, yet he praises many, several under pastoral names which, for us today, effectually conceal their identity.[14] The warmth of his approval may be partly accounted for by his response to their friendliness or by his conviction of their latent talents. Indeed he offers them some wholesome advice, urging Samuel Daniel, for example, to attempt something more ambitious than his sonnets *To Delia.* Under the name Aetion Spenser describes a gentle shepherd " full of high thoughts inuention," whose name has a heroic sound. Though the temptation has been strong to discover here an allusion to Shakespeare, Spenser more probably is referring to Michael Drayton, who gave himself the heroic name of Rowland.[15] With some of these men, Spenser may have renewed the literary symposiums that he had found so absorbing ten years before with Sidney and Dyer, and it seems probable that his happiest hours at court, or within court circles, were spent among the poets.

The nymphs of Cynthia's retinue, as he calls them, also graced him

[12] Gray, *RES* 6. 413-428.

[13] Dedicatory sonnet to Ormonde.

[14] Variorum Edition, *Minor Poems* 1. 463-474.

[15] *Ibid.*, pp. 472-474.

" goodly well." With some he probably associated at court, with others in their own houses, where the elegance and gaiety of Greenwich, Whitehall, Oatlands, Nonsuch, or Richmond were wont to be modestly copied. Among those whose kindness he acknowledges were Mary, countess of Pembroke, Anne, countess of Warwick, Margaret, countess of Cumberland, Helena, marchioness of Northampton, Frances, countess of Essex, the three Spencer sisters, Elizabeth, Anne, and Alice, and two Irish ladies sojourning in England at this time, whom he calls Galathea and Neaera—almost certainly Frances Howard, wife of the earl of Kildare,[16] and Elizabeth Sheffield, wife of the earl of Ormonde. To all these ladies, except the two from Ireland, he dedicated poems within the next few years, in most cases with expressions of warm gratitude for many graces and favors.

At first thought it may seem remarkable that Spenser should so soon have won the regard of these great ladies, but it is not hard to discover a reason for his connection with each one. His friendship with Sidney would of course account for a relationship with the countess of Pembroke, Sidney's sister, and with the countess of Essex, formerly Sidney's wife; and the old service under Leicester would make natural the patronage of Leicester's sister-in-law, the countess of Warwick, and also that of her sister, the countess of Cumberland. Through Raleigh, it seems certain, Spenser met Arthur Gorges, a friend and kinsman of Raleigh's,[17] and through him in turn the marchioness of Northampton, his aunt. Blood relationship and contacts in Ireland would explain his connection with the others. To Spenser, with his aesthetic tastes and strong aristocratic feeling, the kindly attentions of these noble ladies must have given great satisfaction.

In the company of at least one of them, the countess of Pembroke, both his literary enthusiasm and his social gifts might have received equal stimulus. Mary Herbert had enjoyed the good education that high-born women of the Renaissance sometimes received. Like her brother, she had literary talent, which expressed itself mainly in translation—in this year, 1590, she completed two translations, both from the French, " A Discourse of Life and Death," from Mornay, and " Antonius," a Senecan tragedy, from Garnier—and, also like her brother, she was a generous patron of poets. At fifteen she had become the third wife of Henry Herbert, earl of Pembroke, so that at an extremely early age she had found herself mistress of one of England's great country houses, and had also acquired the means

[16] Cf. Henley, *TLS*, July 6, 1933, p. 464.

[17] Sandison, *PMLA* 43. 669-670.

to encourage men of letters. Her beauty and goodness were much celebrated by the poets. Spenser was reminded of her brother by both her looks and her spirit, and indeed doubtless believed that in her own way this oval-faced, auburn-haired, intelligent young woman was perpetuating the ideals for which her brother had stood. In the dedicatory sonnet to her, Spenser says that his remembrance of Sir Philip's heroic spirit

> Bids me most noble Lady to adore
> His goodly image liuing euermore,
> In the diuine resemblaunce of your face;
> Which with your vertues ye embellish more,
> And natiue beauty deck with heuenlie grace. . . .

Still another lady who vouchsafed him grace, according to *Colin Clouts Come Home Againe*, was Rosalind.[18] If his interest may be measured by the number of lines he gives to her, the two passages totaling 70 lines in which he lauds her and defends her rejection of him suggest that the years have not lessened his devotion. Was he graciously received by this Laura of the North, and did the two laugh over the mystification so long maintained? Had his suit, though begun perhaps as something else, become in fact a literary *amour courtois*? The secret remains, as he wished, unrevealed. Certainly no more suitable poem for a return to the Rosalind theme could have been found than this magnificent autobiographic pastoral.

These days of waiting at court for the preferment that might be expected to follow the publication of *The Faerie Queene* would have tempted many to idleness. Court life, except for busy ministers like Burghley or Walsingham, was likely to become a relaxing existence. But Spenser, thanks to his faithful pen and an accommodating printer, was in no danger of yielding to its subtle spell.

While Spenser was still in Ireland, which, as we have seen, he appears to have visited in the spring of 1590, Ponsonby may have conceived the idea of bringing out a collection of Spenser's shorter poems, in order to profit by the favorable reception that had greeted *The Faerie Queene*. Whoever initiated it, such a project was soon under way. Though ostensibly fathered by Ponsonby, as set forth in a short preface entitled "The Printer to the Gentle Reader," it was probably planned and closely supervised by the poet himself. This volume was called *Complaints*, "being," says Ponsonby, "all complaints and meditations of the world's vanity, very grave and profitable." Nine poems or groups of poems are in-

[18] See line 484.

cluded, three of them series of sonnets translated from du Bellay and Petrarch. Portions of the volume represent early work; one poem, *The Ruines of Time*, was written, in large part, at least, after Spenser's coming to England with Raleigh; and others convey no certain indication as to time of composition. For a collection so miscellaneous in theme, purpose, and style, no more satisfactory title could have been found. Elegy, satire, and a more or less conventional lament over the vanity of life provide the volume with at least a degree of unity.

> O vaine worlds glorie, and vnstedfast state
> Of all that liues, on face of sinfull earth,[19]

that is the theme of most of the volume, a theme more appropriate to the intense religiosity of the Middle Ages than to the relatively buoyant, worldly attitude of the Renaissance. Yet this melancholy note continues to be heard often during the Renaissance. Though Spenser composed sufficient works in a minor key to make up this volume, his prevailing temper was serene and hopeful. Life for him contained far more beauty than ugliness, and his great knights of holiness, temperance, and chastity, in spite of terrific battles and even occasional defeats, ultimately achieve their missions.

This volume need not detain us long, since in one connection or another allusion has already been made to *Virgils Gnat*, *Mother Hubberds Tale*, *Visions of the Worlds Vanitie*, du Bellay's and Petrarch's *Visions*, and the visions at the end of *The Ruines of Time*, all of which appear in it. The poem printed first, *The Ruines of Time*, a comprehensive elegy or lament for five members of the Sidney, Dudley, and Russell families, is dedicated to the countess of Pembroke. The fact that these persons had all died since 1585, and that the three noble families were allied by marriage, justified such a joint perpetuating of their memory. One will not soon forget Spenser's picture of the famous city of Roman Britain, Verulamium—once princess " of this small Northerne world," yet now scarcely a memory—which provides his point of departure. Human greatness too, he reminds us, as he passes to the celebration of the dead, may be soon forgotten, and only the poet can save men from oblivion.

> Then who so will with vertuous deeds assay
> To mount to heauen, on *Pegasus* must ride,
> And with sweete Poets verse be glorifide.

The graphic picture of Verulamium, drawn from Holinshed and Camden, and the eloquent presentation of the doctrine of immortality through

[19] *The Ruines of Time* 43-44.

verse, devotedly held by Spenser, as by most men of the Renaissance, furnish this poem with a definite interest quite aside from its eulogies of Sidney, Leicester, and the others, and cause one to forgive the imperfect integration of its parts.

The second poem in the *Complaints* volume, *The Teares of the Muses*, is dedicated to Lady Strange, youngest of the Spencer sisters. This bitter lament of the Muses over the current state of culture in England has raised the question how a man of Spenser's temperament could see only darkness where we, looking back, can perceive a glorious dawn. Several explanations may be offered. For one thing, the pattern of his poem called for a dark view; like a prosecuting attorney, he was obliged to say what he could against the accused. Then he may have written during a mood of dejection, perhaps when, as a man of learning and a poet, he was feeling keenly the indifference of those he had hoped to win as patrons. Moreover, as Dr. Stein has argued, he must have been writing from the point of view of a courtly circle that approved classical standards and elevation of style and was impatient with any literature that did not conform to the learned tradition, as, for example, the romantic dramas of Marlowe and Kyd.[20] Finally, whether *The Teares of the Muses* was composed in 1590 or earlier, the picture is not grossly distorted; relatively little of merit had yet been published. The great literary revival had just begun, and Spenser may be pardoned for failing to detect, as we can in retrospect, its rich promise.

Nearly a third of the volume consists of early translations, among which is the series of sonnets entitled *Ruines of Rome* from du Bellay's *Antiquitez de Rome.* Spenser's translating of du Bellay's *Songe* for van der Noot's *Theatre* years before, probably led him also at about the same time to render into English these melancholy reflections on the fall of Rome. Joachim du Bellay, described by Spenser as "first garland of free Poësie That *France* brought forth," was a member of the Pléiade and, along with Ronsard, its mouthpiece. Du Bellay and Spenser heartily agreed in certain of their theories about poetry; and it is surely significant that Spenser, while still a schoolboy, should have acquired with this brilliant exponent of the new poetry of France such an intimacy as a translator is bound to feel for the man he translates.

The most fanciful and beautiful poem in *Complaints* is *Muiopotmos: or The Fate of the Butterflie.* This little mock-heroic story of the death of Clarion the butterfly at the hands of Aragnoll the spider was dedicated to

[20] Stein, p. 49; cf. also Witherspoon, *The Influence of Robert Garnier on Elizabethan Drama*, pp. 65-83.

Lady Elizabeth Carey with the modest statement that offering it in return for her excellent favors would be like presenting the gods with flowers for their divine benefits. The comparison to flowers is apt, for his elaboration of a trifling theme by means of lavish description, simile, and myth suggests a bouquet, varied in form and color and capable of giving immediate enjoyment. The critic has naturally sought for more than meets the ear, but if there is a mystery, Spenser has failed to provide the key and must indeed have realized that for most readers the whimsicality and sensuous beauty of his poem were sufficient.

As has been said, Spenser apparently relieved the tedium of the later months of 1590 by writing, revising, and assembling the material for *Complaints*, the only collection of his poetry to be published during his life.[21] On December 29, Ponsonby entered the book in the Stationers' Register, as approved by Dr. Staller, who, as later events were to demonstrate, probably gave it scant attention; or can it be that his personal acquaintance with Bishop Young, and perhaps with Young's one-time secretary, made him indulgent?[22] It was printed by Thomas Orwin, whose shop was in narrow Paternoster Row, just north of St. Paul's Churchyard. Here Spenser was probably a faithful visitor while his book was in press, for corrections and revisions that another would hardly have made were introduced during the printing.[23] By March 19, 1591, it was on sale, for on that day a reader by the name of H. Cocke bought a copy for the sum of two shillings and sixpence. At about the same time, or even earlier, Spenser may have sent to the three Spencer sisters copies of the poems dedicated to them, bound separately, each with its own title-page, since title-pages suited to this purpose appear in the *Complaints* volume.[24] Lady Carey's little presentation copy of *Muiopotmos* would have included also, it appears, the three series of visions, which immediately follow *Muiopotmos* in the *Complaints* volume, and which begin and end with references to some one addressed as "faire Ladie."

Another work whose completion belongs to the later months of 1590 is *Daphnaïda*, an elegy on Douglas Howard, wife of Arthur Gorges. In his dedication to Gorges' aunt, the marchioness of Northampton, Spenser

[21] Some of this work he perhaps did in Hampshire. According to Aubrey ('*Brief Lives*' 2. 233), Samuel Woodford, the poet, said that Spenser lived for a time in Hampshire, near Alton, and wrote a good part of his poetry there. Professor Leicester Bradner, in an unpublished paper, suggests that Spenser, during this stay in England, may have visited Sir Henry Wallop at Farleigh Wallop, the Hampshire residence to which Wallop returned in 1589. Farleigh Wallop is but six miles from Alton.

[22] Judson, *A Biographical Sketch of John Young*, p. 7.

[23] Johnson, pp. 27-28.

[24] Stein, pp. 9-10.

says he wrote the poem partly because of the fame of Douglas Howard, partly because of the special good will he bore her husband, but there can be little doubt that Spenser's desire to gratify Raleigh, who was Gorges' kinsman, was influential, not to mention the likelihood of patronage from both Gorges and the marchioness. Arthur Gorges, soldier, courtier, and man of letters, and, as Spenser tells us, grandson to a Howard, had married the great heiress Douglas Howard six years before, when she was not yet fourteen. She had been betrothed one day and married the next, with the consent of her mother but contrary to the wishes of her father, who had hoped to arrange a marriage that would bolster his fortune. She died August 13, 1590, after a long illness, leaving one child, Ambrosia, less than two years old.[25]

Though *Daphnaïda*, in which the shepherd Alcyon laments his loss of Daphne, lacks neither melody nor fine passages, Alcyon's unrestrained and repetitious expression of his grief becomes monotonous. Perhaps Spenser determined to make the poem long enough to be issued as a little book—it occupies twenty-four pages as first printed—or, as Dr. Gottfried suggests, he may have been fascinated by the symmetry of seven groups of seven seven-line stanzas. Whatever the explanation of its length, it could hardly have failed to gain by abridgment.

Much as Spenser must have enjoyed certain aspects of English life, including the opportunity to publish the works at which we have just been glancing, his stay in England was not altogether happy. For one thing, as *Colin Clouts Come Home Againe* makes abundantly clear, he disliked the court. Of course he venerated the queen and admired many courtiers, both for their " spotlesse honestie " and their " profession of all learned arts "; and no eye so sensitive as his to form and color, to rich fabrics and fine armor, and to pageantry could have been blind to the elegance and beauty of its life. But its frivolity, its heartless competition for preferments and honors, it immorality—these were so loathsome to him that the " cold and care and penury " of Ireland seemed good by comparison. He especially resented the scorn visited upon plainly dressed men of learning by courtiers whose superiority was based solely on expensive dress and an overbearing manner; because of their utter lack of solid attainments, such men, in his judgment, were no better than inflated bladders. With no serious occupation to absorb their thoughts, the frequenters of the court were one and all given to love, or what passed for love, but was really a licentious profaning of love's " mightie mys-

[25] Sandison, *PMLA* 43. 648-650.

teries." If Spenser had ever looked with favor on life at court, he was to do so no longer.

But he had another and more particular reason for being unhappy during these later months of 1590. His *Faerie Queene* had been published and had been well received, but the preferment he awaited from the queen did not come. Along with the ethical, patriotic, and artistic motives, and the longing, so nearly universal in his day, for fame, which had prompted the writing of his great epic, there was certainly a hope for the material rewards to which men of letters in Elizabethan England thought themselves entitled. Just what form he expected these rewards to take—a gift of money, a pension, a monopoly or similar source of revenue, or a post of importance in the English or Irish government—we do not know. Certainly his maintenance at court must have been a drain on his resources, and the development of his estate called for large outlays, so that generous gifts of money would be almost imperative. Patronage of some sort he tells us he received from the countess of Pembroke, the Spencer sisters, and others. But the larger reward from the queen was not forthcoming.

To Spenser it seemed clear that the lord treasurer was blocking his preferment. So strong did this conviction become that, with impulsive indiscretion, he several times in his *Complaints* condemned Burghley's parsimony. Spenser's impatience first appears most plainly in his long argument in *The Ruines of Time* where he lauds the poet as the only sure source of immortality. He begins by frankly advising the great to purchase immortality from the poet:

> But such as neither of themselues can sing,
> Nor yet are sung of others for reward,
> Die in obscure obliuion. . . .
>
> Prouide therefore (ye Princes) whilst ye liue,
> That of the *Muses* ye may friended bee. . . .

Presently he refers to good Sir Francis Walsingham, who is "halfe happie" because immortalized by the poet Thomas Watson. But since Walsingham's death, he declares, learning lies unregarded and men of arms wander unrewarded;

> For he that now welds all things at his will,
> Scorns th'one and th'other in his deeper skill.

In *Mother Hubberds Tale* he is still more outspoken against Burghley. This satire includes, it will be recalled, two separate adventures of a fox and an ape at court. The second of these adventures, in which occurs the bitter personal attack on Burghley, is generally thought to have been composed during Alençon's memorable suit for Elizabeth's hand ten years before, but the satire may have been altered or expanded when the old poem was prepared for the press. At any rate, lines like the following surely reflect Spenser's feeling in the autumn of 1590:

> And when he ought not pleasing would put by,
> The cloke was care of thrift, and husbandry,
> For to encrease the common treasures store;
> But his owne treasure he encreased more
> And lifted vp his loftie towres thereby,
> That they began to threat the neighbour sky. . . .
>
> Of men of armes he had but small regard,
> But kept them lowe, and streigned verie hard.
> For men of learning little he esteemed;
> His wisedome he aboue their learning deemed. . . .
>
> Ne would he anie let to haue accesse
> Vnto the Prince, but by his owne addresse:
> For all that els did come, were sure to faile. . . .

The core of Spenser's charge is that Burghley, while shamelessly enriching himself, hinders the proper rewarding of soldiers and scholars, on the grounds of economy, and through his authoritative position in the government is able to prevent their access to the queen.

In declaring that Burghley had little esteem for men of learning, Spenser was unfair to the lord treasurer, who gave his patronage freely to certain classes of writers. Although poets and dramatists did not appeal to him, he encouraged historians and others whose work he thought might benefit the state.[26] Among many works dedicated to him were Grafton's and Holinshed's chronicles, Camden's *Britannia*, and Ascham's *Schoolmaster*, this last by Ascham's widow, with the remark that she was mindful how much all good learning owed him for its defense. Serious books like these certainly appealed to Burghley. It is interesting to speculate on his probable attitude toward *The Faerie Queene* if he could have stolen sufficient time from the " graue affaires " of state to weigh, as Spenser hoped he might, its " deeper sence."

In *Mother Hubberds Tale* occurs a passage that must depict accurately the sort of exasperation that Spenser felt as days stretched into weeks and weeks into months without any sign of the patronage on which he had built high hopes.

[26] D. Nichol Smith in *Shakespeare's England* 2. 191-192.

Full little knowest thou that hast not tride,
What hell it is, in suing long to bide:
To loose good dayes, that might be better spent;
To wast long nights in pensiue discontent;
To speed to day, to be put back to morrow;
To feed on hope, to pine with feare and sorrow;
To haue thy Princes grace, yet want her Peeres;
To haue thy asking, yet waite manie yeeres. . . .

But at last came the word he had so eagerly awaited. On February 25, 1591, he was granted a pension of £50, to be paid annually in four installments as long as he should live.[27] Did this meet his hopes and expectations? It would seem so, for in *Colin Clouts Come Home Againe* he speaks with enthusiasm of the "goodly meed" and "bountie" that the queen had bestowed on her shepherd Colin.

In none of his works, moreover, does he pour out a more lyrical flood of praise upon Elizabeth, though of course we must not assume his pension to be the only or necessarily even the main occasion of this most extravagant of all his eulogies of his queen. She was, to be sure, his recent benefactress, but to this chivalrous, patriotic idealist, she was a symbol of so much more, just as she was to most of his fellow poets.[28] His glowing happiness over her liberality was no short-lived emotion, if we may judge by sonnet LXXIV of the *Amoretti*, penned several years later, in which he refers to

my souereigne Queene most kind,
that honour and large richesse to me lent.

We do not know just when Spenser returned to Ireland, but it seems unlikely that he remained in England long after the granting of his pension. Perhaps he sailed with the first good spring weather. Let us hope that he was gone by the time the strictures on Burghley in *Mother Hubberds Tale* were noticed by those in power. That they were noticed, and that the unsold copies of the book were called in by the authorities, we know from several brief allusions in publications during and after 1592.[29] If Spenser returned to Kilcolman in the spring, he must have been immersed at once in the multifarious matters connected with his estate and other interests, and his absence would give the authorities a good excuse to forget his literary indiscretions, which after all were committed by a man whose devotion to queen and country could not be doubted.

[27] Carpenter, *A Reference Guide*, p. 70.

[28] Wilson, *England's Eliza*, pp. 394 ff.

[29] Stein, pp. 79-86; in 1596 a copy was obtained at the high cost of five shillings; so that its suppression continued, it would seem, but ineffectively (Bennett, *ELH* 4. 60-61).

XIV

COLIN HOME AGAIN

SPENSER RETURNED in 1591 to an estate legally his own, for his grant of Kilcolman had been passed in October of the previous year.[1] And heartily glad he was to be back. Through the delicate veil of pastoral convention with which he drapes the account of his experiences, the reader may penetrate easily to the central fact that Ireland, for all its poverty and unrest, seemed good to Spenser. The well-known passage in *Colin Clouts Come Home Againe* which refers to his luckless lot in being banished into that waste where he was quite forgotten, we should remember, is probably Raleigh's picture of his fate rather than his own. The drawbacks to life in Ireland he knew only too well, but he was glad to resume them in exchange for the tinsel of the court.

Pleasant is the opening picture of *Colin Clouts Come Home Againe* in which he describes the reunion with his Irish associates. We can imagine Lodowick Bryskett and his neighbors Hugh Cuffe, Thomas Saye, and Arthur Hyde, to mention but a few, hastening to Kilcolman for the latest news from England, and we do not wonder at his friends' expressions of deep satisfaction over the return of one whose practical good sense must have been valued quite as much as his warm friendship and literary gifts. Very human was his evident satisfaction in describing his journey. For all his praise of Elizabeth, his narrative as a whole was bound to leave his friends more contented with their lot. The bliss of court life, he assured them, was specious and vain, and no young man who had inured himself to the hard realities of Irish life should leave his quiet home for the uncertainties awaiting the courtier.

During the year or more when he was mainly in England, we need not doubt that he kept himself well informed of the situation in Ireland. Though his years of association with Lord Grey had trained him to think in the larger terms of Ireland's welfare, as is proved by his *View of the Present State of Ireland*, events in Munster would naturally claim his special attention. An event of particular interest to him in 1590 was surely the mutiny of Sir Thomas Norris's company of foot soldiers, a body of men that he must have seen often. Dissatisfaction over lack of pay persuaded them, in May, to march from Limerick to Dublin and appeal in

[1] Fiant 5473, *Sixteenth Report*, p. 137.

person to the lord deputy for a settlement of their grievances. What happened was described in detail by Sir George Carew. When they appeared at the castle bridge on the morning of Ascension Day, the gusty old deputy, Sir William Fitzwilliam, was tempted, if they would not leave, to disperse them with cannon, but instead decided to notify them that they might have part of their pay. This they refused, hoping for full arrears. The deputy then, without further parley, rode forth to church, preceded by Carew, bearing the sword of state.

"Master of the Ordnance," he said to Carew, "I will see whether these fellows will stay me on the bridge; I am sure you will not let them take the sword from you."

"No, sir, they shall scratch for it before they shall get it," replied Carew.

"I think so," said the deputy, "and am glad that it is in a man's hand."

On the appearance of the deputy and his party, the soldiers all besought consideration of their wrongs. One man used offensive language, and on him Fitzwilliam turned fiercely. For a moment a clash seemed imminent, for the deputy's servants drew their swords. But when the deputy cried, "Disarm them!" the men quietly submitted, and were bound and led away.[2] They were, however, soon pardoned and sent back to Munster.

To Spenser, with his idealism in regard to the profession of the soldier, this affair must have been mortifying, though he doubtless recognized that the government was more culpable than the men. Indeed he was convinced that a chief weakness of the Munster plantation was the failure to provide within the province adequate garrisons maintained by a settled allowance from the revenue of the crown lands.[3] Later events were to prove his wisdom in this matter.

During Spenser's ten years in Ireland, English rule had been substantially strengthened and extended except in Ulster. In Ulster, Turlough Luineach O'Neill had been the dominant figure. Another chief of great importance, whose territory lay to the northwest, in Donegal, was Sir Hugh MacManus O'Donnell. Directly or indirectly these chiefs controlled most of northern Ireland. Another leader whose power was steadily growing was Hugh O'Neill. As Spenser says in the *View*, he had been raised up "out of the dust" by Elizabeth, as a counterweight to Turlough; yet destiny was to create in him the most serious of all perils to Elizabeth's rule in Ireland. Spenser in 1596 likened him to a frozen snake picked up

[2] *Cal. Carew MSS.* (1589-1600), pp. 31-33. Carew refers to the dialogue quoted as "these or the like words."

[3] *View*, pp. 162-163.

by a farmer which, growing warm, hisses at his benefactor.[4] But in 1590 there was as yet no clear indication of the great ambitions that were later to possess him.

Hugh O'Neill's father was Mathew O'Neill, first baron of Dungannon; his alleged grandfather, Con O'Neill, first earl of Tyrone. When about twenty-two years of age, Hugh had been taken under the protection of the English government and sent to England, where he had spent six years at court, part of it perhaps in Leicester's household, whose almost regal magnificence would have offered startling contrasts to the primitive environment in which he had passed his boyhood. This sojourn in England was designed to safeguard his life from Turlough Luineach O'Neill, who as chief of Tyrone might have murdered him as he had already murdered Hugh's brother Brian. Incidentally by grounding him thoroughly in English ways and in the English character, it had made him potentially a much more dangerous foe of the English. On his return to Ireland in 1568, he was established by the government on lands in the north comprising what is now the county of Armagh. Almost at once friction developed between him and Turlough, which was not diminished by the obvious desire of the authorities to increase Hugh's prestige. In 1585 he was permitted the title of earl of Tyrone, and through the efforts of the lord deputy Perrot he was enabled to secure from Turlough, in return for an annual payment of 1,000 marks, a large district in the county of Tyrone lying to the northwest of his lands.

In August, 1591, occurred an event which, though in itself of no great importance, certainly contributed to the earl of Tyrone's series of grievances that were finally to place him at the head of Irish opposition to English rule. Having become a widower in January, 1591, he soon fell violently in love with Mabel Bagenal, daughter of Sir Nicholas Bagenal, who had grown old in the Irish service as marshal of the army. As the Bagenal estates were at Newry, north of the Pale and less than thirty miles from Dungannon, the earl easily found the opportunity for meetings with Mabel, and his title, power, and personal charm, outweighing his fifty years, enabled him to win the affection of this English girl of twenty. But Sir Henry Bagenal, her brother, now lord marshal of the army, strenuously opposed the match. The lovers, however, plighted their troth, and Tyrone gave her as pledge a chain of gold. Three weeks later they went separately to the home of a friend of the earl's near Dublin where they were married by the bishop of Meath. Sir Henry Bagenal was furious, and he as well as several who were concerned in the affair promptly sent

[4] *Ibid.*, p. 147.

letters of recrimination or justification to Burghley and to the privy council.[5] At first the marriage seemed to promise happiness. Two years later Tyrone wrote to Burghley that his young English wife was bringing civility into his household and into the country roundabout, as he had hoped she would, but Tyrone sought in vain to conciliate her brother. Sir Henry remained deeply resentful and positively refused to pay the £1,000 that had been specified in Sir Nicholas's will as his daughter's marriage portion. As time went on, the enmity between Tyrone and his brother-in-law deepened, and undoubtedly had a bearing on Tyrone's determination to break with the English, though Sir Henry believed it merely provided an excuse for one who had decided to revolt.

About the end of 1592, Tyrone's animosity for Turlough seems to have given way to larger aims. Spanish intrigue and the influence of Hugh Roe O'Donnell, the handsome, popular, newly inaugurated young chief of neighboring Donegal, helped to foster his larger ambitions. Whatever the precise reasons for Tyrone's determination to oppose English rule in Ireland, the cause of Irish independence acquired its first great leader in him. "Very subtle headed," Spenser calls him,[6] and it is indeed surprising how often he was able to bolster wavering English faith in his loyalty, in order, it would seem, to win needed time for his plans. His great gifts were justly set forth by Camden:

> A strong body he had, able to endure labour, watching, and hunger; his industry was great, his mind great and able for the greatest businesses; much knowledge he had in military skill and a mind most profound to dissemble, insomuch as some did then foretell that he was born to the very great good or hurt of Ireland.[7]

Whether he was born for Ireland's good or harm depends on one's point of view. To many of the Irish he naturally seemed a heaven-sent patriot, to the English a terrible menace. Spenser calls him in the *View* an "arch rebel";[8] could Spenser then have known that Kilcolman would one day be despoiled by men who had pledged allegiance to Tyrone, he might have applied even more bitter language to the earl.

We know little of how Spenser occupied himself after his return to Ireland, but it is safe to assume that his energies were devoted mainly to his estate and to his writing. His deputy clerkship perhaps required some attention, though his discovery that the drudgery of this office could be placed upon the shoulders of another probably caused him to delegate

[5] Meehan, *The Fate and Fortunes of Hugh O'Neill*, pp. 288-300.
[6] *View*, p. 145.
[7] *The Historie of the . . . Princesse Elizabeth*, Book IV, p. 23.
[8] P. 145.

most if not all of its duties from now on. Indeed it may have been about this time that its burdensome detail, through an arrangement with Bryskett, was turned over to Nicholas Curteys, who shortly after Spenser's death declared that he had long served " in that poor and troublesome place of Clerk of the Council of Munster," occupying it " upon the trust of Lodowick Bryskett and Edmund Spenser." [9] From a petition of Lord Roche, dated 1593, we know that Spenser, by an agreement with Curteys, was to " be free in the said office for his causes," or suits, a valuable proviso considering the litigation in which the undertakers were frequently involved.[10] By December 27, 1591, Spenser had finished the first draft of *Colin Clouts Come Home Againe*, a poem evidently written with gusto. In composing it, he relived one of the most stirring and eventful periods of his life.

Heartened by the success of the first installment of *The Faerie Queene*, he undoubtedly devoted as much time as he could spare to a continuation of this great project. He writes of " sloth, that oft doth noble mindes annoy," and playfully assures Raleigh that he is not always idle, but indolence could scarcely have been one of his temptations. He must have accustomed himself early to a highly effective use of his time,

> the threasure of mans day,
> Whose smallest minute lost, no riches render may.[11]

Perhaps demands of his estate caused him to compose under greater pressure than hitherto, for several times in the later books of *The Faerie Queene*, he admits fatigue, comparing himself, for example, at the close of a canto, to a weary ploughman turning his team homeward at the day's end. In his *Amoretti* also he confesses that composition has brought its hours of exhaustion.

> After so long a race as I haue run
> Through Faery land, which those six books compile,
> giue leaue to rest me being halfe fordonne,
> and gather to my selfe new breath awhile.[12]

---

[9] Chichester, Spenser's substitute, was in England on a mission for the deputy in September, 1590, so that Spenser by that time may have settled the duties of the clerkship on another, perhaps Curteys—*C. S. P. Ir.* (1588-1592), p. 363 (25), *C. S. P. Ir.* (1598-1599), p. 484 (61). Among Professor Ray Heffner's papers is a copy of an undated letter from Nicholas Curteys to the privy council (S. P. 63. 139. 62). From it we learn that Curteys was associated as secretary, or chief clerk, with the commission, headed by Justice Anderson, which visited Ireland in the summer of 1588 for hearings of claims against the undertakers. Heffner conjectures that " Spenser probably met Curteys at these hearings."

[10] Hardiman, *Irish Minstrelsy* 1. 320.

[11] *F. Q.* 4. 7. 23; Dedication, *Colin Clouts Come Home Againe*; *F. Q.* 4. 10. 14.

[12] LXXX.

Yet weariness did not diminish his creative powers nor reduce the quality of his work. Unlike most great poets, he was able to soar on in steady flight, and sustained all his life a remarkably high level of excellence.

In 1592 Cuthbert Burby put on sale at his lately opened shop by St. Mildred's Church in the Poultry, London, a small volume containing both the translation of a Platonic dialogue known as *Axiochus* and an oration spoken by a page of the earl of Oxford before the queen at a pageant held at Whitehall. The dialogue is described on the title-page as translated from the Greek by " Edw. Spenser." If a copy of the book came into the hands of Spenser, he was perhaps amused to see the " E." or " Ed." that he had modestly used up to this time expanded into " Edw." The success of *The Faerie Queene*, he must have known, was chiefly responsible for this publishing venture by Burby, as also Burby's description of the translator as " that worthy scholar and poet, Master Edward Spenser, whose studies have and do carry no mean commendation, because their deserts are of so great esteem." The natural assumption that the translator was Edmund Spenser the poet has been vigorously supported by Professor F. M. Padelford, the lucky discoverer and editor, in 1934, of this long-lost work.[13]

The *Axiochus* is a Greek dialogue of unknown authorship, though in Spenser's time generally ascribed to Plato. In it Socrates presents so eloquently the compensations, even blessings, of death that the fears of Axiochus, who has not long to live, are transformed into a positive desire for death. Though Burby asserts that the translation was from the Greek, Professor Padelford has demonstrated that the translator used a Latin version of the dialogue. It would be a satisfaction to know the true history of the translation and the steps that led to its publication by Burby, who virtually began his troubled career as a publisher with this little book.

Spenser may have wished to devote himself whole-heartedly to the Muses after his return to Ireland, but obviously no such course was possible. Much ingenuity was undoubtedly required to make his estate even moderately successful, for the Munster plantation was proving no utopia. Though references to the Munster project are not numerous in the State Papers of the years 1590-1594, there is enough mention to show which way the wind was blowing. Bringing in English settlers to the number

[13] Two arguments have been made for Anthony Munday as the translator, one by Mr. Bernard Freyd, the other by Dr. Marshall W. S. Swan. Dr. Swan bases his conclusions in part on the belief that the oration, missing from Professor Padelford's copy, but lately brought to light, is by Munday. Cf. Freyd, *PMLA* 50. 903-908; Padelford, *ibid.*, pp. 908-913; Swan, *ELH* 11. 161-181.

required was proving impossible: in the autumn of 1592 there were but 245 English tenants on all the seignories. Many Irish tenants had been accepted, and yet the land was sparsely settled, and the revenues were small. The undertakers were experiencing great difficulty in paying even their modest rents. The solicitor-general, Roger Wilbraham, wrote to Burghley on September 7, 1593, that the undertakers grew poorer and poorer, for their revenues were insufficient to supply them with their accustomed English food and apparel, and he predicted that when the full rents became due in 1594 many would leave the keys under the front door and depart.[14] Furthermore, contentions between them over allotments of land, as well as suits on the part of the dispossessed Irish, continued apparently without interruption, so that, though the province as a whole enjoyed, for Ireland, an unusual calm, there were plenty of small local tempests.

Of Spenser's progress with his estate, we know little. In 1592 he paid his rent of £9 14*s.* 16*d.*[15] In the autumn of that same year, when a commission gave more than three months to an inspection of the seignories, he, like a majority of his fellow undertakers, was absent, and hence furnished neither in person nor through an agent any certified list of tenants. The commissioners were of the opinion that those who were absent had met their obligations less well than the rest in the matter of English settlers, and for that reason had delivered no names.[16]

Legal affairs occupied some of Spenser's time. In 1594, for example, we find him sitting twice at Mallow, with others, as justice of the queen for the county of Cork.[17] Moreover, in 1593 and in the year or two following, he and Lord Roche were again in litigation over disputed lands. Lord Roche believed that Spenser, whom he calls his "heavy adversary," was multiplying suits against him because of the arrangement already mentioned with Nicholas Curteys, then acting as clerk of the council of Munster, by virtue of which Spenser had his suits without cost to himself. One case involved the possession of three plowlands of Shanballymore, situated less than three miles from Roche's estate, and another three ploughlands of Ballingerath, which Spenser had occupied and from which he had taken, according to Lord Roche, corn and wood to the value of £200. Spenser, so far as we know, never acquired the former lands, and his failure to appear in connection with the latter suit resulted in a decree

[14] *C. S. P. Ir.* (1592-1596), pp. 58 (44 V), 145 (30).
[15] *Ibid.*, p. 57 (44 IV).
[16] *Ibid.*, p. 58 (44 V).
[17] Berry, *Journal of the Cork Historical and Archaeological Society*, 2nd Series, 12. 2.

giving Roche possession. Still another case concerned two ploughlands of Kilvallinge and Classagny in County Cork; a decree of February 12, 1595, ordered these returned to Roche, and a commission was appointed to inquire into the value of corn and wood taken from these lands by Spenser. Furthermore, Roche declared that a certain Joan Ny Callaghan was his opponent through the support and maintenance of Spenser.[18] We could wish a more complete knowledge of this second series of quarrels with Lord Roche, but if we base our judgment entirely on the scanty evidence surviving, this litigation does not appear to reflect credit on Spenser: seeing matters from the point of view of an opponent could hardly be called one of his virtues.

Some of his biographers have probably laid undue emphasis on these legal duels with his neighbor, and have even supposed that Spenser's satisfaction in Kilcolman was ruined by such contentions. But against our record of them we should balance the long account of country life in Book VI of *The Faerie Queene*, in which its peace and freedom and its quiet pleasures are most engagingly depicted; for may we not here read an expression of his contentment at Kilcolman, his reconciliation with Irish life? The tone of this passage, so like that suffusing much of *Colin Clouts Come Home Againe*, suggests quietude of spirit and a cheerful adjustment to an existence whose discords and hardships might once have seemed unbearable.

> It is the mynd, that maketh good or ill,
> That maketh wretch or happie, rich or poore:
> For some, that hath abundance at his will,
> Hath not enough, but wants in greatest store;
> And other, that hath litle, askes no more,
> But in that litle is both rich and wise.[19]

Undoubtedly this London-bred man was growing ever more attached

[18] Hardiman 1. 320; Atkinson, *Edmund Spenser, A Bibliographical Supplement*, p. 5 (the spelling "Classagny" and the date of the decree verified at the P. R. O. Dublin). Some of Spenser's efforts to increase his holdings near Kilcolman had proved, or were to prove, more successful. An undated document in the British Museum (reproduced by Warner in *Facsimiles of Royal, Historical, Literary and Other Autographs*, No. 92) indicates his possession of Richardstown Castle, which stands less than a mile from the confluence of the Awbeg and Bregoge Rivers near the town of Doneraile. In this document, signed "Ed. Sp[en]ser," the keeping of the woods, rushes, and brakes on the castle lands is assigned to one McHenry, who is to have a house within the fortified court of the castle for himself and his cattle in time of war. He is, besides, to repair the castle within a period of seven years and to show himself a good neighbor to Spenser and his people. A Mr. McHendry attested one of the items in the bill of complaint against Lord Roche, dated October 12, 1589. For lands acquired by Spenser for his son Peregrine, see *infra*, p. 174, and note.

[19] *F. Q.* 6. 9. 30.

to the natural features of his Irish home. He had given the name of Mulla to the Awbeg River, which washed the borders of his estate, and refers to its shining surface, to the alders on its banks, and to the superior trout and pike that bred in its clear depths. " Mulla mine," he terms it in Book IV of *The Faerie Queene.* Toward his more remote surroundings we perceive a similar friendly attitude—toward the large pleasant valley in which Kilcolman was situated, and toward the mountains that walled it on the north. From his estate he could plainly see Galteemore rising twenty miles away, its familiar truncated peak looking to him gray, or hoary, as if still scarred by the previous winter's frosts. He was clearly moved by the majesty of the Galtees, and his allusions to them suggest a feeling for mountain scenery not common in his day.

Unhappily brigands dwelt not far from the earthly paradise of the shepherds in Book VI; and as time passed, Spenser must have been increasingly conscious that beyond the borders of quiet Munster, dangerous trouble was brewing. As early as February 20, 1592, Sir Henry Bagenal wrote Burghley that the more restless and lawless elements of the north were gravitating to Tyrone's country. By the spring of 1593 there were rumors that the northern chiefs under Tyrone's leadership were plotting rebellion. Yet in the autumn Tyrone cooperated with Sir Henry in the suppression of an uprising led by Hugh Maguire, the chief of Fermanagh. This, however, was Tyrone's last service for Elizabeth, and it was performed most likely with somewhat more reluctance than he cared to admit. On July 31, 1594, a new lord deputy, Sir William Russell, arrived to relieve Sir William Fitzwilliam, whose age and bodily ailments had made his continuance in office even thus long a manifestation of heroism. Russell had been a friend of Leicester's and Sidney's, and his appointment must have been of more than passing interest to Spenser, who, in 1596, refers to him as " the honorable gentleman that now governeth there," and speaks with respect of his campaign against the wily old rebel Fiagh MacHugh O'Byrne.[20] Hopes were held that a new deputy might turn Tyrone back from a path that seemed to be leading him straight toward open rebellion.

To many it appeared likely that Tyrone's plotting had the backing of Spain. The defeat of the Armada had by no means ended the danger of a new effort to conquer England, and for years reports had been coming in from merchants and seamen that fleets were assembling in Spanish harbors for a descent on Ireland. Sir William Stanley's name was often coupled with the expected attack, and his thorough knowledge of

[20] *View,* pp. 152-153.

Ireland was reckoned a great asset to the invaders.[21] In Book V of *The Faerie Queene* Spenser portrays the fierce struggle waged by Catholic Spain against England, the Netherlands, and Huguenot France; and it is not unlikely that while this book, or part of it, at least, was being written, rumors of imminent invasion were reaching the poet. After his return from England he could have experienced no great surprise at almost any time to learn that a contingent of the Spanish fleet had anchored in the harbor of Cork, or Kinsale, or Waterford, and it is possible that the virility of his narrative, and the intense feeling that infuses much of it, owe not a little to such well-grounded apprehensions.

But for Spenser even revolution and war must have moved into the background when love and marriage advanced their claims. Spenser's second marriage occurred in all likelihood on June 11, 1594. Of such moment was this even, both in his life and in his poetry, that it deserves a chapter of its own.

[21] *Cal. Carew MSS.* (1589-1600), p. 17 (46); *C. S. P. Ir.* (1588-1592), pp. 386 (22), 452 (2); *C. S. P. Ir.* (1592-1596), pp. 71-72 (8 XI), 93 (22), 244 (48 III).

XV
ELIZABETH BOYLE

MUCH THAT we know about Spenser's marriage to Elizabeth Boyle is found between the covers of a small octavo volume published in 1595 by William Ponsonby with a title-page bearing the words: " Amoretti and Epithalamion. Written not long since by Edmunde Spenser." A young cavalry officer, Sir Robert Needham, then serving in Ireland under Sir William Russell,[1] was honored with the dedication, presumably because of Ponsonby's friendship for Needham. The book was inscribed to him, says Ponsonby, in order to " gratulate " his safe return from Ireland. The choice seemed appropriate to Ponsonby because Needham loved poetry, and also because the manuscript happened to cross to England on the same ship that brought him over. It may seem odd that Spenser did not himself prepare a dedication to one of his friends or patrons, but very likely he was yielding to the convention that made a gentleman reluctant to print, or appear to print, his own works, especially when they were so personal as this volume. In addition to eighty-eight sonnets, placed one on a page between ornamental borders, and the *Epithalamion*, some trifling Anacreontic verses appear after the sonnets, separating them from the *Epithalamion*—as it were, a series of poetical asterisks. Their inclusion may have been Ponsonby's not very happy idea.

Spenser was married on St. Barnabas' Day, June 11, the longest day of the year according to the calendar then in use. Though a line in the *Epithalamion* tells us the day, we do not know certainly the year. Yet because Ponsonby entered the volume in the Stationers' Register on November 19, 1594, it has been customary to assume that the " Written not long since " of the title-page indicates that the marriage occurred in the previous June. This assumption is supported by the fact that, as Sonnet LXXX makes clear, he had finished the first six books of *The Faerie Queene* before his marriage. Considering the immensity of the task of completing the second installment of three books, it is reasonable to assume as long an interval as possible between his return to Ireland in 1591 and his completion of Book VI.

Before looking at the lover's picture of a woman conveyed to us by

[1] *Cal. Carew MSS.* (1589-1600), p. 223.

the *Amoretti* and the *Epithalamion*, we should perhaps ask what historical investigation has to say of this second wife whom Spenser took when he was about forty.

She was the daughter of Stephen and Joan Boyle, of Bradden, a village three miles from Towcester, Northamptonshire.[2] Bradden and Althorp are both but a few miles from Northampton, and Professor Heffner recently discovered the interesting fact that Elizabeth Boyle and the children of Sir John Spencer of Althorp were fourth cousins,[3] so that it is possible that the young Elizabeth may sometimes have been a visitor at Althorp and Wormleighton and have come to know Elizabeth, Anne, and Alice Spencer, though she would have looked up to them as great ladies, beyond her in years as well as rank. Stephen Boyle died in 1582, leaving some £250 as a marriage portion for each of his children.[4] Elizabeth had two brothers, Alexander and George; and Alexander, like Elizabeth, was destined to be transplanted from the quiet English midlands to Ireland. She was also niece by marriage to John Dryden, a great-grandfather of the poet.[5] Still another relative, who was to prove of the very greatest importance to her in her later years, was Richard Boyle, to be known long after this as "the great earl of Cork," one of the most distinguished figures in Ireland during the first few decades of the seventeenth century.

Because this man became after Spenser's death almost a foster father to Elizabeth, and may well have taken an interest in her welfare before she married Spenser, we shall glance briefly at his career and character. He first set foot on Irish soil in the summer of 1588, a young man of twenty-one, possessing, aside from his clothing, only a diamond ring, a great gold ring, a gold bracelet, and in his purse twenty-seven pounds, three shillings.[6] But in his breast was an unquenchable determination to win success in this wild land of opportunity. As escheator, or certifier of lands reverting to the crown, he doubtless saw opportunities for financial gain. Already prosperous by 1595, he added to his wealth by marrying a Limerick heiress. From then on the story of his life reminds one of certain American youths who by persistence and vision and sheer genius for amassing riches have been able quickly to exchange obscurity and poverty for fantastic wealth and the power that so often accompanies such wealth. In 1604 he obtained a patent to Raleigh's great estates on the Blackwater. These he developed rapidly, building harbors, bridges, castles, and towns, establishing mining, weaving, and other industries, and making his

[2] Welply, *NQ* 146. 445-447.
[3] *HLQ* 2. 82.
[4] Welply, *NQ* 146. 446.
[5] *Ibid.*, 162. 166.
[6] Townshend, *The Life and Letters of the Great Earl of Cork*, p. 6; *DNB*.

lands so productive that the original undertakers must have been filled with amazement and envy. In 1603 he was knighted, in 1616 he became Lord Boyle, baron of Youghal; in 1620, Viscount Dungarvan and earl of Cork; and in 1631, lord high treasurer of Ireland.

Our first specific indication of friendship between Richard Boyle and Elizabeth pertains to her second marriage. Since she was younger than Spenser by perhaps fifteen or twenty years,[7] it is not surprising that she married again after his death. Within little more than a year and a half we find her the wife of Roger Seckerstone, by whom she had one child, a son named after Richard Boyle, who was his godfather.[8] A few years later, when she was again a widow, Boyle leased her a house at Kilcoran for the purely nominal rent of two shillings, sixpence, per annum.[9] On March 2, 1612, she was married at Youghal to Captain Robert Tynte. The ceremony was performed in the study of Sir Richard, who himself gave her away, and who recorded in his diary the hope that God would bless the couple with good agreement and many virtuous children.[10] They were blessed, it is thought, with four. Both Seckerstone and Tynte were acquaintances of Boyle, and he probably arranged both marriages. Three letters written by Elizabeth Tynte in 1615, 1616, and 1620 are preserved among the Lismore Papers.[11] In the first of these she refers to Boyle's "ever wonted kindness" toward her, and in the second she thanks him for offering to let her son remain with him for his better education. All three letters, though brief and concerned with specific business, reveal sincere gratitude and friendship.

In view of this intimate association with Richard Boyle during her later years, it is natural to suspect that his presence in Ireland was somehow responsible for Elizabeth's first going there. We know that Boyle persuaded his sisters Mary and Elizabeth to join him and that they both soon married and settled near Youghal.[12] Not yet himself a resident of

[7] The best evidence of her age is that she married Captain Tynte in 1612, and had by him (probably) four children (Welply, *NQ* 165. 114; see also 162. 184-185).

[8] Brady, *Clerical and Parochial Records* 2. 260; *The Lismore Papers* (*First Series*) 1. xvi-xvii.

[9] *Ibid.*, pp. xiv-xvi; the house was not, as Grosart supposed, near Youghal, but fifteen miles to the northwest, on property leased by Boyle for its timber (Henley, *Spenser in Ireland*, p. 198 and note).

[10] *The Lismore Papers* (*First Series*) 1. 8; Robert Tynte attained prominence in County Cork, was knighted in 1620, and resided with his wife at Ballycrenan Castle, overlooking beautiful Ballycottin Bay (Welply, *NQ* 165. 111).

[11] *The Lismore Papers* (*Second Series*) 2. 12, 60, 237.

[12] Townshend, p. 8; Mary married Richard Smith of Ballynetra, as his estate on the river four miles north of Youghal was called, and Elizabeth, Pierce Power, of Lisfinny Castle, which

Sr

Being the time is longe since I saw you, & the distance of my being so far of, I may not be so ungratfull, not to remember with due respect, thankfullnes for your ever wonted kindnes towardes me. which I wish better requytall then either word or linnes: but having no other, I can but imytate the poore womanes with desiring not to be forgotton of you but that you would continue your wonted faviours towardes me: as for my health I thanke god I am much better then I was & have found better contentment then ever I have found befor, & I hope it will so continue & I will put my best indever to the same & shall intreat the help of my best frindes, to enabell my strenketh ther unto: ther is some that hath professed great frinshipe unto me, but I find now what the are & hath bine the caues of ~~my [illegible]~~ all. which I shall tell you at my coming so with my best wishes to your self I remayne

Gillingam this xxj desember 1615

your very loving kinswoman
Eliz: Tynte

Elizabeth Tynte to Sir Richard Boyle. From *The Lismore Papers*, Second Series, edited by A. B. Grosart, Vol. I, 1887.

Youghal, he may nevertheless have influenced Elizabeth and her brother Alexander to make their home in this pretty town at the mouth of the Blackwater. If so, the circumstance would account for the line in *Epithalamion* which speaks of " the sea that neighbours to her neare," and it is pleasant to believe that Spenser's magnificent seventy-fifth sonnet, in which he tells of writing his sweetheart's name upon the strand, has basis in fact, refers indeed to the famous three-mile beach at Youghal, to this day called the Strand.

It would be interesting to know Elizabeth's attitude as stepmother toward Sylvanus and Katherine. A legal document, till lately extant, hints that her relationship with Sylvanus was not of the best. Probably in 1602 or 1603, Sylvanus, having perhaps, as Mr. Hamer believes, just come of age, accused Elizabeth and her husband, Roger Seckerstone, of unjustly withholding the title-deeds of Kilcolman, and petitioned the chancellor of Ireland to require their surrender.[13] Since Seckerstone may have been chiefly responsible for Sylvanus' grievance, we should perhaps refrain from allowing this affair to influence our judgment of Elizabeth.

A better side light on her character may be obtained from her letters. They are lucid and to the point; though they reveal a sense of obligation to Boyle, they are free from any hint of subservience; and they reflect a kind heart—as when she urges Boyle to show his loving favor and countenance to her son whom he is educating, and to excuse his childish actions on the ground of his youth and inexperience; or when she asks Boyle to accept five pounds overdue for her brother Alexander's rent, expressing at the same time the hope that such tardiness will not be repeated. Even her penmanship (if we may, with Grosart, assume the letters to be autograph) tells us something. One of her letters, reproduced in facsimile by Grosart, is in a trained, rapid, flexible hand (the " Italian "), suggestive of one possessing neatness and system, and indicative—especially at that time in the case of women—of education.

When, in our effort to learn more of Elizabeth Boyle, we turn to the *Amoretti*, we find a work differing notably in one respect from the typical sonnet sequence of that day: Spenser wrote about a woman who responded to her lover's suit. At first she is, to be sure, through sixty-one sonnets, a proud, disdainful mistress, a typical Petrarchan lady; but then she yields to love and joins her lover in a mutual affection that looks toward mar-

is now a ruin near Tallow on the Tallow-Fermoy road. Query—when did the sisters first settle in Youghal?

[13] Betham, *Archaeologia* 21. 552-553; Hamer, *RES* 7. 280.

riage, conduct natural enough in real life but quite out of accord with the habits of her prototypes.

In another respect, Spenser's *Amoretti* is different. It tells a clearer story than any other Elizabethan sonnet sequence, one thing that aids the impression of consecutive narrative being the intermittent suggestion of chronology. The courtship begins with the "New yeare forth looking out of Ianus gate." When spring arrives, the lady disobeys the universal precept to love, and remains as hard as iron and as cold as ice all the rest of the year. But with another New Year's day, hope springs in the heart of the lover—a hope well founded, for we hear not one word more of coldness and pride. On Easter day he reminds her that love is a lesson that the Lord has taught. And when spring soon follows, we are sure that she is now in tune with it. Through twenty-three sonnets the happiness of the couple is pictured, or at least implied. But the sequence ends with four sonnets that tell of discord. The lover has been slandered to his mistress; and there follow separation and, for him, loneliness:

> Dark is my day, whyles her fayre light I mis,
> and dead my life that wants such liuely blis.

Great ingenuity has been exercised in trying to read a consecutive story into Sidney's sonnets, and even greater in mending the disorder of Shakespeare's. In what contrast is the intelligible arrangement of this sequence!

A coherent narrative we certainly have, but is it an account of Spenser's courtship of Elizabeth Boyle? Because of the conventional character of many of the sonnets, its integrity as autobiography has been challenged. No one can question the presence of convention: Petrarch, Ariosto, Tasso, Desportes, du Bellay, Ronsard, and others seem to live again in these sonnets, in situation as well as in figure or conceit, though of outright translation there is little. Generally the work of earlier sonneteers has been so well assimilated that it reappears merely like bits of old melody woven into a new musical composition. But that many of the sonnets are firmly rooted in convention is none the less true. Who indeed would care to insist that some of them are not perhaps merely elegant exercises and that others were not written to earlier mistresses? [14]

Be their origin what it may, they were arranged with care to present, as we have seen, a lucid narrative. And we need hardly doubt that this narrative concerns Elizabeth Boyle, for from time to time occur sonnets that are

[14] Scott, *MLR* 22. 189-195. For a discussion of the theory that sonnets of the *Amoretti* were addressed to Elizabeth Carey, see Strathmann, *ELH* 2. 33 ff., and the articles by P. W. Long and J. C. Smith listed by him.

obviously autobiographic, landmarks that show the direction of the whole. Such is sonnet XXXIII, in which Spenser agrees with his friend Bryskett that he is culpable in not carrying forward *The Faerie Queene*, but defends himself by saying that such a task is impossible for one, like himself, distraught over trying to win a proud woman. Such is LX, where he declares that his year of unsuccessful courtship seems longer than all the forty that preceded it. Such too is LXXIV, in which he informs us that his queen, his mother, and his mistress are all named Elizabeth, as also LXXX, where he speaks of laying aside *The Faerie Queene*—now grown to six books—for a while in order to sing his " loues sweet praise." We may then reasonably conclude that, whatever the occasion of certain individual sonnets, the sequence as it stands was intended by the poet to celebrate his courtship of Elizabeth Boyle, and to suggest, at least in a broad general way, the course of this affair.

Though some conception of the real experience that lies behind the sequence adds to its interest, no knowledge of Elizabeth Boyle is needed for an enjoyment of the ideas, the imagery, the technical excellence of the sonnets. Most appealing are those belonging to the second year, after his mistress has been won. They convey the greater sense of freshness and reality, but here too imitation, even translation, has been discovered; LXXII, LXXIII, and LXXXI all have their counterparts in Tasso, to whose sonnets Spenser seems to have been especially drawn. The sequence has been criticized as deficient in passion, but a happier balance could hardly be struck between the claims of flesh and spirit. Certainly Spenser has much to say of the " souerayne beauty " of his mistress, the loveliness of her physical charms; yet he is too thoroughly a Platonist not to insist on the superior beauty of her mind:

> But that which fairest is, but few behold,
> her mind adornd with vertues manifold.[15]

The technical excellence of Spenser's sonnets has always aroused admiration,—the easy management of his rhyme scheme by which he links his quatrains, and his unfaltering lucidity, grace, and melody. Inasmuch as he became familiar with the form as a boy, we ought not to wonder at the exceptional mastery shown in this great collection written long after his apprenticeship had been served.

When we pass to the *Epithalamion*, sequel to the *Amoretti*, we feel closer to biographical fact, yet here too we encounter convention. The marriage hymn, like the love sonnet, had developed a series of traditional

[15] XV.

features, and certainly Spenser knew these well. In this poem he betrays especially his intimacy with the epithalamia of Catullus and certain French poets of the Pléiade,[16] but as usual, he moves freely, aided, not hampered, by the works of others; the principal features of his hymn come from them, but he adds and modifies as he pleases, so that the final achievement is truly his. In one respect he has an enormous advantage over his predecessors: he is celebrating his own marriage. He does not need to imagine the joy of another, but may merely voice his own strong feelings. He could have said with Sidney: " And Love doth hold my hand, and makes me write."

Spenser begins his *Epithalamion* with a reference to the poems he has written to " adorne " others, and he ends it with the statement that this hymn was written " in lieu of many ornaments " that were to have decked his love. It is natural to assume that by " ornaments " he meant " poems." Since his sonnet cycle ends abruptly in misunderstanding and separation, may we not suppose that he intended to round it out with additional sonnets, but for some unexplained reason determined to compose his great marriage hymn instead? If this is the correct interpretation of the somewhat obscure envoy of the *Epithalamion*, we must agree that he has abundantly compensated for any sonnets he failed to write.

The description of the marriage day, which provides the substance of his *Epithalamion*, was written, presumably, in advance of the event. The biographer, searching here for facts will find his greatest reward in the mood of the poem: this second marriage of Spenser's was clearly an event of unalloyed joy, even ecstasy. " So I vnto my selfe alone will sing," he declares, and the reader feels throughout the poem an extraordinary depth of sincerity. Beyond this clear revelation of Spenser's emotions, we must recognize that the poem oscillates between reality and imagination. Fanciful he is when he sends the nymphs of river and lake, of forest and sea, to awaken his bride, but factual, in a sense, when he includes the nymphs of the Awbeg River and of his own little reedy lake lying near his castle. Reality we have probably when he describes her flower-strewn path, her white attire and loose, flowing golden hair adorned with a garland, as also the music played while she goes to the church and the feasting that follows, for here we meet nothing contrary to the social customs of the day. Details of Roman origin we certainly have when he describes the boys running up and down the street, shouting " Hymen io Hymen," or tells of posts and walls sprinkled with wine, and Bacchus and Hymen crowned

[16] Van Winkle in his ed. of *Epithalamion*; McPeek, *JEGP* 35. 183-213.

with vine wreaths; and something as far from realism as the Song of Songs when he pictures his bride with eyes like sapphires, forehead like ivory, cheeks like ruddy apples, a neck like a marble tower, and a breast like a bowl of uncurdled cream. As usual he is the true poet of the Renaissance, weaving into his splendid, colorful web strands of the most varied origin, yet giving to the whole a harmonious texture. His theory of art and sense of reserve govern the selection and management of his material, but the spirit of the event he shares fully with us.

Spenser seems to have been finishing the later cantos of *The Faerie Queene* while his courtship was in progress. The strange episode of cantos vii and viii of Book VI involving proud, heartless Mirabella, obliged to journey on her mangy ass through the wide world till she had saved as many lovers as she had destroyed, was probably written before his efforts were crowned with success. He hopes proud ladies who rule men's hearts will learn a lesson from Mirabella's fate:

> Ye gentle Ladies, in whose soueraine powre
> Loue hath the glory of his kingdome left,
> And th'hearts of men, as your eternall dowre,
> In yron chaines, of liberty bereft,
> Deliuered hath into your hands by gift;
> Be well aware, how ye the same doe vse,
> That pride doe not to tyranny you lift;
> Least if men you of cruelty accuse,
> He from you take that chiefedome, which ye doe abuse.

We surely need not suppose that Mirabella is a representation of Elizabeth Boyle, but she may very well owe her being to Spenser's impatience over Elizabeth's reluctance to accept him.

If his spirits were low when he conceived Mirabella and appointed her an almost interminable penance, they had risen to the joyous level of the *Epithalamion* by the time he had finished another canto or two. In canto x, the writing of which we may safely assign to the last triumphant half year of his courtship, he introduces himself and his love into his poem just as the Italian painters of the Renaissance sometimes chose a corner of their great canvases for a representation of themselves. And much indeed like a painting of Botticelli's is the picture of Colin piping to his lass, with the three Graces dancing and singing about her, while an "hundred naked maidens lilly white" dance in a ring around this inner group. Said Colin of the fourth maiden:

> Another Grace she well deserues to be,
> In whom so many Graces gathered are,

Excelling much the meane of her degree;
Diuine resemblaunce, beauty soueraine rare,
Firme Chastity, that spight ne blemish dare;
All which she with such courtesie doth grace,
That all her peres cannot with her compare,
But quite are dimmed, when she is in place.
She made me often pipe and now to pipe apace.

The last line seems to imply that a good deal of the *Amoretti* was inspired directly by Elizabeth Boyle.

Feeling evidently that some apology was needed for having so highly complimented his love, a country girl without noble rank, in a book designed to celebrate his queen, Spenser continued with this direct address to Queen Elizabeth:

Sunne of the world, great glory of the sky,
That all the earth doest lighten with thy rayes,
Great *Gloriana*, greatest Maiesty,
Pardon thy shepheard, mongst so many layes,
As he hath sung of thee in all his dayes,
To make one minime of thy poore handmayd,
And vnderneath thy feete to place her prayse,
That when thy glory shall be farre displayd
To future age of her this mention may be made.

At the close of the *Epithalamion,* Spenser expresses the hope that he and Elizabeth may raise a large posterity, which will long possess the earth in happiness and eventually, for their "glorious merit," inherit heavenly tabernacles. As far as we know, this union was blessed with only one child, a boy whom they called Peregrine. Of him we catch several glimpses, as in a letter he wrote in 1618 from London to his kinsman Lord Boyle. He has obtained, so this letter tells us, a place as gentleman usher, but he sees no future in such service, and wishes with the aid of Boyle, who has been kindness itself in the past, to enter upon a more promising career.[17] Subsequently Peregrine returned to Ireland and married Dorothy Tynte, a step-daughter of his mother's.[18] Though Kilcolman passed to Sylvanus, Peregrine was not forgotten, for his father had invested £200 in the castle and lands of Renny and in other properties for this younger son, and these Peregrine enjoyed after his mother's death.[19] Renny was situated in the beautiful valley of the Blackwater some six miles up the river from

[17] *The Lismore Papers* (*Second Series*) 2. 139.
[18] Welply, *NQ* 162. 204.
[19] *Ibid.*, p. 169; Brady 2. 260.

Fermoy, and tradition has it that Spenser himself enjoyed sometimes residing on this pleasant estate.[20] Peregrine died in 1642.[21] Mr. Welply has traced his descendants far enough to establish the fact that Spenser's hope of a large progeny was realized.[22]

Spenser's first wife, whose very existence was long in doubt, is still hardly more than a shadow. In contrast Elizabeth Boyle has acquired a remarkable degree of reality. Thanks to patient investigation, we now feel in some sense acquainted with this beautiful, dignified, golden-haired English woman, who possessed both character and education, and who was related to the noble Althorp family whom Spenser so revered, and hence was at least a distant kinswoman of Spenser himself. Her most notable achievement, from our point of view, was serving as inspiration for some of the finest love poetry in the English language. Spenser was confident that he could make her immortal by his verses, but even he might have been surprised at how enduring a monument he was to erect to her in the form of a diminutive volume entitled *Amoretti and Epithalamion*.[23]

[20] Howitt, *Homes and Haunts of the Most Eminent British Poets* 1. 25.

[21] Welply, *NQ* 162. 204.

[22] *Ibid.*, pp. 239-240, 257. For a full account of Spenser's descendants, see *ibid.*, pp. 186-187, 202-206, 220-224, 239-242, 256-259 (pedigree on pp. 257-259).

[23] Elizabeth Tynte died August 23, 1622. In 1636, Sir Robert erected the church of Kilcredan, seven miles southwest of Youghal, near Ballycottin Bay; and here, till 1924 or 1925, when the Tynte monuments were destroyed, there existed in marble a representation of the woman to whom Spenser had given a more enduring memorial. See Welply, *NQ* 162. 169; Lee, *Journal of the Cork Historical and Archaeological Society*, 2nd Series, 31. 86.

XVI

LONDON REVISITED

WITH THE passing of the long summer day that brought to a climax perhaps the deepest emotional experience of his life, Spenser could turn his thoughts once more to his manuscript of *The Faerie Queene*, now awaiting the printer. But it is hardly to be supposed that he would wish to send this precious second installment of his poem to England by a messenger or allow its publication without his personal supervision. If, however, we are correct in dating his marriage in 1594, and if he himself took the manuscript to London and caused it to be entered promptly in the Stationers' Register, a year and a half were to pass before he was ready to undertake the journey. Why he waited so long, we do not know, but there may have been many reasons for his reluctance to leave Ireland, one of them perhaps the disturbing activities of the earl of Tyrone.

Indeed, Tyrone remained the great riddle to which nobody could find a convincing answer. He was like a ship for ever taking a new tack: one day he seemed bent on revolt in spite of English efforts at conciliation, and the next he declared that he intended no undutifulness toward his prince during his life. On June 24, 1595, the government decided to drop all efforts at appeasement, and proclaimed him a traitor. Three months later he formally assumed the title of "the O'Neill," a designation which carried with it tremendous prestige because of its association with an ancient kingly tradition, and which in the judgment of many of the Irish legitimatized whatever he might do. Then in less than a month we find him agreeing to a truce and soon after offering a humble submission to the queen, presumably to gain time, for he knew he could accomplish nothing very effective without Spanish aid. He was, in fact, as Spenser recognized, a master of craft.

The seriousness of the situation was clear to the English, but the measures they adopted to meet it were far from effective. They did, to be sure, replace Lord Deputy Fitzwilliam with the younger and more active Sir William Russell; and, the following year, they sent over Sir John Norris, still an awe-inspiring figure because of his distinguished military record, to assume command of all the forces in Ireland. But these men disliked one another so heartily that real cooperation was impossible; and the army placed at their disposal was small and ineffective. Though it contained some fifteen hundred capable men fresh from service in Brittany, certain new levies sent direct from England were as usual of poor quality. Of two such companies, Norris complained that not twenty men were likely to prove soldiers, most being poor old ploughmen or rogues. But a more serious cause of the army's inefficiency was its appalling lack of food and clothing. When the men realized that they were not to be decently fed, clothed, and paid, they deserted in such numbers that the companies fairly melted away; of those who did not disappear, many became ill, and the vigor of the rest was so impaired that they were unsuited to the hard conditions of Irish warfare. Tyrone, on the other hand, was training and equipping such an army as no Irish chief had ever before commanded.

Meanwhile, even if the second installment of *The Faerie Queene* remained for a time unpublished, other volumes were being issued by Ponsonby. A composite volume consisting of *Colin Clouts Come Home Againe* and a collection of seven elegies on the death of Sir Philip Sidney, these latter introduced by Spenser's *Astrophel*, bears the date 1595, as does also *Amoretti and Epithalamion.* The *Amoretti* volume was probably published early in 1595, since it had been entered in the Stationers' Register on November 19, 1594, but the volume including *Astrophel*, in view of the fact that its date is old style, may have appeared as late as March, 1596. Of these volumes, that containing the love poetry did not receive a unanimous welcome. To Burghley, love poetry was trivial, or worse, and he took no pains to conceal his displeasure. This we know from certain lines in the Proem of Book IV and from the conclusion of Book VI of *The Faerie Queene*, where Spenser answers his critics, one of the most prominent of whom was evidently Burghley: frozen hearts incapable of love, declares Spenser, have no right to pass judgment on love poetry. Again we marvel at the poet's temerity.

When Spenser composed his lament for Sidney we do not know, but apparently some years after his friend's death, since he confessed in his dedication to *The Ruines of Time* that he had hitherto allowed Sidney's name "to sleep in silence and forgetfulnesse." It seems strange that the news of Sidney's death did not prompt Spenser at once to embody his sorrow in verse, but probably, like some of Sidney's other friends, he had hesitated to join the too voluble chorus of grief.

Spenser's elegy is a thoroughly characteristic work. It presents enough of the facts of Sidney's life to give the whole an air of solidity and truth. But mere fact did not satisfy Spenser's Renaissance conception of beauty and interest. There must be fictitious detail, some of it dictated by literary tradition, the rest by his own fancy. And so he draws on the pastoral convention, on his reading—in this case the Adonis story—and on his ever fertile imagination. Spenser's attractive picture of his friend's boyhood and youth corresponds in the main with what we know of Sidney, though Spenser's insistence on his gayety and fondness for society hardly accords with the facts.[1] The elegy makes a good deal of the mutual devotion of Sidney and his wife, Frances Walsingham,[2] to whom *Astrophel* is dedicated. She could hardly have been other than pleased by the account of her late husband's fervent and undeviating regard for her, though possibly she felt that Spenser was making rather free use of poetic license when he declared that she was the object of all Sidney's verses, and her pleasure may well have given way to surprise upon her learning in the latter part of the elegy that she, who for five years had been the wife of Robert Devereux, earl of Essex, had died of grief immediately after Sidney's death, and that the two had been transformed into a small red and blue flower, with a star-like center, called Astrophel.

The second elegy, purporting to be the work of Sidney's sister, is almost certainly also by Spenser, as both meter and style link it with the opening elegy.[3] It follows the elegiac pattern of contrasting moods, sorrow turned to joy toward the last by the consoling thought that Sidney's spirit "liues for aie, in blisfull Paradise." Of the remaining five elegies, two by Bryskett are especially fitting additions to the collection, for Bryskett had been Sidney's intimate associate during two years of Continental travel, and the reader receives an impression of true sorrow even in lines that embody the worn images of weeping rivers, hills, dales, and stars.

We may be reasonably sure that Spenser was in London by the winter of 1595-1596 and that his first concern was arranging for the reprinting of Books I-III of *The Faerie Queene*, and for a first printing of his lately completed Books IV-VI. The new installment was entered by Ponsonby in the Stationers' Register on January 20, 1596. Both were issued as quartos, and on the title-page of each appears the date 1596 and the *Anchora Spei* device of Richard Field, the printer. Once more we may think of Spenser as close to the center of England's book trade and not at all averse to exchanging for a time the fields of Kilcolman for the narrow streets of Blackfriars, where Field had his shop,[4] only a few

[1] Wallace, *The Life of Sir Philip Sidney*, pp. 45, 71, 111, 197, 222, 276.

[2] The Stella of Spenser's *Astrophel* is surely Sidney's wife; see the conclusions of Hoyt H. Hudson and of Walter G. Friedrich, Variorum Edition, *Minor Poems* 1. 493-494.

[3] *Ibid.*, pp. 500-505.

[4] McKerrow, *A Dictionary of Printers*, p. 102.

moments' walk from Ponsonby's dwelling in St. Paul's Churchyard. Field was a Stratford boy and probably an intimate friend of Shakespeare's; and his shop represents a sort of physical link between the two poets, for here within the previous three years *Venus and Adonis* and *Lucrece* were printed, and during this very year a third edition of the earlier poem was produced. Yet we do not know that these two literary geniuses, each supreme in his own field, ever met amid the presses and bales of paper in Field's shop, or, for that matter, anywhere else.

Books I-III were reset from the first edition, with a few corrections and changes. The dedication to Elizabeth was expanded to cover virtually a page, with phrasing that accentuates the grandeur of the queen and the humility of the poet, as if a bud had now become a full-blown flower—"To the most high, mighty, and magnificent empress renowned for piety, virtue, and all gracious government, Elizabeth by the grace of God queen of England, France, and Ireland and of Virginia, defendour of the faith, &c. her most humble servant Edmund Spenser doth in all humility dedicate, present, and consecrate these his labours to live with the eternity of her fame." Another noteworthy change concerns the five stanzas originally concluding Book III, which describe the joyful reunion of Sir Scudamore and his bride, Amoret, snatched away from him on the very day of his wedding by the magician Busirane and held in durance for seven months. By eliminating these five stanzas and substituting three new ones, Spenser defers the meeting of husband and wife to Book IV, so that the reader's interest may be whetted, in the manner of a modern serial. The omission of the seventeen dedicatory sonnets can perhaps be justified on the ground that they had served their purpose in helping to launch the work impressively six years before, but the failure to reprint the useful prefatory letter to Raleigh seems an unfortunate oversight.

The books constituting the second installment must have been published some time before November 12, 1596, since a message sent on that date from Edinburgh by Robert Bowes, formerly English ambassador and still often a diplomatic representative at the Scotch court, indicated that the book was being read there. King James, according to Bowes, was outraged at the treatment accorded his mother in the ninth canto of Book V, and insisted that Spenser be duly tried and punished.[5] In this canto the trial of Mary Stuart is portrayed with virtually no disguise. The harshest lines concern the summoning of witnesses by Zele, the prosecuting attorney:

> Then brought he forth, with griesly grim aspect,
> Abhorred *Murder*, who with bloudie knyfe

[5] Carpenter, *A Reference Guide*, p. 41.

Yet dropping fresh in hand did her detect,
And there with guiltie bloudshed charged ryfe:
Then brought he forth *Sedition*, breeding stryfe
In troublous wits, and mutinous vprore:
Then brought he forth *Incontinence* of lyfe,
Euen foule *Adulterie* her face before,
And lewd *Impietie*, that her accused sore.

Early in 1598 it was said that Walter Quin, a brilliant young Irish protégé of James, who later became tutor to his children, was "answering Spencer's book whereat the k[ing] was offended."[6] But there is no evidence that James's complaint ever came to anything or that Quin's answer was published. As a matter of fact, James very likely professed more rancor than he felt, for he had lost sympathy with his mother after being disinherited by her, and even his protests over her execution do not seem to have been very determined.[7]

Readers who had enjoyed the first installment of *The Faerie Queene* were probably eager buyers of the new volume when it appeared in Ponsonby's shop. Because Spenser was such a faithful, ardent friend, we might expect him to excel in writing of friendship, the theme of Book IV. Yet he is generally thought to have been less successful here than in the two books that follow. A chief defect, in the opinion of many, is the lack of a hero—at least a hero who dominates the narrative. Spenser tells us that this book contains the legend of Cambell and Triamond; yet these friends hold the stage but briefly and then vanish for good. In places his theme is lifted to cosmic proportions by the introduction of such figures as Ate, goddess of discord, representing the disruptive forces in the world, including political anarchy and treason, and her antithesis, Dame Concord, who is responsible, not only for friendship, but for the very order and harmony of the universe:

By her the heauen is in his course contained,
And all the world in state vnmoued stands,
As their Almightie maker first ordained,
And bound them with inuiolable bands. . . .[8]

His ending the book with three cantos in each of which marriage is the

[6] *Ibid.*, p. 42.

[7] Grosart (ed. of Spenser 1. 215) suggests that James's complaint may have been intended to offset Elizabeth's recent protest concerning the liberation from the Castle of Carlisle, by Sir Walter Scott of Buccleuch, of the freebooter "Kinmont Willie"—see *Acts of the Privy Council* (1595-1596), p. 470.

[8] 4. 10. 35.

theme seems justified by his belief that marriage best typifies the harmonious union of two spirits—for him, the essence of friendship.

Book V, with its treatment of world politics, takes us into a quite different atmosphere. Though the theme of Book V is justice, and though Spenser illustrates the administration of justice and equity in many different relationships of life, he is thinking especially of justice as involved in the great struggle currently going on between Catholic Spain and Protestant England. Almost inevitably, therefore, he includes Spain's support of the Irish rebels, her sponsoring of the league against Henry IV and the Huguenots, and her establishment of the Inquisition in the Low Countries, nor could he forget the plotting within England through Mary Stuart or the huge military effort against England by means of the Armada. The exceedingly happy outcome given by him to all these adventures must have warmed the hearts of patriotic Englishmen, who, in spite of their successes against Spain, were still awed by the thought of her imperial wealth and power.

In a curious episode, written perhaps after Spenser's arrival in England and first included in canto xii but shifted at the last moment to canto xi, we are shown Artegall in France aiding hard-pressed Burbon, who patently is Henry IV. Artegall as champion of Henry IV, if he is to be recognized here as anything more than English policy and power, ought to be either Essex or Sir John Norris,[9] for these two were the most prominent figures associated with the aid Elizabeth extended to the great French king. Spenser's known enthusiasm at about this time for the earl would seem to indicate Essex, whose inclusion might be accounted for by Spenser's growing conviction that this popular young noble, now that Leicester and Sidney and Grey were all dead, was the logical leader of the party that stood for British imperialism and for a strong, aggressive championship

[9] Dr. Josephine Waters Bennett argues that Artegall in France is Sir John Norris rather than Essex (*SP* 37. 177-200; *The Evolution of "The Faerie Queene,"* pp. 191 ff.). Norris did, to be sure, accomplish more in France than did Essex, but can we be certain that Spenser's readers would be reminded sooner of quiet, effective Norris than of dazzling Essex? Moreover, there is ground for believing that Spenser valued Essex above Norris in 1590, and that his confidence in Essex grew while his admiration for Norris waned. In 1590, Spenser put Essex immediately after Hatton at the beginning of his first series of dedicatory sonnets in *The Faerie Queene,* Norris next to the end in his second series, a group written as an afterthought. The *View* shows Spenser's sense of Essex' greatness in 1596, but there is no mention of Norris in that work, though Lord Deputy Russell, then quarreling with Norris, is referred to with respect. *Prothalamion* also shows the great faith Spenser was placing in Essex. Dr. Bennett takes the impassioned last stanzas in Book V (28-43), in which Spenser attacks Artegall's slanderers, as a defense of Norris, but again the *View* proves Spenser's persistent anxiety over Grey's reputation, while we can only speculate as to his attitude in regard to efforts to discredit Norris.

of Protestantism in Europe, a cause to which Book V, for all its treatment of other phases of justice, is manifestly dedicated.[10]

In Book VI, whose theme is courtesy, Spenser turns from policies of state to the essence of individual conduct. Several times in this book he defines courtesy in language similar to that found in the popular books of conduct of his day, which viewed it as the maintenance of a proper attitude toward the several ranks and classes of society. Thus, for example, he declares that the Three Graces teach us

> all the complements of curtesie:
> They teach vs, how to each degree and kynde
> We should our selues demeane, to low, to hie;
> To friends, to foes, which skill men call Ciuility.[11]

But though Spenser may offer us the conventional definition of courtesy, he illustrates something quite different in Calidore's actions. In the case of this knight and also the other exponents of this virtue, including the naked, inarticulate man of the woods, courtesy is synonymous with kindness. And, save in the opening stanzas, we are never taken to court, where the courtesy of the books was reputed best to flourish.

The fact that Calidore's mission was the pursuit of the Blatant Beast may be taken as evidence that Spenser considered slander a particularly odious violation of courtesy. We first hear of this hundred-tongued dog in connection with Artegall, and it may be that the slander Spenser believed had been heaped on Lord Grey bred in his mind the conception of the monster. But in that day, when success depended so largely on the personal favor of the great, and when the best of men had to struggle madly for patronage, slander was a particularly useful weapon of the unscrupulous, and he had doubtless seen something of its baleful effect long before he knew Lord Grey. Recently his good friend Raleigh had felt its poisonous tooth. In Book IV he had glanced at Raleigh's secret marriage in his description of Belphoebe's wrath at Timias' over-solicitous care of the wounded Amoret. Here in Book VI he returns to the theme. The odd episode in which Timias and the lady Serena, after being bitten, are nursed to health by the good hermit of the woods is probably as transparent an account as Spenser cared to give of the experience of Raleigh and Elizabeth Throckmorton. Spenser indicates clearly enough that he does not condone their action,[12] but he also shows his disgust with the malicious talk that greeted the disclosure. He himself had suffered from

[10] Heffner, *ELH* 3. 68. [11] 6. 10. 23. [12] Cf. Sorensen, *SP* 33. 196-197.

the Blatant Beast, as we learn in his *Amoretti*, and it is probable that the "Venemous toung" that separated him from his love heightened the bitterness of his picture of the beast toward the end of Book VI.

The thought of slander seems to have been uppermost in Spenser's mind for some time, since in Book IV he provides an allegorical representation of it hardly less powerful than the Blatant Beast of Books V and VI. This is the old hag Sclaunder, who sits on the ground in her little cottage, biting her nails and pouring out streams of poison against all who profess truth and virtue.

> Her nature is all goodnesse to abuse,
> And causelesse crimes continually to frame,
> With which she guiltlesse persons may accuse,
> And steale away the crowne of their good name;
> Ne euer Knight so bold, ne euer Dame
> So chast and loyall liu'd, but she would striue
> With forged cause them falsely to defame;
> Ne euer thing so well was doen aliue,
> But she with blame would blot, and of due praise depriue.[13]

As he wrote these last lines, Spenser was probably thinking of the misconstructions that his poetry had suffered, especially from Burghley. Obviously Spenser had ceased to hope for good will from that quarter, and his expectations, for himself as well as for England, were doubtless fixing themselves on the knightly young person of Essex.

Perhaps Sir Calidore was intended as a representation of Essex.[14] Not that Sidney could ever cease to be a precedent of "noblesse and of cheualree" to Spenser, but England surely might produce more than one pattern of courtesy, and the man whom he addressed as

> Magnificke Lord, whose vertues excellent
> Doe merit a most famous Poets witt,[15]

and whom he was soon to characterize with the words

> Faire branch of Honor, flower of Cheualrie,[16]

had become in popular estimation the embodiment of those graces and courtly qualities for which Sidney had stood; so that it is hardly conceivable that Spenser was not mindful at times of Essex as he composed the story of his knight of courtesy.

[13] 4. 8. 25.
[14] Heffner, *ELH* 1. 7-36; Harrison, *The Life and Death of . . . Essex*, pp. 70, 275.
[15] Dedicatory sonnet, *F. Q.*
[16] *Prothalamion* 150.

After the drudgery involved in the publication of *The Faerie Queene* was over, we may think of Spenser's enjoying some leisure, and it is interesting to speculate on how he occupied his time. If some of it was dedicated to his friends, he surely visited Gabriel Harvey at Saffron Walden, and we can imagine his regret at seeing him disappointed, broken, penniless, though still conserving a few sparks of the old ambition.[17] Another friend whom he doubtless sometimes saw was the bishop of Rochester, for we can hardly conceive of Spenser's attending Elizabeth at Greenwich without riding the five or six miles to Bromley for a call on his former patron. Young, though only sixty-two, regarded himself as already an old man and seems to have been no longer active in public affairs; [18] for that reason he might have welcomed the picture of court and colonial life that his one-time secretary could bring him. Still another friend whose society Spenser must have enjoyed was Raleigh, who in August, 1595, had returned from his first voyage to Guiana, where he had sought in vain the fabulous city of El Dorado. Into Book IV of *The Faerie Queene* Spenser had put a reference to the "conquest of that land of gold," and he would have been deeply interested in Raleigh's experiences there. Not yet had Raleigh won back the full favor of Elizabeth, and Spenser's publication at this time of *Colin Clouts Come Home Againe*, with its expressions of appreciation and commendation of Raleigh, was perhaps in part Spenser's effort to reinstate his friend in the queen's regard.[19] In June, 1596, Raleigh sailed on the memorable expedition to Cadiz, undoubtedly with Spenser's blessing, since offensive war on Philip was precisely what Spenser most wanted to see, and nobody could have been more delighted than he at the brilliant achievements of Raleigh on this voyage.

Friendly contacts with literary men of kindred interests may be implied by his writing two commendatory sonnets at about this time, one for Nenna's *Nennio, Or A Treatise of Nobility*, translated by William Jones; the other for Lavardin's *Historie of George Castriot, Surnamed Scanderbeg, King of Albanie*, translated by Z. I., and published by Ponsonby. In the sonnet written for *Nennio*, Spenser approves Nenna's democratic contention that true nobility derives from virtuous conduct rather than from blood, a position not, by the way, maintained in Book VI of *The Faerie Queene*, where he touches often on this much-debated question. Daniel and Chapman also wrote commendatory sonnets for *Nennio*, which was dedicated to the earl of Essex. Perhaps the sonnet

[17] Smith in Harvey, *Marginalia*, pp. 68-74.
[18] Judson, *A Biographical Sketch of John Young*, pp. 32-33.
[19] Koller, *ELH* 1. 43.

commending *The Historie of George Castriot* was composed at Ponsonby's request; at any rate, a better invitation to read the book could hardly have been devised. Z. I. dedicated his translation to Elizabeth Carey's husband, Sir George Carey, with praise of his matchless hospitality.

Still another commendatory sonnet, though not published till 1599, may have been composed during this sojourn in London. It was prefixed to *The Commonwealth and Gouernment of Venice*, written by Cardinal Contarini and translated by Lewes Lewkenor.[20] Spenser praises Venetian justice but also the architectural beauty of the city. Any one familiar with Contarini's opening paragraph, where he describes the wonder and delight often seen by him on the faces of strangers newly arrived in Venice, must regret that Spenser never had the opportunity to observe the strange situation and rich, fantastic beauty of the city which, even today, seems akin to his fairy visions.

Social contact with his friends, attendance at court, and the writing of an occasional sonnet could not long satisfy a man of Spenser's restless energy, and again we find him taking up his pen as he had done six years before. A labor that must have occupied many spare hours was composing his *View of the Present State of Ireland*, to which reference has so often been made.[21] This orderly, elaborate treatise—cast into the form of a dialogue for the sake of interest—professes to set forth, first, the many evils present in Elizabethan Ireland and, secondly, his program for redressing them. Incidentally it provides us with our best picture of Irish life during the last decade of the sixteenth century. More than half the treatise is devoted to the evils, such, for example, as relate to the old Brehon law that still prevailed in many localities and to customs involving dress, warfare, and religion. This portion of the work reflects his passion for the antique, and gives us a glimpse of him happily devoting spare moments, over a period of years, to the "many sweet remembrances of antiquities"—looking (uncritically) [22] into books on Irish history, comparing the manners and customs of earlier days with those about him, studying the derivation of words, and examining such historical relics as churches and tombs.[23] Space is lacking, he says, for all the material he has gathered, and some of it is being reserved for another treatise on the subject of Irish antiquities.

[20] See Perkinson, *MLR* 35. 15, note 1. The volume was dedicated to Anne, countess of Warwick. The sonnet is signed "Edw."

[21] Gottfried, *MLN* 52. 176-180.

[22] Covington, University of Texas *Studies in English*, No. 4, p. 37; Gottfried, *Transactions of the Wisconsin Academy of Sciences, Arts and Letters* 30. 325-326.

[23] Pp. 48, 51-52.

The latter part of the work, in which he offers detailed plans for completing the conquest of Ireland, and for organizing it so that it might remain at peace and gradually become thoroughly English in culture and temper, shows him to be an opponent of compromise and a firm believer in the severe course of action approved by most of the officials in the Irish government during his closest association with it. Spenser's proposal that the irreconcilable elements in the population be exterminated [24] has often been condemned. He himself, for that matter, did not regard such a course with complacency, but he undoubtedly felt it would be more humane than a policy that wavered between conciliation and severity and thus made the agony of conquest an almost interminable process. The idea of permitting the Irish to work out their salvation in their own way probably never occurred to him, partly because of the loyal groups scattered through the country, especially in the towns, but even more because of the danger that Ireland might become an appendage of Spain and hence a base for attacks on England.

One of his proposals is of especial interest. He had seen the effectiveness of the Irish government constantly jeopardized by unintelligent interference from England, or at least by lack of adequate support, and he therefore suggested the revival of the lord lieutenancy. In the past, lord lieutenants had intermittently governed Ireland, but Spenser would continue the deputy as governor, giving him even more ample powers, while the lord lieutenant watched the interests and protected the policies of the Irish government from England. Spenser wanted a great man for the place, one who could easily awe the army of mischief-makers at home: "such an one I could name," he says "upon whom the eye of all England is fixed and our last hopes now rest." [25]

It can hardly be doubted that he was thinking of the earl of Essex. At this time Essex was at the pinnacle of his career. On August 10, 1596, he had returned from the capture of Cadiz with prizes valued at £13,000 and with his reputation as a soldier heightened. On this expedition he had displayed courage, from the time, before the attack had begun, when he had excitedly thrown his plumed hat into the sea, till the hour when his three thousand soldiers had caused the surrender of the city. Moreover, he had increased his reputation for courtesy and chivalry. Pillage was by custom a part of such affairs, but he had strictly ordered his troops to offer no violence to man, woman, or child, on pain of death, and so well were his commands observed that commendation was evoked from Philip him-

[24] P. 134.

[25] P. 217.

self. Highly pleasing to Spenser must have been the fact that Raleigh and Essex cooperated successfully throughout the voyage and returned with a new respect for each other, and nobody could have been more delighted than Spenser at the blow administered to Philip's prestige. Into the *Prothalamion*, written after Essex' return, Spenser put a large measure of his joy over the victory and his faith in the heroic part that he believed Essex was to play in his country's annals: in the town house on the bank of the Thames once occupied by Leicester, he says, there

> now doth lodge a noble Peer,
> Great *Englands* glory and the Worlds wide wonder,
> Whose dreadfull name, late through all *Spaine* did thunder,
> And *Hercules* two pillors standing neere,
> Did make to quake and feare:
> Faire branch of Honor, flower of Cheualrie,
> That fillest *England* with thy triumphes fame,
> Ioy haue thou of thy noble victorie,
> And endlesse happinesse of thine owne name
> That promiseth the same:
> That through thy prowesse and victorious armes,
> Thy country may be freed from forraine harmes:
> And great *Elisaes* glorious name may ring
> Through al the world, fil'd with thy wide Alarmes,
> Which some braue muse may sing
> To ages following. . . .

On April 14, 1598, Matthew Lownes, a London bookseller, entered a copy of Spenser's *View of the Present State of Ireland* in the Stationers' Register, with the understanding that he get further authority before it be printed, but such authority seems not to have been obtained. The treatise was, however, no doubt inspected by some of those whom Spenser hoped it might influence: of many manuscript copies, several are thought to have found their way into the hands of Elizabeth's principal ministers, and one copy significantly was found among the papers of Greene, Essex' secretary.[26] The *View* was finally published in 1633 at Dublin by the Irish historian Sir James Ware, with a dedication to Lord Deputy Thomas Wentworth, who later became earl of Strafford.

Several of Spenser's notable poems may be assigned to this period of waiting for the preferment he hoped from the new installment of *The Faerie Queene.* On September 1, 1596, at Greenwich, where court was being held, he completed the dedication for a little book entitled *Fowre*

[26] Bennett, *SP* 37. 182, note 11; Heffner, *MLQ* 3. 509.

Hymnes. This volume was inscribed to two noble sisters, Margaret, countess of Cumberland, and Anne—through an odd error her name appears as " Marie "—countess of Warwick. Both these women had been kind to him on his previous visit to England, and now they were again his patrons. Indeed his dedicating of this book to them was a modest recognition, he says, of the " great graces and honourable favours " that they were daily showing him.

With the *Fowre Hymnes* was included a second edition of *Daphnaïda*; they were issued by Ponsonby as a slender quarto, with the date 1596. The four hymns—hymns in the sense of stately paeans to god or hero—have caused in our time much speculation and comment, and many a page in the scholarly journals would have been saved if Spenser had been a trifle more explicit in the wording of his dedication. Here he informs us that the first two hymns had been composed in the " greener times " of his youth, and that because "those of like age and disposition" had drawn from them poison for their strong passion rather than honey for their honest delight, one of the sisters to whom the hymns were later dedicated had urged him to call them in. When he found that this could not be done on account of the large number of copies in circulation, he resolved " at least to amend, and by way of retractation to reform them, making, instead of those two hymns of earthly or natural love and beauty, two others of heavenly and celestial."

This dedication has raised the question as to when these first two hymns were written, for the " greener times " of his youth is a vague expression, and also whether they were revised at the time of publication, or amended merely by being offset through the addition of the hymns of heavenly love and beauty. Their style[27] certainly does not convey the impression of early workmanship, but their content may very well have been drawn in part from some of his early love poetry. How reasonable, for instance, is the conjecture that a stanza like the following from *An Hymne in Honour of Loue* owes a debt to *The hell of louers, his Purgatorie*, a work casually named by Ponsonby in his Foreword to the *Complaints*:[28]

> The gnawing enuie, the hart-fretting feare,
> The vaine surmizes, the distrustfull showes,
> The false reports that flying tales doe beare,
> The doubts, the daungers, the delayes, the woes,

[27] Bennett, *SP* 32. 153-157.

[28] Cf. Buck, *PMLA* 23. 98; Sandison, *ibid.* 25. 143-144.

The fayned friends, the vnassured foes,
With thousands more then any tongue can tell,
Do make a louers life a wretches hell.

Several times in the hymns Spenser asserts that he, who had long since experienced the mighty power of love, is now distraught by a new flame; and he repeatedly prays that the heart of the disdainful woman whom he now adores may be softened and his suit blessed with success. These complaints, along with the mature style, suggest that the two earlier hymns may have been composed, in their present form, during his first year of unsuccessful courtship of Elizabeth Boyle. But what of revision? Perhaps he did, in fact, soften the eroticism of certain passages objected to by one of the noble ladies; but, more probably, with his words of apology, he was merely yielding to the familiar convention of turning from secular to religious poetry with a disparagement of the former, in which case we need not take seriously his reference to ardent young men sucking poison from his verses.

It would be interesting to know what reception the public gave the hymns. Like so many of Spenser's works, they are rich in suggestion because of their various sources of inspiration, so that they were bound to appeal to men of different tastes and degrees of learning, just as they do, for that matter, today. Those familiar with the fashionable neo-Platonic thought of Italy would be attracted by Spenser's obvious familiarity with the literature of that field, and might attempt to trace in the four hymns the famous *scala* by which a man ascended from the love of a woman to the love of God. Lovers who had never dabbled in philosophy would find in many passages of the hymns in honor of love and beauty an analysis of their own experiences, reading the depths of their disappointments, perplexities, and joys, no doubt, into some lines that admit of other interpretations. And persons fervently religious would certainly respond to the hymns of heavenly love and beauty, and in the case of the first of these might be amazed to discover Christian theology epitomized in lines of such exceptional grace.

Another poem whose composition belongs to 1596 is *Prothalamion*, a hymn made in honor of the double marriage of the eldest daughters of Edward Somerset, earl of Worcester. The earl, whose ancestral seat was beautiful Raglan Castle near Monmouth, Wales, was a favorite with the queen and a warm friend of the earl of Essex [29]—though not warm enough to follow him into revolt a few years later. The marriage was celebrated

[29] Harrison, *The Life and Death of . . . Essex*, pp. 249, 279, 284.

at Essex House, November 8, 1596.[30] The poem will be recalled as a melodious, highly fanciful narrative of the passage of the sisters by water to Essex' mansion, which stood on the bank of the Thames next the law courts. As Professor Manly has suggested, they had come perhaps to take part in their betrothal ceremony. Was Spenser, the reader wonders, a member of the great company, led by Essex and the bridegrooms, who issued from the stately mansion and went down to the river's edge to receive them?

Prothalamion, quite aside from its lyric beauty, which has long made it a favorite with anthologists, is notable for certain highly personal revelations. From it we learn, as was remarked in an earlier chapter, that Spenser was born and brought up in London, and that he had once "gayned giftes and goodly grace" from Leicester, when the earl dwelt in this mansion now occupied by his stepson. We also learn that Spenser was growing very weary of waiting for the preferment to which he doubtless felt his new books of *The Faerie Queene* entitled him. In the first stanza he writes:

> When I whom sullein care,
> Through discontent of my long fruitlesse stay
> In Princes Court, and expectation vayne
> Of idle hopes, which still doe fly away,
> Like empty shaddowes, did aflict my brayne,
> Walkt forth to ease my payne
> Along the shoare of siluer streaming *Themmes*. . . .

One longs to know just what the idle hopes were that were always flying away like shadows. Almost certainly they did not concern a post in the English government. The second installment of *The Faerie Queene* repeatedly indicates how distasteful any calling would have been that required his more or less constant presence at court. Moreover, his interests were now in Ireland, and his thoughts had no doubt been fixed there with increasing intensity as he had labored on his *View of the Present State of Ireland*, with its elaborate plans for bringing tranquillity to that troubled land. A grant of property, a means of revenue like Bryskett's controllership of the customs on wines, possibly a responsible, well-paid position in the Irish government, may have been the object of his suits, though it seems hardly possible that he would have accepted a post likely to deprive him of leisure for superintending his estate and especially for pursuing his literary interests.

[30] *DNB.*

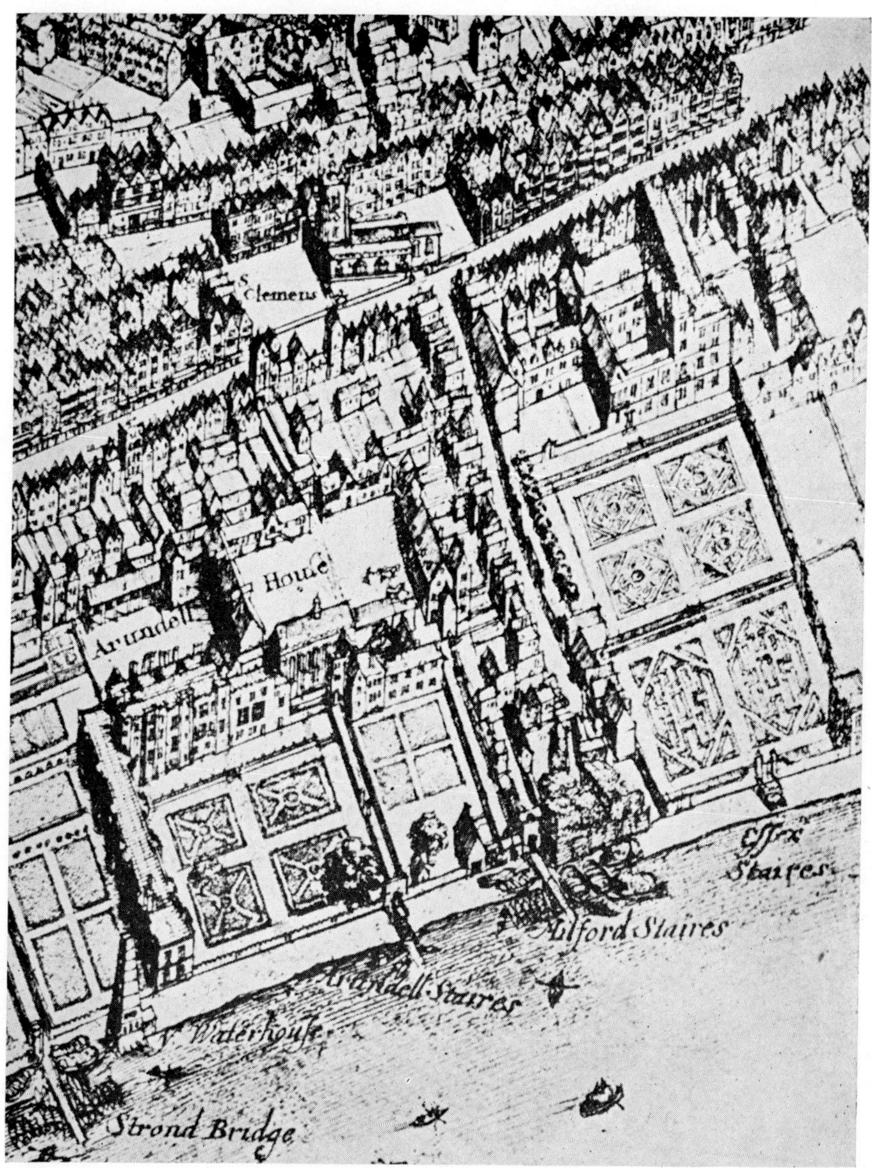

Essex House, its stately façade rising beyond large formal gardens that were reached from the Thames by Essex Stairs. Detail from Hollar's "View of West Central London" (about 1658?), reproduced in *Archaeologia*, Vol. LXXIII.

Prothalamion mentions his sense of woeful lack in possessing no such patron as Leicester had once been. From Leicester he turns to Essex and bursts into the joyous eulogy of the young earl already quoted. Essex was England's hope, but he was Spenser's too. Just how Spenser came to write the *Prothalamion* we do not know, but this handsome thin quarto in large type surely has all the appearance of a gracious invitation to Essex to become his patron, and seems the more tactful and persuasive because the praise of the earl is made incidental to a courtesy shown the earl's friends.

Less than two weeks after the marriage of Worcester's daughters, Spenser had an opportunity to make use of the legal knowledge that the vicissitudes of Irish life had forced him to acquire. Some three years before, Elizabeth Boyle and her brothers had sought in vain to recover £100 left them by their father in 1582, but lent at interest soon after his death, when they were far under age and hence not yet entitled to their patrimony. On November 20 a new effort was made for its recovery, through a suit in chancery entered on that day, with Spenser, his wife, and her two brothers as plaintiffs. Inasmuch as this legal action, according to Mr. Welply, would have required the presence of Spenser's wife in London,[31] she had perhaps accompanied him to England; if so, did the long period of waiting prove as tedious to her as to her husband? The documents relating to this suit carry us back in thought several years to Spenser's marriage; since part of the £100 involved should have been applied to Elizabeth's marriage portion, it is clear that the full sum of £250 left by her father as her dowry was not available when she married Spenser. How this suit was finally settled we do not know.

We have no evidence of when Spenser went back to Ireland,[32] nor has any record been preserved of immediate rewards from the great; yet in the end his long stay may not have proved fruitless. With many passages of Book VI in mind, we may rest assured that he left the court with profound relief, and, in spite of anxieties about Tyrone, set out eagerly for the land that had become in a true sense his home.

[31] *NQ* 162. 184-185. Probably Spenser and his wife spent a part of 1596 at Bradden, Northants, from which frequent visits to her first cousin, Erasmus Dryden, at Canons Ashby, distant but four or five miles, would have been easy (see Variorum Edition, *Minor Poems* 1. 654, and Aubrey, '*Brief Lives*' 2. 232).

[32] Mr. Hamer argues that Spenser's suit would not necessarily have prolonged his stay in England into 1597 (*ibid.*, p. 382).

XVII

LAST YEARS

If SPENSER'S STAY in England terminated, as it may well have done, in the late autumn of 1596, he had been absent from Ireland about a year. During that time the combined efforts of Lord Deputy Russell and Lord General Sir John Norris had not improved matters. How indeed could these men hope to achieve much, considering their disagreements in policy and the inadequacy of their military forces? Russell had no faith in Tyrone's promises; yet Norris, who through most of his life had placed a soldier's trust in the sword, was now deeply committed to appeasement. Meanwhile Tyrone and O'Donnell accepted pardons with their right hands, while with their left they sent letters to Philip II and seditious messages to chiefs throughout Ireland. In Connaught, as well as in Ulster, the spirit of revolution was now rampant, largely through the efforts of O'Donnell, who shared with Tyrone chief responsibility for the tremors that were now beginning to shake the land.

Hugh Roe O'Donnell had personal reasons for his ardent desire to end English rule in Ireland. In 1587, when his father, Sir Hugh MacManus O'Donnell, chief of Donegal, failed in some of his promises to the Irish government, Lord Deputy Perrot sent a ship laden with wine, as if from Spain, to Lough Swilly, with directions that O'Donnell, or his son Hugh Roe, be lured aboard and then borne away by force to Dublin. The stratagem worked, and the son thus became a hostage in Dublin Castle at about the age of sixteen. During the adolescent years when a boy most craves freedom and activity he was held there a prisoner. Twice he made his escape. The first time he was quickly captured and brought back, but his second gamble for liberty proved successful, though he almost lost his life in the snowy Wicklow Mountains, and later had to have his great toes, which were frost-bitten, amputated. O'Byrne gave him refuge in Glenmalure, and eventually he reached his own country. He soon became chief of Donegal, and from then on devoted his resources and ability to the overthrow of the English.

O'Donnell's efforts at fanning Connaught into rebellion had been vainly resisted by Sir Richard Bingham, its governor. Bingham had ruled the province for twelve years with an iron hand, and now his enemies insisted that its revolt had been caused by his harshness and greed. In May,

1596, he was detained in Dublin, and in his absence Sir John Norris attempted the pacification of the province. Although Norris remained there from June to mid-December, he was unable, with O'Donnell hovering in the north, to achieve anything of permanent value.

Munster, at this time, was quieter and more prosperous than any other part of Ireland. Not that even here occasions for anxiety were lacking. The troublesome MacSheehys, who had been driven out of the province, were returning, and though Vice President Norris had hanged ninety of them in ten days, the danger had not been eliminated.[1] Both the Norrises felt concern for such English settlers as lived in scattered, thatched dwellings, and well they might, since every night saw outbreaks of violence somewhere, and the armed forces of the state were as usual inadequate and unpaid. Moreover, signs of disloyalty were present. Bishop Lyon, for example, was shocked to discover the " style and title " of the queen torn out of all the grammars—seventy-four in number—in one school.[2] Yet the province no longer resembled the waste into which the Desmond rebellion had turned it. Mattocks and ploughirons, instead of weapons, had become the concern of the country people, with the result that corn and beef were better and cheaper there than in England, and indeed a hungry Ireland was being fed from a surplus produced in Munster.[3]

The growing prosperity of Munster did not, however, blind its inhabitants to the generally dangerous situation. Clearly the winds of revolt were rising, and a violent storm seemed likely soon to break. Spenser, of course, had kept himself informed of Irish affairs while he was in England and was only too well aware of the situation. In the *View* he wrote of it: " . . . all have their ears upright, waiting when the watchword shall come that they should all rise generally into rebellion and cast away the English subjection." [4] From the showy, artificial life of the court, which had attracted him so little, we may think of his coming once more into an Ireland vibrant with deep, primitive, hardly concealed emotions.

The following year, 1597, was filled with events of serious consequence for Ireland. In January Sir Conyers Clifford, a hero of the memorable Cadiz expedition, arrived to replace Sir Richard Bingham as governor of Connaught; and in May a new deputy, Thomas Lord Burgh, received the sword of state from Lord Deputy Russell, who, though disappointed in his efforts to subdue Tyrone, had at least the satisfaction before leaving Ireland of compassing the death of Fiagh MacHugh O'Byrne. Sir John

[1] *C. S. P. Ir.* (1596-1597), p. 161 (15).
[2] *Ibid.*, p. 17 (8 I).
[3] *Ibid.*, pp. 13 (8), 33 (20), 155 (57).
[4] P. 122.

Norris, after amicable discussions with the new deputy, retired into Munster, to inspect its fortifications; and there, at Mallow, as a result of old wounds, he died in the arms of his brother Thomas.[5] Since Sir Thomas Norris's castle was less than eight miles from Spenser's, one is tempted to guess that Spenser visited his old friend and superior, and in the shadow of death forgot what must have been his bitter disappointment over this last Irish chapter of the famous soldier's career. Bagwell suggests that Norris's futile resort to negotiation instead of war may have been the result of his ill health. On September 20, Sir Thomas Norris, who had for so long governed Munster, became its lord president.

Soon after arriving, Lord Burgh, bent on vigorous prosecution of the war, sent Clifford to attempt the recovery of important Ballyshannon Castle on the borders of Donegal, while he himself led his troops against Tyrone. Neither effort proved successful. Clifford suffered a disastrous defeat at O'Donnell's hands, and Lord Burgh, after some successes, died suddenly "of an Irish ague" at Newry on October 13, to the great dismay of the English. The rule of Ireland was assigned temporarily by the privy council to Archbishop Loftus and Chief Justice Gardiner, while the earl of Ormonde became lieutenant general of the army. On December 22, Ormonde secured "humble and penitent submission" from Tyrone, who, as usual, seems to have been merely sparring for time, in perennial hope of substantial Spanish aid.

In the absence of records touching Spenser's activities during 1597, we may conjecture that he was residing quietly at Kilcolman, working as he could at his epic, increasing his holdings of land, and certainly hearing with the keenest interest reports of the events that were agitating so deeply all the other provinces of Ireland. Munster continued to be blessed with relative quiet and with agricultural productivity, in contrast to the rebellion, want, and even famine elsewhere. Yet in the background of men's thoughts was for ever the possibility of a Spanish invasion, which, because of the good harbors of Munster, might be undertaken there; and, moreover, those most familiar with the province, like the Norris brothers, were subtly conscious of an undercurrent of disaffection on the part of the Irish that might rise quickly to the surface.[6] In midsummer the queen expressed concern for her Munster plantation. She had been informed that requirements as to English settlers on the seignories were not being

[5] Bagwell says "before Sept. 9" (*Ireland under the Tudors* 3. 288, note); the date of July 3 given by *DNB* is manifestly erroneous, since the Irish state papers include a letter written by Norris on July 21.

[6] *C. S. P. Ir.* (1596-1597), pp. 313 (96), 349 (42).

observed, and that certain undertakers had failed to pay their rents. She ordered these matters investigated and directed that the patentees dwelling near one another cooperate for their mutual defense.[7]

On February 7, 1598, Spenser was granted permission to postpone till the beginning of the following Easter term arrearages of rent due on Buttevant Abbey, " for that at this present, by reason of trouble in the way, he durst not bring down any money." [8] Buttevant Abbey was one of the properties acquired by Spenser for his son Peregrine. The picturesque ruins of this Franciscan abbey, founded, or perhaps restored, by David de Barry in the thirteenth century, rise on the main street of Buttevant. Spenser's primary interest in leasing the abbey was presumably the half ploughland attached to it,[9] but he was too much a lover of beauty not to have sighed now and then over the remnants of its delicate window tracery and well-executed capitals, for it was in his day a ruin. Buttevant Abbey and the neighboring abbey of Ballybeg must have been in his thoughts when, in *Colin Clouts Come Home Againe*, he referred to the town of Buttevant,

> Whose ragged ruines breed great ruth and pittie,
> To trauailers, which it from far behold.

In spite of Tyrone's submission to Ormonde, it became increasingly evident that all Ireland was in a dangerous mood. On April 18, the bishop of Meath, who had lately conferred with Tyrone and O'Donnell, wrote Burghley that he was sure these two northern chiefs could not be reclaimed from their rebellious course, adding the saying that " a traitor will be a traitor, do what a man can." [10] On the same day one of the O'Connors reported an assertion of Tyrone's that within a month he would kindle such a fire in Munster that Ormonde would have no leisure to trouble the Irish in Ulster and Leinster.[11] Two days later, Secretary Sir Geoffrey Fenton, for many years one of the warmest friends of the Irish among English officials at Dublin, reluctantly confessed that he believed Tyrone could never be conciliated, an opinion expressed by Spenser two years before in his *View*.[12] Norris, conscious of the growth of revolutionary sentiment in Munster, asked pledges of noblemen and gentlemen whose loyalty he had reason to question, held general musters, and armed the

[7] *Ibid.*, pp. 329-330 (2), 331-332 (4).
[8] Ferguson, *The Gentleman's Magazine*, 1855, 2. 606.
[9] *Ibid.*, p. 607.
[10] *C. S. P. Ir.* (1598-1599), p. 119.
[11] *Ibid.*, p. 125 (16 I).
[12] *Ibid.*, pp. 123-124 (16); *View*, p. 145.

inhabitants, with some apprehension, to be sure, lest these same weapons might later be turned against the government.[13] On June 7, Ormonde's truce with Tyrone expired, and Tyrone proceeded promptly to lay siege to an important frontier fort that the English had established on the Ulster Blackwater in order that they might control a main pass into his country; he also sent forces into Cavan and toward the borders of Leinster.[14] Thus, early in June, 1598, the great rebellion of Tyrone, so long awaited, began, though nobody as yet could have guessed the proportions it was to assume.

For a few weeks nothing of special consequence occurred. Tyrone's soldiers indeed made some headway, and his secret agents more. These emissaries appeared in every province, quietly preaching the gospel of revolution, and promising, as the rewards of patriotic adherence to the cause, a recovery of forfeited lands and a re-establishment of the Catholic faith,[15] to which the great majority, thanks in part to the earnest and intelligent efforts of Jesuit missionaries, were now genuinely devoted.

Because the fort on the Blackwater could not hold out indefinitely, the council decided that Sir Henry Bagenal, marshal of the army, should lead some 3,500 foot and 300 horse to its relief. Had the wiser and more skilful Ormonde directed in person this critical mission, who can tell what the outcome might have been? On August 14, Sir Henry's forces were defeated by Tyrone in the fateful Battle of the Yellow Ford, so called from the color of the bed of the little Callan River at a ford which the army used as it marched from Armagh to the neighboring fort on the Blackwater. Sir Henry moved his forces up in six regiments divided from one another by intervals of several hundred feet, an arrangement that Ormonde thought only a man bewitched would have adopted.[16] As they approached, the first contingent was thrown into confusion before the second could give it aid, and soon the whole English army was in full retreat. Half of it was lost. So serious a defeat had never before been suffered by the English in Ireland. Sir Henry was killed by a bullet in his forehead. Tyrone could hardly have been grieved at news of his brother-in-law's death, for the two men had been bitter enemies almost from the time of Tyrone's elopement with Mabel Bagenal seven years before.

Two days later, on the morning of August 16, news of the disaster reached Dublin, to the consternation of the government officials. If even a minor reverse was likely to cause sporadic revolts, what could be expected to follow a defeat of this magnitude? Messages of warning were dis-

[13] *C. S. P. Ir.* (1598-1599), pp. 161-162 (51).

[14] *Ibid.*, p. 173.

[15] *Ibid.*, p. 182.

[16] *Ibid.*, p. 279 (95).

patched at once to all parts of the realm, and Ormonde was urged to hasten from Kilkenny to Dublin.

As soon as Norris heard of the defeat, he directed the gentlemen and nobles of Munster, Irish as well as English, to meet on the frontiers with their forces, and the towns to give such aid as they could, for he feared that the rebels of Leinster, for some time in revolt, would now be encouraged to extend their depredations into his province. The results of his efforts were discouraging; as the province had grown in wealth, its martial spirit had waned, and those who responded were either unwilling to co-operate whole-heartedly or incapable of giving effective service. Of regular troops he had but 100 foot and 42 horse, and his munitions were insufficient.[17] It would be interesting to know whether Spenser heeded this first summons.

In the month that followed, Norris's worst fears were realized. His province suffered many incursions, in the course of which great spoils were taken; and he learned, moreover, that large bodies of rebels were gathering on the border. Meanwhile, his urgent appeals to Dublin for men and munitions brought no response.[18]

By early October, 2,000 insurgents had crossed from Leinster into Munster and were beginning to drive away cattle and lay siege to castles. Among their leaders were Captain Richard Tyrrell, described by Moryson as " of English race, but a bold and unnatural enemy to his country and the English," and Owen MacRory O'More, both of whom were acting under Tyrone's direction.[19] Norris, besides his own company of foot, and 140 soldiers who had joined him by way of Youghal, had only the noblemen, gentlemen, and others of the province, with forces raised by them, amounting to 100 horse and 300 kern, " weakly armed, and accordingly minded; and of the undertakers not any to be accounted of "; no wonder he felt unable to oppose so large a force. The rebels, he heard, were moving toward Connello or Aherlow, whence it would be easy to pass into the northern parts of County Cork; evidently they expected soon to control the whole province.[20] A large portion of the population was going over to them, part out of sympathy, the rest from a natural desire to forestall the spoiling of their lands.

Reports of the rebels' approach in force sent most of the undertakers in flight toward the protection of city walls, especially of the coast towns, and Cork was soon crowded with refugees. Among fleeing undertakers

[17] *Ibid.*, pp. 245-246 (43). [18] *Ibid.*, p. 270 (82).
[19] Moryson, *An Itinerary* 2. 218; Four Masters, *Annals of the Kingdom of Ireland* 6. 2077.
[20] *C. S. P. Ir.* (1598-1599), pp. 280-281 (96).

was Hugh Cuffe, Spenser's neighbor to the north. Justice Goold, who on October 6 reported Cuffe's flight, professed knowledge of no undertakers who were able to keep their seignories.[21] What happened on the estate of Arthur Hyde, another neighbor of Spenser's, to the east, was recorded by Hyde himself in a letter written at Cork on October 28. His detailed account bears quoting, since something very like this may have occurred on Spenser's estate.

After the Ulster rebels had entered the Province, . . . the rebels of Munster, all the Province through, rose instantly before noon, and made spoil and prey, with fire and sword, upon all English subjects. At which time my wife, for safety of her life, with her children fled to Cork, most dangerously escaping their hands, being assisted with the help of the Lord Barry; in which morning the rebels took all such cattle, which were upon my lands, of mine and my English tenants. But my wife having left a ward in my castle for the defence of the same with all my goods therein, my goods were all preserved till the 19th of this month, on which day I landed from England at Youghal. On which day, also, in the morning, the new proclaimed Earl of Desmond, Derby M'Owen, son-in-law to the Lord Roche, now called Earl of Clancarty, Donogh M'Cormac, son-in-law to the White Knight, called M'Donogh of Doallo, and Piers Lacy, new made Seneschal of Imokilly, which are the chief of Munster rebels, together with Onie M'Rory O'Moraghe [O'More], [and others] . . . , chief leaders and Captains of Ulster rebels, being in all of Munster and Ulster four thousand, came to the castle and assaulted it, and played against it with their shot, till the 22nd following; and, having burnt the town by it, with the houses and corn about it, and also burnt down the top of the castle, and also 'moymd' [breached] the wall through, the warders, divers of them wounded, and all wearied out with watching and fighting, and having no possible means to be assisted by any of Her Majesty's forces, and the Lord General then being passing from them out of the Province, were compelled to yield the castle, upon Desmond's promise that they should depart with their lives, and the carrying away of their own wearing apparel; who, being passed but a mile from the castle toward Cork, were robbed, and stripped to their naked bodies, by the Lord Roche's tenants, but were not slain, as at their first taking it was bruited. The warders were eighteen.[22]

Only two brief allusions to the destruction wrought at Kilcolman have been preserved. The first, in an anonymous history of the time, calendared among the Irish state papers as of October, 1598, is as follows: "Edmund [MacSheehy] was killed by an Englishman at the spoil of Kilcolman."[23] The second is Jonson's statement to Drummond of Hawthornden twenty years later "that the Irish having robbed Spenser's goods and burnt his house and a little child new born, he and his wife escaped, and after, he

[21] *Ibid.*, p. 282 (99). [22] *Ibid.*, p. 302. [23] *Ibid.*, p. 322.

died for lack of bread in King Street" etc.[24] The earlier statement suggests that the rebels encountered at least some resistance in this spoiling of his "fair stone house," of which no trace remains today, and of his castle. In connection with Jonson's remarks, natural yet unwarranted inferences have been made: Jonson did not say that the child burnt by the rebels was Spenser's, and the escape referred to may as well have been out of Ireland as from Kilcolman. All that may confidently be said about Spenser's flight is that most of the undertakers, seeing no prospect of adequate military aid, left their castles ahead of the advancing army of insurgents, and that many of them, including Spenser, found refuge in Cork.

On October 11, Ormonde was at Kilmallock, in southern Limerick, where he was joined by Norris and some of the noblemen and gentlemen of the province. From there the lord general passed by way of Mallow and Cork to Youghal; at Youghal on October 21 he wrote letters to the privy council, to Sir Robert Cecil, and to Elizabeth in each of which he alluded to the cowardice of the undertakers. To the privy council he wrote: "I may not omit to acquaint your Lordships that, at my coming into this Province, I found that the greatest part of the undertakers had most shamefully quitted and forsaken their castles and houses of strength before even the traitors came near them, leaving all to their spoils. . . ."[25] Probably the flight of the undertakers was made necessary by their failure through the preceding years to people their seignories with sufficient English families. The more easily obtained and more profitable Irish had been accepted as tenants, and consequently now, in this hour of need, the defensive strength that had been intended was lacking.

On October 23, Norris, other officials of Munster, and many undertakers and other refugees were at Cork, and there they had to stay for weeks awaiting reinforcements to the small body of soldiers Norris had with him. This period of waiting must have been almost unbearable. The crowding from so great an influx of refugees, the insolence of the citizens, many of whom secretly sympathized with the rebellion, the news of the defection of some of the leading men of the province, as the White Knight, Patrick Condon, John Barry (brother of Lord Barry), and David Roche (son of Lord Roche), all must have conspired to make these days black indeed.[26]

[24] Herford and Simpson's ed. of Jonson 1. 137.

[25] *C. S. P. Ir.* (1598-1599), pp. 290-291 (117), 293 (118, 119).

[26] *Ibid.*, pp. 298 (124), 299 (125). A ten-page manuscript calendared in the Irish State Papers, 1598-1599, pp. 431-433 (59), as "A briefe note of Ireland," and endorsed as by Spenser, was reprinted in full by Grosart in his edition of Spenser (1. 537-555). According

Did Spenser at this time first receive the ironical news that he had been made sheriff of Cork? On September 30, 1598, the privy council wrote to the lords justices warmly urging them to appoint Spenser to that office. The letter refers to him as " a gentleman dwelling in the county of Cork, who is so well known unto your lordships for his good and commendable parts (being a man endowed with good knowledge in learning and not unskilful or without experience in the service of the wars) as we need not use many words in his behalf." [27] According to William Saxey, chief justice of Munster, the eagerly sought and important office of sheriff was often filled by self-seeking, unscrupulous men, whose least interest was the promotion of justice.[28] The author of the Legend of Justice, we may assume, would have been an exception to the type depicted by Saxey, but he certainly had no chance to perform the duties of his office, and indeed the request for his appointment may never have been acted upon by the busy lords justices at Dublin.[29] In fact, it is possible that Spenser, prior to his arrival in England, did not hear of this honor, which, in all likelihood, was a tardy response to his efforts for preferment when last in London. In urging his appointment, Essex or Elizabeth may have taken the initiative, though it is worth noting that two others whose patronage he had sought, Lords Howard and Buckhurst, were present when the letter was authorized, as was also Sir George Carey.

On December 9 Norris was able to report to the privy council that the imperatively needed reinforcements had arrived: 1,000 men had landed at Cork, 600 at Kinsale, and 400 at Waterford. Biscuit, butter, and cheese had also come, along with munitions. He had believed at first that the ambitions of James Fitzthomas of Desmond for the earldom of Desmond and of Derby MacOwen for the earldom of Clancarty underlay the uprising in Munster, but now religion was being alleged as its cause. Four

to Grosart, the manuscript is " in the well-known handwriting of Sir Dudley Carleton" (*ibid.*, p. 230). Its primary aim was to reveal the causes of the rebellion, to depict the unhappy state of the refugees, and to spur Elizabeth to the thorough conquest of Ireland. Grosart and others have assumed the manuscript to be a fruit of Spenser's enforced leisure at this time, but because some of the ideas in it are contrary to his previously expressed opinions, his authorship has been questioned. Perhaps this document—really three documents, different from each other in tone—is the joint work of several refugees, and its endorsement a result of Spenser's having brought it to England along with Norris's dispatches. Cf. Renwick, *View*, pp. 329-330; Heffner, *MLN* 52. 58; Hulbert, *MP* 34. 345-353.

[27] *Acts of the Privy Council* (1598-1599), pp. 204-205.

[28] *C. S. P. Ir.* (1598-1599), p. 395.

[29] It seems doubtful whether the letter of December 8 from Captains Southwell and Cottrell to the privy council, in which it is stated that the sheriff of County Cork, among others, went to Cork at the beginning of the rebellion, can refer to Spenser—*Ibid.*, p. 398 (12).

castles only still held out, including his own at Mallow. Four days later he wrote to Sir Robert Cecil that the rebellion in his province had gained such headway, and been so strengthened by the daily efforts of priests, that he believed extreme measures would be necessary to bring the people back to loyalty. To the relief of Kilmallock, besieged now for twenty days, he hoped soon to march. Norris's letters to the privy council and to Cecil were taken to England by Spenser and delivered at Whitehall, where court was being held, on Sunday, December 24.[80]

[80] *Ibid.*, pp. 399-401 (15), 404-405 (22), 414 (36), 467 (24).

XVIII

SLEEP AFTER TOIL

ON DECEMBER 30, six days after his arrival at Whitehall, Spenser was paid £8 for bringing over Norris's letters. The warrant was signed by Secretary Sir Robert Cecil.[1] On January 13,[2] two weeks later, Spenser died in Westminster—in King Street, if we may trust Ben Jonson. King Street, which disappeared about the end of the past century, was the main thoroughfare of Westminster. It paralleled the Thames and extended through the royal palace of Whitehall, which today, except for a banqueting hall of later date, is but a name. During the twenty days following Spenser's arrival, the privy council sat at Whitehall in almost daily sessions. As might be supposed, their business mainly concerned the critical situation in Ireland—the raising, equipping, and transporting of troops for service there, and the coaxing of loans for this purpose from reluctant citizens.[3] The portentous decision to send Essex to Ireland crystallized during this time. On January 4 Essex wrote to Lord Willoughby: "Now for myself. Into Ireland I go. The Queen hath irrevocably decreed it; the Council do passionately urge it; and I am tied in mine own reputation to use no tergiversation."[4] As a member of the council, Essex attended its meetings faithfully during this period, and we may be sure took a prominent part in its deliberations. To Spenser, its weighty decisions touching Irish affairs would normally have been of profound interest, but perhaps his physical and mental state forbade his concerning himself with such matters.

Spenser had suffered terrible losses. His home had been ruined and his cattle stolen; and the houses and possessions of his English tenants had probably met a similar fate. Moreover, Renny, Buttevant, and his other lands in County Cork had, for all he knew, been "spoiled" with the same thoroughness. His ready funds may well have been exhausted by himself and his family during their painful two months in Cork. The testimony is overwhelming that he arrived in England a poor man, poor at least in available assets, and with just such uncertainty about the future as

[1] Bennett, *MLN* 52. 400.

[2] Zeitler, *ibid.* 43. 322.

[3] *Acts of the Privy Council* (1598-1599), pp. 397-462.

[4] Harrison, *The Life and Death of . . . Essex*, p. 212.

tens of thousands of European refugees experienced when, in 1940, the tidal wave of German armies inundated Holland, Belgium, and France.

But did he " die of want," as was several times alleged in the years following his death? [5] A sober, detailed account of his last days would be a boon indeed. The only contemporary allusion to his death is that of John Chamberlain in a letter to his friend Dudley Carleton written four days after the event. If Chamberlain had heard of any extraordinary circumstances, he would undoubtedly have put them into this long, gossipy letter. He says merely: " Spenser, our principal poet, coming lately out of Ireland, died at Westminster on Saturday last." [6] Although we do not know what pressing obligations Spenser may have had to meet, we should expect him to have been safely protected from immediate want by Sir Robert's generous payment. From three years later, dates the first extant assertion that he died because of neglect and want,[7] and from twenty years later the story reported by Ben Jonson and John Lane that he refused help offered by Essex on the ground that it came too late; " he died for lack of bread in King Street," Jonson told Drummond, " and refused 20 pieces sent to him by my Lord of Essex, and said he was sorry he had no time to spend them." [8] It was, of course, a frequent complaint of sixteenth-century poets that literary men and scholars were neglected by those who should have gloried in the opportunity, as patrons, of supplying their needs; and it may well be that the story of Spenser's death from neglect and want was embroidered on the fact of his death while in the grip of the sudden poverty wrought by Tyrone. Elizabethan poets do not seem to have been backward in appealing for financial aid, and it is hard to believe that Spenser, had he lacked the absolute necessities of life, would have hesitated to ask them of Essex, Sir George Carey, or even Lords Buckhurst and Howard, all of whom, as members of the privy council, were daily at Whitehall; and it is equally improbable that these men, who had so lately expressed their high regard for his worth, would have failed to respond. There were also, no doubt, at court many of the friends and patrons acquired during his previous visits to England. Moreover, dying of want and neglect would usually be regarded as a process, not of two or three weeks, but of months or years.

Whatever the circumstances of Spenser's last days, it is a satisfaction to remember that no long period of suffering could have preceded the coming

[5] See Heffner, *MLN* 48. 221-226.

[6] *The Letters of John Chamberlain* 1. 64-65.

[7] *The Return from Parnassus*, p. 11.

[8] Herford and Simpson's ed. of Jonson 1. 137.

of that rest and peace which had inspired some of his most eloquent lines. His extremely busy life in a turbulent land may account for his inclination to describe death as a dispenser of quietude and rest. What may be the last line of poetry he ever wrote [9] is an expression of his longing for rest:

> Then gin I thinke on that which Nature sayd,
> Of that same time when no more *Change* shall be,
> But stedfast rest of all things firmely stayd
> Vpon the pillours of Eternity,
> That is contrayr to *Mutabilitie*:
> For, all that moueth, doth in *Change* delight:
> But thence-forth all shall rest eternally
> With Him that is the God of Sabbaoth hight:
> O! that great Sabbaoth God, graunt me that Sabaoths sight.

This stanza, designated as the second of the eighth canto, concludes the fragment on Mutabilitie. His Mutabilitie cantos—two complete and two stanzas of a third—first appeared in the 1609 edition of *The Faerie Queene*, the First Folio. How they got into the hands of the printer, Matthew Lownes, we cannot be sure, but entries in the Stationers' Register indicate that Ponsonby's rights in *The Faerie Queene*, on his death, probably from the plague, in 1603, passed to Simon Waterson and from him to Matthew Lownes; [10] these cantos, therefore, no doubt came first into Ponsonby's hands and then successively to the other two men. Lownes apparently knew no more about them than we do, for he introduced them merely with this brief note: "Two Cantos of Mutabilitie which, both for form and matter, appear to be parcel of some following book of the *Faerie Queene* under the legend of Constancy. Never before imprinted." An allusion in them to the river myth of Mulla and Bregog, whose luckless loves, he says, Colin has made well known, is good evidence that they were composed in or after 1595, when *Colin Clouts Come Home Againe* was published. Without considering here the many theories to which these cantos have given rise, we may conjecture that they were intended as part of a later book of *The Faerie Queene*, and that they were found among Spenser's effects after his death. They would naturally be handed over to the man who had been his publisher for so many years. With an entire book of his poem in mind, Spenser probably for some reason felt moved to compose first of all this portion near the center, for the cantos are numbered vi, vii, and viii. His writing them ahead of the book as a whole might account for their constituting a unified, symmetrical poem, more

[9] Padelford, *PMLA* 45. 704-711.

[10] Johnson, *A Critical Bibliography*, p. 22.

perfect in structure than many of his independent compositions. They represent, moreover, one of his finest works in both imagery and thought, a fitting crown for his poetic career.

Mutabilitie, as we may call them, is concerned with the impermanence of all things in the universe. A sense of the instability of man and nature, and the pensiveness, even melancholy, induced by this thought, appear often in the literature of the Renaissance, as in the lyrics of Nashe and Raleigh and in the sonnets of Shakespeare. Through myth-like tale and pageant, Spenser presents his meditations on this theme.

Perhaps nowhere does he create more impressive figures than Mutability, the beautiful Titaness who ruled over the earth, and who did not hesitate to contend with Jove himself for dominion of the heavens; or than great Dame Nature, far taller than the other gods, mysterious, veiled, who was obliged to settle the controversy. Arresting is Dame Nature's verdict, that change is indeed everywhere, yet that through this very change continuity, permanence, perfection are attained; more arresting, perhaps, is her added thought that a time will come when this permanence through change will give way to a permanence of another sort, devoid of change.

The philosophical conceptions here presented with such grandeur and sweep seem chiefly indebted to the neo-Platonic thought current in Spenser's day, but the very diversity of the "sources" that have been proposed indicates, as usual, his thorough assimilation of his reading and his freedom from slavish imitation. In addition to the underlying metaphysical ideas, there is much narrative interest, much rich descriptive detail. Especially pleasing are the mythical tale about Molanna and Fanchin, a companion piece to the love story of Mulla and Bregog in *Colin Clouts Come Home Againe*, and the pageant of the Months, Days, and Hours, reviewed by Dame Nature from her throne on "Arlo," highest of the Galtees. Spenser's peculiar gift for creating with a few lines the vivid personification of an abstraction was never more brilliantly displayed than in this pageant.

Mutabilitie brings us close to the Spenser of these last years in Ireland. It breathes his love of the country, his pleasure in its rivers and mountains and woods. Who can read this poem without picturing him as he traces the Behanagh to its double source high in the Galtees or stands on the top of Galteemore, gazing at the peaks and slopes around him and then off toward the fertile plain of Tipperary,

> The richest champian that may else be rid,
> And the faire *Shure*, in which are thousand Salmons bred?

Not Kilcolman only but the surrounding region has cast its spell upon him. Yet a curse lies on the land. Wolves and thieves dwell in the forests of Arlo. Restless change tyrannizes as never before, and life seems tragically uncertain. Can we doubt that the condition of Ireland from 1595 on was partly responsible for his expression of loathing for " this state of life so tickle " and for his satisfaction in the thought of the stability represented by " Him that is the God of Sabbaoth hight "?

Spenser was buried in the south transept of Westminster Abbey in what is now known as Poets' Corner. He was interred, we are told by Camden, " near to Chaucer, at the charge of the earl of Essex; his hearse being attended by poets, and mournful elegies and poems, with the pens that wrote them, thrown into his tomb," [11] interesting variations from the sprigs of evergreen (to symbolize immortality) or handkerchiefs wet with tears that were sometimes thrown into the grave. A number of epitaphs and epigrams are extant, some of which may be copies of these very poems.[12] In the fall of 1938 permission was granted to open the grave of Spenser on the slender chance that the lyrics which had lain in oblivion for nearly three and a half centuries might be recovered, especially, it was hoped, verses by Shakespeare. Spenser enthusiasts enjoyed a pleasurable sense of expectancy for a few days, but the quest was stopped by public protest, and there was no certainty even that Spenser's coffin had been found. Though we possess only Camden's brief description of the funeral, we may assume that it was accompanied by the usual pageantry so much enjoyed by the London populace, since the earl of Essex met the cost. Just at this time Essex' mind was deeply engrossed by the great new Irish undertaking, his appointment as governor of Ireland having been made the day after Spenser's death—a fact which may account for the statement of John Lane that the earl would not have provided Spenser's funeral except for the efforts of Lane's friend Lodowick Lloyd, a minor poet and the queen's sergeant-at-arms.[13]

Queen Elizabeth, according to William Browne in his *Britannia's Pastorals*, employed an agent to erect a magnificent monument to Spenser, but Avarice ambushed the agent and " robbed our Colin of his monu-

[11] *The Historie of the . . . Princess Elizabeth*, London, 1688, p. 565.

[12] Camden, *Reges, Reginae, Nobiles, & alij in Ecclesia . . . Westmonasterij sepulti*, pp. I, 2^{v}-3^{r}; id., *Remains Concerning Britain*, p. 427; Breton, *Works* 1, " Melancholike Humours," pp. 15-16; Thynne, *Emblemes and Epigrames*, p. 71; Fitzgeoffrey, *The Poems of*, pp. xix-xx, xxiii; Carpenter, *A Reference Guide*, p. 229 (for verses by William Alabaster), and p. 240 (for verses by R. H.); Manningham, *Diary*, p. 2; Weever, *Epigrammes*, p. 101.

[13] Heffner, *MLN* 48. 223.

Spenser's monument in Westminster Abbey. Engraving by Louis du Guernier. From John Hughes' *The Works of Mr. Edmund Spenser*, London, 1715.

ment." [14] A less poetic account of what happened would be welcome. No monument was erected till Anne Clifford, countess of Dorset, some twenty years later, made good the lack. She may have been prompted partly by the fact that her mother and her aunt were Spenser's patrons—Spenser, it will be recalled, dedicated his *Fowre Hymnes* to them—and partly by her passion for restoring castles, churches, and chapels and for erecting monuments. To the poet Samuel Daniel, who had been her tutor, she set up a monument at Beckington, in Somersetshire, with an inscription beginning as does Spenser's: "HERE LYES EXPECTINGE THE SECOND COMMING OF OUR LORD & SAUIOUR JESUS CHRIST YE DEAD BODY OF SAMUELL DANYELL ESQ THAT EXCELLENT POETT AND HISTORIAN. . . ." Spenser's simple monument was constructed, at a cost of £40, by the master mason and statuary Nicholas Stone, who is remembered for his many monuments and other works, including Inigo Jones' Banqueting Hall and the celebrated effigy of John Donne in St. Paul's.[15] The inscription on Spenser's monument, with its curious errors in the dates of both birth and death, was as follows:

HEARE LYES (EXPECTING THE SECOND
COMMINGE OF OVR SAVIOVR CHRIST
JESVS) THE BODY OF EDMOND SPENCER,
THE PRINCE OF POETS IN HIS TYME;
WHOSE DIVINE SPIRRIT NEEDS NOE
OTHIR WITNESSE THEN THE WORKS
WHICH HE LEFT BEHINDE HIM.
HE WAS BORNE IN LONDON IN
THE YEARE 1510. AND
DIED IN THE YEARE
1596.[16]

In 1778, the monument, which had been constructed of freestone, and was much decayed, was restored "in durable marble" through the efforts of William Mason, the friend and biographer of the poet Gray.[17] Mason's interest in Spenser had probably been quickened by election to a fellow-

[14] *Works* 1. 193-194.

[15] The Walpole Society, *Seventh Volume*, p. 54. Although Stone's notebook does not date the erection of Spenser's monument, the year 1620, which heads the preceding group of items, has been generally accepted. A date earlier than 1613 is impossible, since in that year Stone began his career in London.

[16] Dart, *Westmonasterium* 1. 74; Professor Long reminds us that a confusion between *5* and *1* is common in MSS. of Spenser's day (*MLN* 31. 179).

[17] The Walpole Society, *Seventh Volume*, p. 54.

ship in Pembroke College and by Gray's and Richard Hurd's enthusiasm for Spenser. The portrait of Spenser now hanging in the hall of Pembroke College was given to the college by Mason.[18] The original inscription on the monument was retained except that the dates were changed to 1553 and 1598, and no alteration was made in the design of the monument.

Unfortunately Stone's design included no bust or other likeness of the poet, though effigies of various sorts appear on many of Stone's monuments. Had such a likeness been provided, the fascinating question of Spenser's appearance would very likely have been answered. We have, to be sure, John Aubrey's well-known statement: "Mr. Beeston says he was a little man, wore short hair, little band and little cuffs,"[19] but since William Beeston was born after Spenser's death, even this meager description must be accepted with caution. We have also portraits, engravings, and busts that have been accepted as likenesses of the poet, but proof that any one of these is authentic is lacking.

Because several of Spenser's portraits have for so long received general acceptance, a brief glance at the history of his likenesses may be profitable. Apparently no portrait of him was commonly recognized as such till about the end of the first quarter of the eighteenth century. During the seventeenth century small engravings purporting to be Spenser appeared, on the title-page of John Cotgrave's *Witts Interpreter*, 1655, and of Edward Phillips' *The New World of Words*, 1670, but in each case the artist was obviously without a portrait to work from, and depicted, not an Elizabethan, but a seventeenth-century gentleman with flowing hair. Before 1732 Michael Rysbrach executed a bust of the poet, and this, it is believed, is the handsome marble bust now gracing the Rare Book Room of the Yale University Library.[20] The sculptor has given his figure a ruff; but again the long hair suggests the lack of an authentic original, and the result bears little resemblance to any other reputed likeness of Spenser.

In the year 1727 the so-called Chesterfield portrait—now owned by Lord Harewood—was engraved with Spenser's name above it by the able engraver and antiquary George Vertue.[21] This thoroughly English face,

[18] Attwater, *Pembroke Collge*, p. 102.

[19] '*Brief Lives*' 2. 233; Aubrey undoubtedly got his information not as Grosart and others say, from Christopher Beeston, who died when Aubrey was only thirteen years old, but from William Beeston, the actor's son (see Aubrey 1. 96 and Nungezer, *A Dictionary of Actors*, pp. 36-38, 39-42).

[20] *New York Times*, May 13, 1934, sec. 2, p. 2.

[21] O'Donoghue, *Catalogue of Engraved British Portraits* 4. 166. Mr. Douglas Hamer, of Sheffield University, kindly contributes this history of the portrait: "The Chesterfield portrait originally belonged to Edward Harley, 2nd Earl of Oxford. At the sale of his effects, 8

Mezzotint by J. C. Le Blon, after the Chesterfield portrait.
From a copy in the British Museum.

with short, curly hair, straight nose, and short, soft beard, through which the well-formed, rounded chin is easily seen, has been most often reproduced as Spenser; but on what grounds Vertue, van der Gucht, Kyte, Simon, and Le Blon were convinced at about this time that they had in this portrait an authentic likeness of Spenser, who can say? The portrait at Pembroke College and that of Lord Harcourt reveal the same face, and even when, in this large group of prints and paintings, minor differences of feature and expression appear, the dress—the soft white collar with square corners and the simple, tight-fitting, slashed doublet—betrays a common original.

In the Plimpton Library at Columbia University hangs a small portrait which in features and dress is definitely related to this group. Dr. Julius S. Held, of New York, is inclined to think that "it was painted in the early 17th century although a slightly earlier date (very late 16th) is not impossible." On it appears the single word "Spencer," apparently added later, perhaps in the eighteenth century. Can this portrait, unmentioned in the discussions of Spenser's likenesses, be the origin of the important family of portraits generally known by the name of Lord Chesterfield? [22]

In 1772 the traveler Thomas Pennant visited Dupplin Castle, Perthshire, seat of the earl of Kinnoull, and there, as he reports in his "Second Tour in Scotland," saw "several very fine pictures," including a "head of Spenser." [23] In 1805 this portrait was engraved for H. J. Todd's variorum edition of Spenser. Todd in his preface mentions securing permission to have the portrait copied, but apparently did not question its authenticity or notice that it portrays quite another person from the subject of the Chesterfield painting, so often engraved during the previous three quarters of a century. Notably different are the sloping forehead, the slightly aquiline nose, and the prominent chin, whose forward thrust is accentuated by a narrow, pointed beard. The dress is a large lace ruff and loose cloak. At Althorp hangs an attractive copy of this portrait, said to have been made by Henry Raeburn in 1820.[24]

March 1741/2, it was bought by Philip Dormer, 4th Earl of Chesterfield, for £2. 6. 0, and remained in the library of Chesterfield House, London, until 1869, when the house was sold. The portrait passed into the hands of the Earl of Carnarvon, who took it to Bretby Hall. Bretby Hall was sold in 1916, and the portrait was then acquired by the Earl of Harewood, who replaced it in Chesterfield House when he purchased that property. A few years ago Harewood sold Chesterfield House, and the portrait is now at Goldsborough Hall."

[22] Judson, *HLQ* 6. 203-204.

[23] In Pinkerton, *A General Collection of the Best and Most Interesting Voyages and Travels* 3. 398.

[24] Shelley, *The Outlook* 61. 46.

In 1865 a special exhibition of portrait miniatures was held at the South Kensington Museum. Here Lord FitzHardinge showed a miniature that was catalogued as a painting of Edmund Spenser by Nicholas Hilliard.[25] When Dr. Grosart published Spenser's works in 1882-1884, he caused this miniature and a handsome portrait long in the family of the Reverend Sabine Baring-Gould to be engraved for certain large-paper copies of his edition, and in Volume I he insists emphatically on the authenticity of these two pictures and also of the Chesterfield portrait, but dismisses the Kinnoull portrait as a " Spaniard's haughty face," and declares that it " ought never to have been engraved as Spenser." Great would be the surprise of Dr. Grosart to learn that Mr. C. H. Collins Baker, formerly of the National Gallery, London, and now of the Huntington Library and Art Gallery, believes the Baring-Gould portrait to be Spanish, a work of the school of Velazquez, and hence obviously not Spenser. The miniature bears little resemblance to the Chesterfield portrait, the face being broader, the head rounder, and the hair longer and parted. Unfortunately there seems to be no documentary proof that this interesting little picture is Spenser or that, as Grosart avers, it belonged to Queen Elizabeth and passed to Elizabeth Carey by way of her husband's family. In Mr. Baker's judgment, the Hilliard attribution is extremely doubtful.[26] The Chesterfield, Kinnoull, and FitzHardinge pictures may any one of them conceivably represent Spenser, but until better evidence is found, we should probably do well to content ourselves with the vivid impression of his personality conveyed by his works and create an image of him from our own fancy.

And what a sharply defined personality emerges from a close study of his works and life! As a foundation there is poise, sanity, persistence in attaining worthy ends, traits often not associated with the poetic temperament. With patience he moves forward toward goals early chosen. He gains learning, he founds a house, he acquires, a decade before his death, the reputation of being England's principal poet, and he employs his poetic gifts, partly, it is true, to win patronage and renown, but not less to set forth the good and attack what he considers the bad and vicious, and to celebrate on a grand scale the achievements of England. The charity schoolboy and sizar could hardly have had visions of much

[25] *Catalogue of the Special Exhibition of Portrait Miniatures on Loan at the South Kensington Museum*, p. 133.

[26] Mr. Baker's comments were made in personal conference. His judgment of the FitzHardinge miniature was based on a photograph which shows a damaged and retouched painting and permits no sound opinion on its original status.

The Kinnoull portrait. From a photograph in the British Museum.

more. His sane and logical thinking appears in the *View*, and indeed in his poetry as well, which, for all its romanticism, is almost always marked by restraint and an observance of decorum born of his classical training. His business sense is perhaps best demonstrated by the fact that he could maintain Kilcolman and at the same time acquire an estate of good proportions for his son Peregrine. "Rich" is a relative term and possibly should not be applied to him, but his success in gaining a competence appears to be at least comparable with Shakespeare's. Though he had restless and impatient days while waiting for preferment at court, and though the sorrows common to existence, especially perhaps the sense of instability natural to those living in a half-conquered land, induced at times a mood of melancholy, the total impression made by his life is one of serenity. The carefree boy becomes a cheerful man, unembittered by serious checks or frustrations, conscious of his powers, and happy, we cannot doubt, over his well-earned fame.

Combined with his fundamental poise and balance were enthusiasms, ardors, loyalties. He loved books, read widely, and made their contents so thoroughly his own that he was easily able to transform what he had read "into something rich and strange." Closely coupled with his fondness for books were his antiquarian interests, which included naturally the chronicles of England, but also the old Irish culture all about him. The past, thanks to his idealism, he was prone to gild: he cherished the myth of Ovid's golden age, and liked to dwell on the bright and noble side of chivalry. His idealism predisposed him to Platonism, which entered ever more and more into his thought and feeling. He was devoted to his friends, minimized their faults, and, calmly indifferent to his own interests, eagerly praised them whether they were in or out of favor with the great. Conversely, those whom he disliked seemed blacker than they were, though the bitterness of his scorn so far as it was visited on particular persons was largely confined to those whom he regarded as the foes of England and Protestantism. Love and marriage were important alike in his life and in his poetry. What a contrast between the cautious weighing by Bacon of the benefits and liabilities of love and Spenser's conviction that it is a prime source of worthy action:

> Then forth he casts in his vnquiet thought,
> What he may do, her fauour to obtaine;
> What braue exploit, what perill hardly wrought,
> What puissant conquest, what aduenturous paine,
> May please her best, and grace vnto him gaine:
> He dreads no danger, nor misfortune feares,
> His faith, his fortune, in his breast he beares

Beauty for him was a ruling passion. He felt its magic in nature, in tapestry and armor and architecture, in man and especially in woman, and his Platonism gave him logical grounds for the reverence it inspired. Finally his love for his country must not be forgotten, nor for his queen as its symbol; his affection for the past in no sense hindered his intense preoccupation with the great events that were from year to year shaping the destiny of England.

" He was not of an age but for all time," said Ben Jonson of Shakespeare. Spenser was " for all time " too, as his influence— subtle, powerful, persistent, especially on men of poetic tastes—proves; but he was also peculiarly a man of his age. His attitude toward the Irish, his aristocratic point of view, his acceptance of current scientific and political theories, his belief in the ethical function of poetry, his thirst for fame, his ardent Protestantism, his love of beauty—all these were thoroughly representative of his epoch. Moreover, if not so versatile as Raleigh and Sidney, he was broad in the Elizabethan way—a man of affairs as well as a scholar and a poet. His distinction probably consists less in his innovations, notable as some of these were, than in his remarkably complete embodiment of the spirit of his age in poetry of lavish profusion and extraordinary beauty.

The FitzHardinge miniature. From an engraving made by W. J. Alais for Grosart's edition of the works of Spenser.

BIBLIOGRAPHY

C. S. P.	Calendar of State Papers
C. S. P. Sp.	Calendar of State Papers, Spanish (see Calendar of Letters and State Papers . . . in the Archives of Simancas)
Cal. Carew MSS.	Calendar of the Carew Manuscripts
DNB	Dictionary of National Biography
ELH	ELH: A Journal of English Literary History
F. Q.	The Faerie Queene
HLQ	The Huntington Library Quarterly
JEGP	The Journal of English and Germanic Philology
MLN	Modern Language Notes
MLQ	Modern Language Quarterly
MLR	The Modern Language Review
MP	Modern Philology
NQ	Notes and Queries
PMLA	Publications of the Modern Language Association of America
RES	The Review of English Studies
SP	Studies in Philology
S. P.	State Papers
TLS	The Times Literary Supplement (London)

Acts of the Privy Council of England. New Ser. London, 1890-.

Arber, Edward, ed. A Transcript of the Registers of the Company of Stationers of London; 1554-1640 A. D. 5 vols. London, 1875-1894.

Atkinson, Dorothy F. Edmund Spenser, A Bibliographical Supplement. Baltimore, 1937.

Attwater, Aubrey. Pembroke College, Cambridge: A Short History. Ed. S. C. Roberts. Cambridge, 1936.

Aubrey, John. 'Brief Lives.' Ed. A. Clark. 2 vols. Oxford, 1898.

Bagwell, Richard. Ireland under the Tudors. 3 vols. London, 1885-1890.

Bakeless, John. The Tragicall History of Christopher Marlowe. 2 vols. Cambridge, 1942.

Baker, George. The History and Antiquities of the County of Northampton. 2 vols. London, 1822-1830, 1836-1841.

Baldwin, T. W. The Genesis of Some Passages Which Spenser Borrowed from Marlowe. ELH 9 (1942). 157-187.

Banks, Theodore H. Spenser's Rosalind: A Conjecture. PMLA 52 (1937). 335-337.

Baroway, Israel. The Imagery of Spenser and the *Song of Songs*. JEGP 33 (1934). 23-45.

Bennett, Josephine Waters. The Allegory of Sir Artegall in *F. Q.* V, xi-xii. SP 37 (1940). 177-200.

———. A Bibliographical Note on *Mother Hubberds Tale.* ELH 4 (1937). 60-61.

———. Did Spenser Starve? MLN 52 (1937). 400-401.

———. The Evolution of " The Faerie Queene." Chicago, [1942].

———. Spenser and Gabriel Harvey's *Letter-Book.* MP 29 (1931-1932). 163-186.

———. Spenser's *Fowre Hymnes*: Addenda. SP 32 (1935). 131-157.

Berry, Henry F. The English Settlement in Mallow under the Jephson Family. Journal of the Cork Historical and Archaeological Society. 2nd Ser. 12 (1906). 1-26.

Betham, Sir William. Communication to Archaeologia: or, Miscellaneous Tracts Relating to Antiquity. 21 (1827). 551-553.

Botting, Roland B. The Composition of the *Shepheardes Calender.* PMLA 50 (1935). 423-434.

Brady, W. Maziere, ed. Clerical and Parochial Records of Cork, Cloyne, and Ross. 3 vols. Dublin and London, 1863-1864.

Breton, Nicholas. The Works in Verse and Prose of. Ed. A. B. Grosart. 2 vols. Privately printed, 1879.

A Briefe Discouerie of Doctor Allens seditious drifts . . . Concerning the yeelding vp of the towne of Deuenter. London, 1588.

Browne, William. The Whole Works of. Ed. W. Carew Hazlitt. 2 vols. Printed for the Roxburghe Library, 1868-1869.

Bryan, Donough. Gerald Fitzgerald, the Great Earl of Kildare (1456-1513). Dublin and Cork, 1933.

Bryskett, Lodowick. A Discourse of Ciuill Life: Containing the Ethike part of Morall Philosophie. Fit for the instructing of a Gentleman in the course of a vertuous life. London, 1606.

Buck, Philo M., Jr. Spenser's Lost Poems. PMLA 23 (1908). 80-99.

Byrom, H. J. Edmund Spenser's First Printer, Hugh Singleton. The Library. 4th Ser. 14 (1933-1934). 121-156.

Caius, John. The Works of. Ed. E. S. Roberts. Cambridge, 1912.

Calendar of Letters and State Papers Relating to English Affairs, Preserved Principally in the Archives of Simancas . . . Elizabeth, 1580-1586. Ed. Martin A. S. Hume. London, 1896.

Calendar of State Papers, Domestic Series, of the Reign of James I. 1603-1610. Ed. M. A. E. Green. London, 1857.

Calendar of the Carew Manuscripts Preserved in the Archiepiscopal Library at Lambeth. 1575-1588. Ed J. S. Brewer and William Bullen. London, 1868.

Calendar of the Carew Manuscripts, Preserved in the Archiepiscopal Library at Lambeth. 1589-1600. Ed J. S. Brewer and William Bullen. London, 1869.

Calendar of the State Papers Relating to Ireland, of the Reign of Elizabeth, 1574-1585. Ed. H. C. Hamilton. London, 1867.

Calendar of the State Papers Relating to Ireland, of the Reign of Elizabeth, 1586-1588, July. Ed. H. C. Hamilton. London, 1877.

Calendar of the State Papers, Relating to Ireland, of the Reign of Elizabeth, 1588, August–1592, September. Ed. H. C. Hamilton. London, 1885.

Calendar of the State Papers, Relating to Ireland, of the Reign of Elizabeth, 1592, October–1596, June. Ed. H. C. Hamilton. London, 1890.

Calendar of the State Papers, Relating to Ireland, of the Reign of Elizabeth, 1596, July–1597, December. Ed. E. G. Atkinson. London, 1893.

Calendar of the State Papers, Relating to Ireland, of the Reign of Elizabeth, 1598, January–1599, March. Ed. E. G. Atkinson. London, 1895.

The Cambridge Modern History. 13 vols. Cambridge, 1902-1911.

Cambridge University Statutes. See The Statutes of Queen Elizabeth for the University of Cambridge.

Camden, William. Britain. Tr. Philemon Holland. London, 1610.

———. The Historie of the Most Renowned and Victorious Princesse Elizabeth, Late Queene of England. London, 1630.

———. Reges, Reginae, Nobiles, & alij in Ecclesia Collegiata B. Petri Westmonasterij sepulti. London, 1600.

———. Remains Concerning Britain. London, 1870.

Campion, Edmund. A Historie of Ireland (1571). Introduction by Rudolf B. Gottfried. New York, 1940. (Scholars' Facsimiles & Reprints.)

Carpenter, Frederic Ives. A Reference Guide to Edmund Spenser. Chicago, 1923.

———. Spenser in Ireland. MP 19 (1921-1922). 405-419.

Catalogue of the Special Exhibition of Portrait Miniatures on Loan at the South Kensington Museum, June, 1865. London, 1865.

Chamberlain, John. The Letters of. Ed. N. E. McClure. 2 vols. Philadelphia, 1939.

Chambers, Sir E. K. The Elizabethan Stage. 4 vols. Oxford, 1923.

Cheyney, Edward P. A History of England From the Defeat of the Armada to the Death of Elizabeth. 2 vols. New York and London, 1926.

Colvile, Frederick Leigh. The Worthies of Warwickshire Who Lived between 1500 and 1800. Warwick and London, n.d.

Cooper, Charles Henry, and Cooper, John William. Annals of Cambridge. 5 vols. Cambridge, 1842-1908.

Cooper, Charles Henry, and Cooper, Thompson. Athenae Cantabrigienses. 3 vols. Cambridge, 1858-1913.

Copinger, W. A. Historical Notes. Journal of the Cork Historical and Archaeological Society. 1st Ser. 2 (1893). 344-348.

Corbett, Julian S. Drake and the Tudor Navy. 2 vols. London, 1898.

Covington, Frank F., Jr. Biographical Notes on Spenser. MP 22 (1924-1925). 63-66.

Covington, Frank F., Jr. Spenser's Use of Irish History in the *Veue of the Present State of Ireland*. University of Texas Studies in English, No. 4 (1924).5-38.

Dart, John. Westmonasterium. Or The History and Antiquities of the Abbey Church of St. Peters Westminster, Containing . . . A Survey of the Church and Cloysters, taken in the Year 1723. 2 vols. London, n.d.

Derricke, John. The Image of Irelande, with A Discouerie of Woodkarne, . . . 1581. Ed. John Small. Edinburgh, 1883.

Desiderata Curiosa Hibernica: or A Select Collection of State Papers. [Ed. John Lodge.] 2 vols. Dublin, 1772.

Documents Relating to the University and Colleges of Cambridge. 3 vols. London, 1852.

Dunlop, Robert. The Plantation of Munster 1584-1589. The English Historical Review. 3 (1888). 250-269.

———. An Unpublished Survey of the Plantation of Munster in 1622. The Journal of the Royal Society of Antiquaries of Ireland. 54 (1924). 128-146.

Dymmok, John. A Treatice of Ireland in Tracts Relating to Ireland. Printed for the Irish Archaeological Society. Vol. 2. Dublin, 1843.

Eccles, Mark. Spenser's First Marriage. TLS, December 31, 1931, p. 1053.

Edwards, Edward. The Life of Sir Walter Ralegh. 2 vols. London, 1868.

Erskine, John. The Virtue of Friendship in the *Faerie Queene*. PMLA 30 (1915). 831-850.

Falkiner, C. Litton. Illustrations of Irish History and Topography, Mainly of the Seventeenth Century. London, 1904.

Farr, W. C., and Others. Merchant Taylors' School: Its Origin, History and Present Surroundings. Oxford, 1929.

Ferguson, James F. Memorials of Edmund Spenser the Poet, and His Descendants, from the Public Records of Ireland. The Gentleman's Magazine, 1855, 2. 605-609.

Fiants, Calendar of, in The Twelfth Report of the Deputy Keeper of the Public Records in Ireland. Dublin, 1880. The Thirteenth Report. Dublin, 1881. The Fifteenth Report. Dublin, 1883. The Sixteenth Report. Dublin, 1884. The Twenty-second Report. Dublin, 1890.

Fitzgeoffrey, Charles. The Poems of. Ed. A. B. Grosart. Privately printed, 1881.

Fitzgerald, Lord Walter. New Abbey of Kilcullen. With a sketch of the life of the founder, Sir Roland FitzEustace, Baron Portlester. Journal of the Co. Kildare Archaeological Society and Surrounding Districts. 3 (1902). 301-317.

Flood, William H. Grattan. Enniscorthy Castle. The Journal of the Royal Society of Antiquaries of Ireland. 35 (1905). 177-178.

Four Masters. Annals of the Kingdom of Ireland. Ed. and tr. John O'Donovan. 7 vols. Dublin, 1856.

Freyd, Bernard. Spenser or Anthony Munday?—A Note on the *Axiochus*. PMLA 50 (1935). 903-908.

Friedland, Louis S. Spenser's 'Wrenock.' The Shakespeare Association Bulletin. 18 (1943). 41-47.

Friedrich, Walter G. The Stella of Astrophel. ELH 3 (1936). 114-139.

Fuller, Thomas. The History of the Worthies of England. 3 vols. London, 1840.

Gerber, A. All of the Five Fictitious Italian Editions of Writings of Machiavelli and Three of Those of Pietro Aretino Printed by John Wolfe of London (1584-1589). MLN 22 (1907), 129-135.

Gollancz, Sir Israel. Summary. Spenseriana in Proceedings of the British Academy, 1907-1908. London, n. d.

Gotch, J. Alfred. The Old Halls & Manor-Houses of Northamptonshire. London, [1936].

Gottfried, Rudolf. The Date of Spenser's "View." MLN 52 (1937). 176-180.

———. The "G. W. Senior" and "G. W. I." of Spenser's *Amoretti*. MLQ 3 (1942). 543-546.

———. Irish Geography in Spenser's *View*. ELH 6 (1939). 114-137.

———. Spenser as an Historian in Prose. Transactions of the Wisconsin Academy of Sciences, Arts and Letters. 30 (1937). 317-329.

Grace Book Δ. Ed John Venn. Cambridge, 1910.

Gray, M. M. The Influence of Spenser's Irish Experiences on *The Faerie Queene*. RES 6 (1930). 413-428.

Greenlaw, Edwin A. *The Shepheards Calender*. PMLA 26 (1911). 419-451.

———. Spenser and the Earl of Leicester. PMLA 25 (1910). 535-561.

Greville, Fulke. Life of Sir Philip Sidney. Oxford, 1907.

Grey, Arthur Lord. A Commentary of the Services and Charges of William Lord Grey of Wilton, K. G. Ed. Sir Philip De Malpas Grey Egerton. Printed for the Camden Society, 1847.

Grosart, A. B., ed. . . . The Spending of the Money of Robert Nowell of Reade Hall, Lancashire: Brother of Dean Alexander Nowell. 1568-1580. Privately printed, 1877.

Hamer, Douglas. Edmund Spenser: Some Further Notes. NQ 162 (1932). 380-384.

———. Some Spenser Problems. NQ 180 (1941). 183-184, 220-224, 238-241.

———. Spenser's Marriage. RES 7 (1931). 271-290.

Hard, Frederick. Princelie Pallaces: Spenser and Elizabethan Architecture. Sewanee Review. 42 (1934). 293-310.

Hardiman, James. Irish Minstrelsy, or Bardic Remains of Ireland; with English Poetical Translations. 2 vols. London, 1831.

Harington, Sir John. The Metamorphosis of Ajax; A Cloacinean Satire: with the Anatomy and Apology. Chiswick, 1814.

Harris, Brice. The Ape in *Mother Hubberds Tale*. HLQ 4 (1940-1941). 191-203.

Harris, Mary Dormer. Unknown Warwickshire. London, [1924].

Harrison, G. B. The Life and Death of Robert Devereux, Earl of Essex. London, [1937].

Harrison, T. P., Jr. The Relations of Spenser and Sidney. PMLA 45 (1930). 712-731.

Harvey, Gabriel. Gabriel Harvey's Marginalia. Ed. G. C. Moore Smith. Stratford-upon-Avon, 1913.

———. Letter-Book of, A. D. 1573-1580. Ed. E. J. L. Scott. Printed for the Camden Society, 1884.

———. The Works of. Ed. A. B. Grosart. 3 vols. Privately printed, 1884-1885.

Heffner, Ray. Did Spenser Die in Poverty? MLN 48 (1933). 221-226.

———. Edmund Spenser's Family. HLQ 2 (1938-1939). 79-84.

———. Essex and Book Five of the *Faerie Queene*. ELH 3 (1936). 67-82.

———. Essex, the Ideal Courtier. ELH 1 (1934). 7-36.

———. Review of B. E. C. Davis's Edmund Spenser: A Critical Study. MLN 50 (1935). 192-195.

———. Review of W. L. Renwick's edition of A View of the Present State of Ireland. MLN 52 (1937). 57-58.

———. Spenser's Acquisition of Kilcolman. MLN 46 (1931). 493-498.

———. Spenser's *View of Ireland*: Some Observations. MLQ 3 (1942). 507-515.

Henley, Pauline. Galathea and Neaera. TLS, July 6, 1933, p. 464.

———. Spenser in Ireland. Dublin and Cork, 1928.

Hennessy, Sir John Pope. Sir Walter Ralegh in Ireland. London, 1883. (Transcriptions of important State Papers in the Appendix.)

Hewlett, James H. Interpreting a Spenser-Harvey Letter. PMLA 42 (1927). 1060-1065.

Heywood, James, and Wright, Thomas, ed. Cambridge University Transactions during the Puritan Controversies of the 16th and 17th Centuries. 2 vols. London, 1854.

Hind, Arthur M. Wenceslaus Hollar and His Views of London and Windsor in the Seventeenth Century. London, 1922.

Historical Manuscripts Commission. Fourth Report. London, 1874.

A History of Hampshire and the Isle of Wight. (The Victoria History.) 6 vols. Westminster, 1900-1914.

Holinshed, Raphael. . . . Chronicles. [London, 1586-1587.]

Howitt, William. Homes and Haunts of the Most Eminent British Poets. 2 vols. London, 1849.

Hudson, Hoyt H. Penelope Devereux as Sidney's Stella. The Huntington Library Bulletin, No. 7 (1935). 89-129.

Hulbert, Viola Blackburn. Diggon Davie. JEGP 41 (1942). 349-367.

———. Spenser's Relation to Certain Documents on Ireland. MP 34 (1936-1937). 345-353.

Hume, Martin A. S. The Courtships of Queen Elizabeth. New York, 1898.

Jenkins, Raymond. Spenser and the Clerkship in Munster. PMLA 47 (1932). 109-121.

———. Spenser: The Uncertain Years 1584-1589. PMLA 53 (1938). 350-362.

Jenkins, Raymond. Spenser with Lord Grey in Ireland. PMLA 52 (1937). 338-353.

Johnson, Francis R. A Critical Bibliography of the Works of Edmund Spenser Printed before 1700. Baltimore, 1933.

Jonson, Ben. Ben Jonson. Ed. C. H. Herford and Percy and Evelyn Simpson. 7 vols. Oxford, 1925-1941.

Judson, Alexander C. Another Spenser Portrait. HLQ 6 (1942-1943). 203-204.

———. A Biographical Sketch of John Young, Bishop of Rochester, with Emphasis on His Relations with Edmund Spenser. Indiana University Studies, Bloomington, 1935.

———. Spenser in Southern Ireland. Bloomington, 1933.

———. Thomas Watts, Archdeacon of Middlesex (and Edmund Spenser). Indiana University Publications, Humanities Series, Bloomington, 1939.

———. Two Spenser Leases. MLQ 5 (1944). 143-147.

The Kalender of Shepherdes: The Edition of Paris 1503 in Photographic Facsimile, A Faithful Reprint of R. Pynson's Edition of London 1506. Ed. H. Oskar Sommer. 3 vols. London, 1892.

Kingsford, C. L. Essex House, formerly Leicester House and Exeter Inn. Archaeologia or Miscellaneous Tracts Relating to Antiquity. 73 (1923). 1-54.

Koller, Kathrine. Abraham Fraunce and Edmund Spenser. ELH 7 (1940). 108-120.

———. Spenser and Ralegh. ELH 1 (1934). 37-60.

Kuersteiner, Agnes Duncan. E. K. Is Spenser. PMLA 50 (1935). 140-155.

Leadam, I. S. The Domesday of Inclosures, 1517-1518. 2 vols. London, 1897.

Lee, Philip G. The Ruined Monuments of Sir Robert Tynte and Sir Edward Harris in Kilcredan Church, Ballycrenane, near Ladysbridge. Journal of the Cork Historical and Archaeological Society. 2nd Ser. 31 (1926). 86-87.

Lewis, Samuel. A Topographical Dictionary of Ireland. 2 vols. London, 1847.

Liber Munerum Publicorum Hiberniae. 2 vols. [London, 1852.]

The Lismore Papers (First Series). Ed. A. B. Grosart. 5 vols. Privately printed, 1886.

The Lismore Papers (Second Series). Ed. A. B. Grosart. 5 vols. Privately printed, 1887-1888.

Long, Percy W. Spenser and the Bishop of Rochester. PMLA 31 (1916). 713-735.

———. Spenseriana: *The Lay of Clorinda.* MLN 31 (1916). 79-82.

———. Spenser's Birth-date. MLN 31 (1916). 178-180.

———. Spenser's Visit to the North of England. MLN 32 (1917). 58-59.

MacCarthy, Daniel. The Life and Letters of Florence MacCarthy Reagh. London, 1867.

McKerrow, R. B., and Others. A Dictionary of Printers and Booksellers in England, Scotland and Ireland, and of Foreign Printers of English Books 1557-1640. London, 1910.

McPeek, James A. S. The Major Sources of Spenser's *Epithalamion.* JEGP 35 (1936). 183-213.

Manningham, John, Diary of. Ed. John Bruce. Westminster, 1868. (Camden Society Publication.)

Meehan, C. P. The Fate and Fortunes of Hugh O'Neill, Earl of Tyrone, and Rory O'Donel, Earl of Tyrconnel; Their Flight from Ireland, and Death in Exile. Dublin, n. d.

[Milles, Thomas.] The Catalogue of Honor. London, 1610.

Millican, C. Bowie. Notes on Mulcaster and Spenser. ELH 6 (1939). 214-216.

———. The Supplicats for Spenser's Degrees. HLQ 2 (1938-1939). 467-470.

Moffet, Thomas. Nobilis; or, A View of the Life and Death of a Sidney, and Lessus Lugubris. Ed. Virgil B. Heltzel and Hoyt H. Hudson. San Marino, 1940.

Moryson, Fynes. An Itinerary. 4 vols. Glasgow, 1907-1908.

Mulcaster, Richard. Positions. Ed. Robert Hebert Quick. London, 1888.

———. Mulcaster's Elementarie. Ed. E. T. Campagnac. Oxford, 1925.

Mullinger, James Bass. The University of Cambridge. 3 vols. Cambridge, 1873-1911.

Murdin, William, ed. A Collection of State Papers Relating to Affairs In the Reign of Queen Elizabeth, from the Year 1571 to 1596. London, 1759.

[Murray, John.] Handbook for Travellers in Ireland. 7th ed. Ed. John Cooke. London, 1906.

Nashe, Thomas. The Works of. Ed. R. B. McKerrow. 5 vols. London, 1904-[1910].

Neale, J. E. Queen Elizabeth. London, [1934].

Nichols, John. The Progresses, and Public Processions of Queen Elizabeth. 3 vols. London, 1788-1805.

Noot, Jan van der. Theatre for Worldlings. Introduction by Louis S. Friedland. New York, 1939. (Scholars' Facsimiles & Reprints.)

Nungezer, Edwin. A Dictionary of Actors. New Haven, 1929.

O'Connor, G. B. Elizabethan Ireland. Dublin, n. d.

O'Donoghue, Freeman. Catalogue of Engraved British Portraits Preserved in the Department of Prints and Drawings in the British Museum. Vol. 4, 1914.

Oliphant, James. The Educational Writings of Richard Mulcaster (1532-1611), Abridged and Arranged, with a Critical Estimate. Glasgow, 1903.

O'Rahilly, Alfred. The Massacre at Smerwick (1580). Journal of the Cork Historical and Archaeological Society. 2nd Ser. 42 (1937). 1-15; 65-83. Reprinted Cork, 1938.

Osgood, Charles G. The 'Doleful Lay of Clorinda.' MLN 35 (1920). 90-96.

———. Spenser's English Rivers. Transactions of the Connecticut Academy of Arts and Sciences. 23 (1920). 67-108.

Pacata Hibernia. Compiled by direction of Sir George Carew. Ed. Standish O'Grady. 2 vols. London, 1896.

Padelford, Frederick M. The *Cantos of Mutabilitie*: Further Considerations Bearing on the Date. PMLA 45 (1930). 704-711.

Parmenter, Mary. Spenser's *Twelue Aeglogues Proportionable to the Twelue Monethes.* ELH 3 (1936). 190-217.

Payne, Robert. A Brief Description of Ireland: 1590. Ed. Aquilla Smith. Reprinted for the Irish Archaeological Society in Tracts Relating to Ireland, Vol. 1. Dublin, 1841.

Pearson, A. F. Scott. Thomas Cartwright and Elizabethan Puritanism, 1535-1603. Cambridge, 1925.

Perkinson, Richard H. 'Volpone' and the Reputation of Venetian Justice. MLR 35 (1940). 11-18.

Pforzheimer Library, The Carl H. 3 vols. New York, 1940.

Pinkerton, John, ed. A General Collection of the Best and Most Interesting Voyages and Travels. 17 vols. London, 1808-1814.

Plomer, Henry R. Edmund Spenser's Handwriting. MP 21 (1923-1924). 201-207.

Plomer, Henry R., and Cross, Tom Peete. The Life and Correspondence of Lodowick Bryskett. Chicago, n.d.

Privy Council. See Acts of the Privy Council of England.

Raines, F. R. In Lancashire Funeral Certificates. Ed T. W. King. Printed for the Chetham Society, 1869.

The Return from Parnassus or the Scourge of Simony. Ed. Edward Arber. London, 1879.

Rich, Barnabe. The Fruites of long Experience. London, 1604.

——. A New Description of Ireland. London, 1610.

Rix, Herbert David. Spenser's Rhetoric and the "Doleful Lay." MLN 53 (1938). 261-265.

Robinson, Charles J. A Register of the Scholars Admitted into Merchant Taylors' School, From A. D. 1562 to 1874. 2 vols. Lewes, 1882-1883.

Ronan, Myles V. The Reformation in Dublin, 1536-1558. London, 1926.

Round, J. Horace. Studies in Peerage and Family History. Westminster, 1901.

Sandison, Helen E. Arthur Gorges, Spenser's Alcyon and Ralegh's Friend. PMLA 43 (1928). 645-674.

——. Spenser's "Lost" Works and Their Probable Relation to His *Faerie Queene.* PMLA 25 (1910). 134-151.

Sargent, Ralph M. At the Court of Queen Elizabeth: The Life and Lyrics of Sir Edward Dyer. London, 1935.

Scott, Janet G. The Sources of Spenser's 'Amoretti.' MLR 22 (1927). 189-195.

Shakespeare's England. 2 vols. Oxford, 1916.

Shelley, H. C. Edmund Spenser: a Tercentenary Survey. The Outlook (N. Y.). 61 (1899). 35-46.

Sidney, Philip. The Correspondence of Philip Sidney and Hubert Languet. Ed. William A. Bradley. Boston, 1912.

——. The Defense of Poesy. Ed. Albert S. Cook. Boston, n.d.

Smith, G. Gregory, ed. Elizabethan Critical Essays. 2 vols. Oxford, 1904.

Smith, Roland M. The Irish Background of Spenser's *View.* JEGP 42 (1943). 499-515.

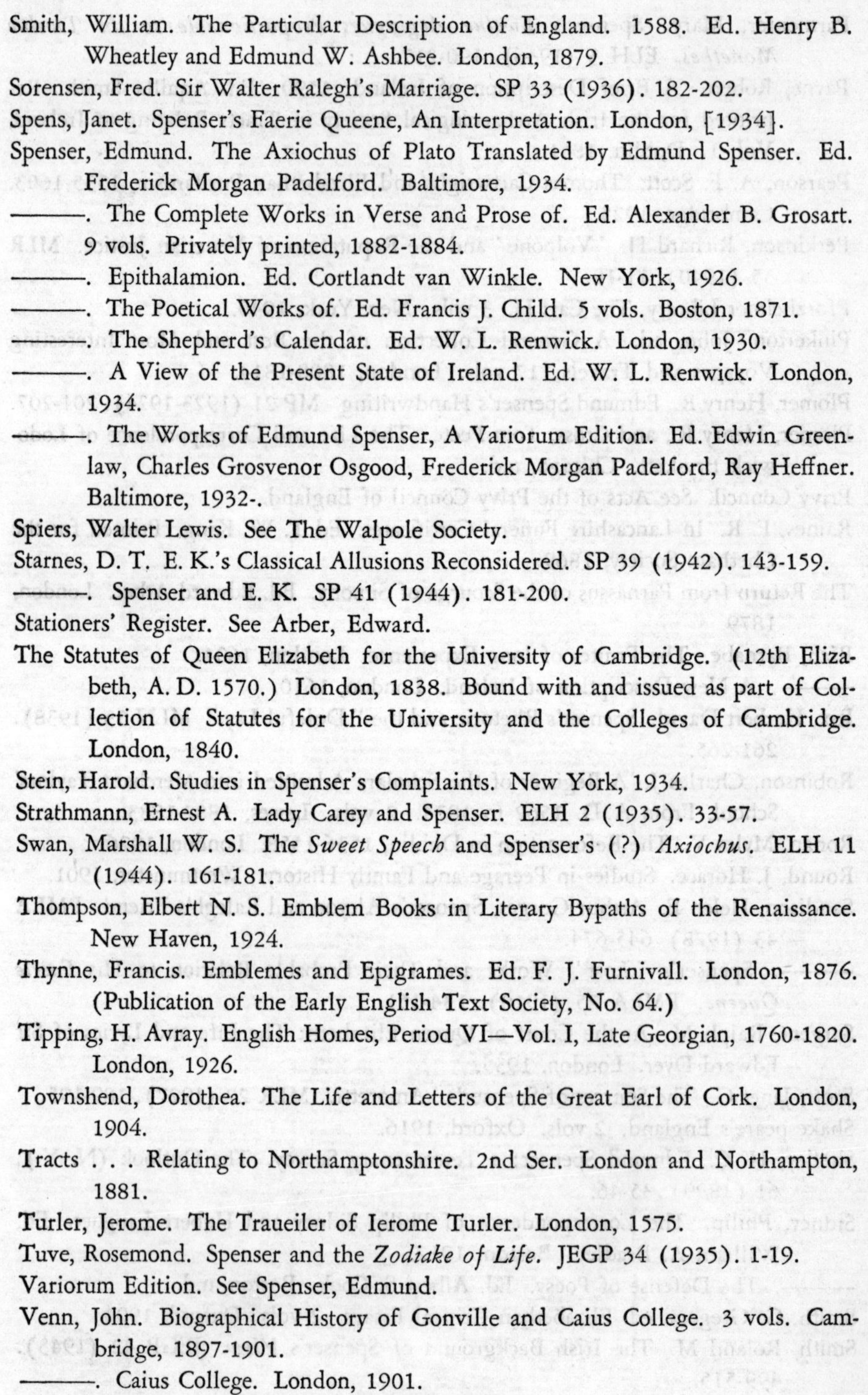

Smith, William. The Particular Description of England. 1588. Ed. Henry B. Wheatley and Edmund W. Ashbee. London, 1879.

Sorensen, Fred. Sir Walter Ralegh's Marriage. SP 33 (1936). 182-202.

Spens, Janet. Spenser's Faerie Queene, An Interpretation. London, [1934].

Spenser, Edmund. The Axiochus of Plato Translated by Edmund Spenser. Ed. Frederick Morgan Padelford. Baltimore, 1934.

———. The Complete Works in Verse and Prose of. Ed. Alexander B. Grosart. 9 vols. Privately printed, 1882-1884.

———. Epithalamion. Ed. Cortlandt van Winkle. New York, 1926.

———. The Poetical Works of. Ed. Francis J. Child. 5 vols. Boston, 1871.

———. The Shepherd's Calendar. Ed. W. L. Renwick. London, 1930.

———. A View of the Present State of Ireland. Ed. W. L. Renwick. London, 1934.

———. The Works of Edmund Spenser, A Variorum Edition. Ed. Edwin Greenlaw, Charles Grosvenor Osgood, Frederick Morgan Padelford, Ray Heffner. Baltimore, 1932-.

Spiers, Walter Lewis. See The Walpole Society.

Starnes, D. T. E. K.'s Classical Allusions Reconsidered. SP 39 (1942). 143-159.

———. Spenser and E. K. SP 41 (1944). 181-200.

Stationers' Register. See Arber, Edward.

The Statutes of Queen Elizabeth for the University of Cambridge. (12th Elizabeth, A. D. 1570.) London, 1838. Bound with and issued as part of Collection of Statutes for the University and the Colleges of Cambridge. London, 1840.

Stein, Harold. Studies in Spenser's Complaints. New York, 1934.

Strathmann, Ernest A. Lady Carey and Spenser. ELH 2 (1935). 33-57.

Swan, Marshall W. S. The *Sweet Speech* and Spenser's (?) *Axiochus*. ELH 11 (1944). 161-181.

Thompson, Elbert N. S. Emblem Books in Literary Bypaths of the Renaissance. New Haven, 1924.

Thynne, Francis. Emblemes and Epigrames. Ed. F. J. Furnivall. London, 1876. (Publication of the Early English Text Society, No. 64.)

Tipping, H. Avray. English Homes, Period VI—Vol. I, Late Georgian, 1760-1820. London, 1926.

Townshend, Dorothea. The Life and Letters of the Great Earl of Cork. London, 1904.

Tracts . . . Relating to Northamptonshire. 2nd Ser. London and Northampton, 1881.

Turler, Jerome. The Traueiler of Ierome Turler. London, 1575.

Tuve, Rosemond. Spenser and the *Zodiake of Life*. JEGP 34 (1935). 1-19.

Variorum Edition. See Spenser, Edmund.

Venn, John. Biographical History of Gonville and Caius College. 3 vols. Cambridge, 1897-1901.

———. Caius College. London, 1901.

———. Early Collegiate Life. Cambridge, 1913.

Venn, John, and Venn, J. A. Alumni Cantabrigienses. Part I, 4 vols. Cambridge, 1922-1927.

The Victoria History of the County of Northampton. Westminster, 1902-.

View. See Spenser. A View of the Present State of Ireland.

Wallace, M. W. The Life of Sir Philip Sidney. Cambridge, 1915.

The Walpole Society, The Seventh Volume of (Spiers, Walter Lewis, The Note-Book and Account Book of Nicholas Stone). Oxford, 1919.

Walter, J. H. 'The Faerie Queene': Alterations and Structure. MLR 36 (1941). 37-58.

Ware, Sir James. De Scriptoribus Hiberniae. Dublin, 1639.

Warner, George F., ed. Facsimiles of Royal, Historical, Literary and Other Autographs in the Department of Manuscripts, British Museum. Series I.-V. 1899.

Watson, Foster. The English Grammar Schools to 1660: their Curriculum and Practice. Cambridge, 1908.

Webbe, William. A Discourse of English Poetrie. Ed. Edward Arber. London, 1871.

Wedel, Lupold von. Journey through England and Scotland Made by Lupold von Wedel in the Years 1584 and 1585. Transactions of the Royal Historical Society. New Ser. Vol. 9. London, 1895.

Weever, John. Epigrammes in the Oldest Cut and Newest Fashion, . . . 1599. Ed. R. B. McKerrow. Stratford-upon-Avon, [1922].

Welply, W. H. Edmund Spenser: Being an Account of Some Recent Researches into His Life and Lineage, with Some Notice of His Family and Descendants. NQ 162 (1932). 110-114; 165-169; 182-187; 202-206; 220-224; 239-242; 256-260.

———. Edmund Spenser. Some New Discoveries and the Correction of Some Old Errors. NQ 146 (1924). 445-447.

———. Edmund Spenser's Brother-in-law, John Travers. NQ 179 (1940). 74-78; 92-96.

———. More Notes on Edmund Spenser. NQ 165 (1933). 92-94; 111-116.

———. Some Spenser Problems. NQ 180 (1941). 74-76; 92-95; 436-439; 454-459.

Willis, Robert, and Clark, John Willis. The Architectural History of the University of Cambridge, and of the Colleges of Cambridge and Eton. 4 vols. Cambridge, 1886.

Wilson, Elkin Calhoun. England's Eliza. Cambridge, 1939.

Wilson, F. P. Spenser and Ireland. RES 2 (1926). 456-457.

Wilson, H. B. The History of Merchant-Taylors' School. London, 1814.

Witherspoon, Alexander M. The Influence of Robert Garnier on Elizabethan Drama. New Haven, 1924.

Wood, Herbert. A Guide to the Records Deposited in the Public Record Office of Ireland. Dublin, 1919.

Zeitler, W. I. The Date of Spenser's Death. MLN 43 (1928). 322-324.

Venn, John, and Venn, J. A. *Alumni Cantabrigienses.* Part I. 4 vols. Cambridge, 1922-1927.

The Victoria History of the County of Northampton. Westminster, 1902.

View. See Spenser, *A View of the Present State of Ireland.*

Wallace, M. W. *The Life of Sir Philip Sidney.* Cambridge, 1915.

The Walpole Society. *The Seventh Volume of* (Spiers, Walter Lewis, *The Note-book and Account Book of Nicholas Stone*). Oxford, 1919.

Walter, J. H. "The Faerie Queene: Alterations and Structure," MLR 36 (1941), 37-58.

Ware, Sir James. *De Scriptoribus Hiberniae.* Dublin, 1639.

Warner, George F., ed. *Facsimiles of Royal, Historical, Literary and Other Autographs in the Department of Manuscripts, British Museum.* Series I-V. 1899.

Watson, Foster. *The English Grammar Schools to 1660: Their Curriculum and Practice.* Cambridge, 1908.

Webbe, William. *A Discourse of English Poetrie.* Ed. Edward Arber. London, 1871.

Wedel, Lupold von. "Journey through England and Scotland Made by Lupold von Wedel in the Years 1584 and 1585," *Transactions of the Royal Historical Society,* New Ser. Vol. 9. London, 1895.

Weever, John. *Epigrammes in the Oldest Cut and Newest Fashion.* 1599. Ed. R. B. McKerrow. Stratford upon Avon, 1922.

Welply, W. H. "Edmund Spenser. Being an Account of Some Recent Researches into His Life and Lineage, with Some Notice of His Family and Descendants," NQ 162 (1932), 110-114, 165-169, 182-187, 202-206, 220-224, 239-242, 256-260.

—. "Edmund Spenser: Some New Discoveries and the Correction of Some Old Errors," NQ 146 (1924), 445-447.

—. "Edmund Spenser's Brother-in-law, John Travers," NQ 179 (1940), 74-78, 92-96.

—. "More Notes on Edmund Spenser," NQ 165 (1933), 92-94, 111-116.

—. "Some Spenser Problems," NQ 180 (1941), 74-76, 92-95, 436-439, 454-459.

Willis, Robert, and Clark, John Willis. *The Architectural History of the University of Cambridge and of the Colleges of Cambridge and Eton.* 4 vols. Cambridge, 1886.

Wilson, Elkin Calhoun. *England's Eliza.* Cambridge, 1939.

Wilson, F. P. "Spenser and Ireland," RES 2 (1926), 456-457.

Wilson, H. B. *The History of Merchant Taylors' School.* London, 1814.

Witherspoon, Alexander M. *The Influence of Robert Garnier on Elizabethan Drama.* New Haven, 1924.

Wood, Herbert. *A Guide to the Records Deposited in the Public Record Office of Ireland.* Dublin, 1919.

Zeitler, W. I. "The Date of Spenser's Death," MLN 43 (1928), 322-24.

INDEX